T0222825

Building Xamarin.Forms Mobile Apps Using XAML

Mobile Cross-Platform XAML and Xamarin.Forms Fundamentals

Dan Hermes

with Contributions by Dr. Nima Mazloumi

apress®

Building Xamarin.Forms Mobile Apps Using XAML: Mobile Cross-Platform XAML and Xamarin.Forms Fundamentals

Dan Hermes
Boston, MA, USA

Nima Mazloumi
San Francisco, CA, USA

ISBN-13 (pbk): 978-1-4842-4029-8
https://doi.org/10.1007/978-1-4842-4030-4

ISBN-13 (electronic): 978-1-4842-4030-4

Library of Congress Control Number: 2019930581

Managing Director, Apress Media LLC: Welmoed Spahr
Acquisitions Editor: Todd Green
Development Editor: James Markham
Coordinating Editor: Jill Balzano

Cover designed by eStudioCalamar

Cover image designed by Freepik (www.freepik.com)

Distributed to the book trade worldwide by Springer Science+Business Media New York, 233 Spring Street, 6th Floor, New York, NY 10013. Phone 1-800-SPRINGER, fax (201) 348-4505, e-mail orders-ny@springer-sbm.com, or visit www.springeronline.com. Apress Media, LLC is a California LLC and the sole member (owner) is Springer Science + Business Media Finance Inc (SSBM Finance Inc). SSBM Finance Inc is a Delaware corporation.

For information on translations, please e-mail rights@apress.com, or visit http://www.apress.com/rights-permissions.

Apress titles may be purchased in bulk for academic, corporate, or promotional use. eBook versions and licenses are also available for most titles. For more information, reference our Print and eBook Bulk Sales web page at http://www.apress.com/bulk-sales.

Any source code or other supplementary material referenced by the author in this book is available to readers on GitHub via the book's product page, located at www.apress.com/9781484240298. For more detailed information, please visit http://www.apress.com/source-code.

Printed on acid-free paper

For your apps.

And for my fiancée, Ginger.

.

Table of Contents

Foreword xv

About the Authors..xvii

About the Technical Reviewer xix

Acknowledgments..xxi

Introduction xxiii

Chapter 1: Building Apps Using Xamarin...1

  Understanding Xamarin.Forms 2

    XAML vs. C#... 3

    Xamarin.Forms Solution Architecture.. 4

  Understanding the Platform-Specific UI Approach 6

    Platform-Specific UI Solution Architecture 6

  Choosing Xamarin.Forms or a Platform-Specific UI.. 7

    Using Custom Renderers, Effects, and Native Views.. 9

  Exploring the Elements of Mobile UIs 10

  Using the Xamarin.Forms UI 11

    Page.. 12

    Layout... 12

    View.. 13

  Creating a Xamarin.Forms Solution 14

    Xamarin.Forms Project... 16

    Xamarin.Android... 19

    Xamarin.iOS.. 20

    Core Library.. 21

    Setting the App's Main Page... 21

Adding Xamarin.Forms Views 23

    Label View 23

    Placing Views Using StackLayout 24

    Background Color and Font Color 25

    Using Fonts 25

    Using Platform-Specific Fonts 26

    Button View 26

    Setting View Alignment and Size: HorizontalOptions and VerticalOptions 29

    Entry View for Text Input 30

    BoxView 31

    Image View 32

    ScrollView 36

    Padding Around the Entire Page 37

    CODE COMPLETE: Adding Xamarin.Forms Views 38

Summary 41

Chapter 2: Building Xamarin.Forms Apps Using XAML 43

Basic Syntax 44

XML Syntax 44

    Element 44

    Attribute 45

    Hierarchy 45

    XML Namespaces 46

XAML Syntax 46

    Classes and Members 47

    Markup Extensions 48

    Constructors 55

    XAML Terms 60

Xamarin.Forms Syntax 61

    Property Element Syntax 62

    Content Property Syntax 62

    Enumeration Value Syntax 63

Event Handler Syntax 63

Collection Syntax 65

Attached Property Syntax 65

Anatomy of XAML Files 67

XAML Compilation 68

XAML Standard 69

Summary 71

Chapter 3: UI Design Using Layouts 73

Xamarin.Forms Layouts 73

Using Xamarin.Forms Layouts 74

StackLayout 74

Padding Around the Entire Layout 75

Stacking with Vertical Orientation 76

Stacking with Horizontal Orientation 77

Nesting Layouts 79

Expanding and Padding Views by Using LayoutOptions 79

CODE COMPLETE: StackLayout 81

FlexLayout 82

Position Views Using Axes 82

FlexLayout Patterns 86

Grid 87

Sizing Rows and Columns 90

Sizing to Fit Views 90

Setting Exact Size 91

Expanding Views to Fit Available Space 92

Expanding Views Proportionally 93

Creating Multicell Views 94

Padding Between Cells 96

CODE COMPLETE: Grid 97

RelativeLayout 98

    Setting View Location and Size 99

    Using Constraints 99

    CODE COMPLETE: RelativeLayout 104

AbsoluteLayout 106

    Creating Bounding Objects with SetLayoutBounds 107

    CODE COMPLETE: AbsoluteLayout 111

ContentView 112

    CODE COMPLETE: ContentView 114

Frame 115

Understanding Custom Controls 116

Summary 117

Chapter 4: Styles, Themes, and CSS **119**

Creating a Page Without Style 119

    Styling Manually Using View Formatting Properties 123

Resources and Dictionaries 126

    Defining Resources 127

    Static Resource Lookup 128

    Dynamic Resource Lookup 134

    Reusable Resource Dictionaries 140

    Lookup Behavior 143

    Overriding Resources 143

    Merging Dictionaries 143

Styles 144

    Style Lookup 145

    Explicit Styles 146

    Implicit Styles 148

    Overriding Styles 149

    Using Resources in Styles 151

    Style Inheritance 153

Styles Overview...157

Device Styles..163

Themes 165

Using Themes..165

Theme Styling Options..167

Dark Theme 168

Light Theme 169

Custom Themes...171

Cascading Style Sheets (CSS)...174

Selectors 175

Using CSS 175

Xamarin.Forms CSS Definition 181

Summary..185

Chapter 5: User Interaction Using Controls 187

Xamarin.Forms Views 187

Picker 188

DatePicker 191

TimePicker..193

Stepper..195

Slider 196

Switch...197

Scale, Rotation, Opacity, Visibility, and Focus 198

CODE COMPLETE: Xamarin.Forms Views..199

Custom Controls..201

Control Templates 202

Commands...204

CommandParameters..206

Triggers 207

TargetType 207

Property Trigger 208

Data Trigger 209

Multi Trigger 209

Event Trigger.. 210

CODE COMPLETE: Triggers.. 211

Behaviors 214

Attached Properties... 214

Behavior 216

Summary... 218

Chapter 6: Making a Scrollable List 219

Xamarin.Forms ListView 219

Binding to a List of Strings.. 220

Selecting an Item 222

Binding to a Data Model 225

CODE COMPLETE: Binding to a Data Model 227

Adding an Image 229

Customizing List Rows... 232

CODE COMPLETE: Customizing List Rows 236

Adding Buttons.. 238

Using Button Views.. 238

Using Context Actions.. 242

Grouping Headers 245

Customizing the Group Header 249

Creating a Jump List.. 253

ListViews Scroll Automatically 254

Pull-to-Refresh.. 255

Optimizing Performance 255

ListView Caching 256

ListView Optimization 257

Summary... 258

Chapter 7: Navigation **259**

  Navigation Patterns... 259

    Hierarchical 260

    Modal.. 261

    State Management 262

  Xamarin.Forms Navigation... 262

  Hierarchical Navigation Using NavigationPage 263

    Pushing and Popping Screens on the Navigation Stack.................... 266

    Setting the Page Title 267

    Customizing the Navigation Bar 268

    Handling the Back Button... 269

    Creating a Drop-Down Menu 269

  Modal 271

    Full-Page Modal Using NavigationPage... 271

    User Notification Using Alerts 271

    Pop-Up Menu Using Action Sheets 273

  Managing State... 274

    Passing Data into Page Parameters 274

    Disk Persistence Using the Properties Dictionary 275

    Using a Static Global Class.. 275

    Using a Static Property on the Application Object 277

  Drill-Down Lists.. 277

    Using ListView by Item 278

    CODE COMPLETE: Drill-Down List... 280

    Using ListView by Page 283

    Using TableView for Grouping Pages 284

    Navigation Drawer Using MasterDetailPage...................................... 287

  Tabs Using TabbedPage 292

    Creating Data-Bound Tabs... 294

    Putting NavigationPages Inside a TabbedPage.................................. 296

Springboard 297

    Making Icons Tappable by Using Gesture Recognizers 299

Carousel Using CarouselPage 300

Summary.. 301

Chapter 8: Custom Renderers, Effects, and Native Views................................... 303

Custom Renderer 303

    When to Use a Custom Renderer... 304

    Creating and Using a Custom Renderer 305

    Creating the Custom Element... 307

    Creating the Custom Renderer 309

Android Custom Renderer.. 310

    CODE COMPLETE: Android Custom Renderer.. 313

iOS Custom Renderer.. 315

    CODE COMPLETE: iOS Custom Renderer 317

Which Renderer and View Do You Customize?... 318

Effects.. 321

    Creating and Using Effects 322

    Text Validator Effect... 325

Native Views 337

    CODE COMPLETE: Native View Declaration.. 340

    Using Factory Methods.. 341

    CODE COMPLETE: Non-Default Constructors and Factory Methods 344

Summary.. 345

Chapter 9: Data Access with SQLite and Data Binding 347

What Is SQLite?.. 347

What Is SQLite.NET?.. 348

Data Binding.. 348

Xamarin.Forms Data Binding 349

    Binding to a Data Model 351

    Using INotifyPropertyChanged.. 354

CODE COMPLETE: Using INotifyPropertyChanged... 358

Understanding ViewModels and MVVM 360

Binding to ViewModels and Data Models 361

Binding a Read-Only ListView 366

Binding an Editable ListView 369

Binding a View to Another View 380

String Formatting 381

Value Converter 381

Using SQLite.NET 382

Locking Is Key 384

Creating a Database 384

Building the Database Path 385

Creating a Table 389

Creating the Data Access Layer 394

CODE COMPLETE: Creating a DAL by Using SQLite.NET... 406

Database Creation Options... 410

Web Services 411

Enterprise Cloud Data Solutions 411

Microsoft Azure Mobile Apps 412

Visual Studio App Center (VSAC).. 414

IBM Mobile Foundation.. 414

Summary.. 415

Index.. **417**

Foreword

It has been a long road since the day in 2001 when we began migrating .NET to non-Windows platforms. In 2009 we brought the first .NET platform to the mobile platforms by introducing a static compiler for .NET and the bindings that allowed it to work and leverage everything that Apple's phoneOS platform had to offer (later renamed iOS).

I am proud to have worked with many talented developers in the course of this effort, on the Xamarin team, and on the Mono, MonoTouch, MonoDroid, and Forms projects, which laid the foundation for cross-platform .NET. Our work helped to convince Microsoft, one of the largest software corporations in the world, of the value of open source and cross-platform.

Xamarin's acquisition by Microsoft helped cement the Xamarin Platform in Visual Studio. Xamarin is now Microsoft's flagship cross-platform mobile app development solution. All of this is great news for C# developers building mobile apps. The popular Xamarin DevOps tools such as Xamarin Test Cloud and Xamarin Insights are finding a new home in Visual Studio App Center, a suite for teams that build, test, and deploy applications to users and to the Play Store and the App Store.

Xamarin.Forms has grown to be Xamarin's most popular cross-platform offering. With Xamarin.Forms we allow developers to write their UI code once and have it leverage the native controls everywhere. Many developers build Xamarin.Forms apps using XAML, which is what this book is about.

XAML is important to many of us coding in C# with Visual Studio, which is the main reason we offer it in Xamarin.

The XAML language has a long history, starting with WPF, continuing with Silverlight and finally in UWP. Xamarin XAML reuses the same XAML concepts and maps them into the cross-platform UI framework. It includes additions such as FlexLayout, Effects, Themes, Styles, and CSS. We remain committed to making Xamarin.Forms the easiest platform to build mobile applications.

Dan Hermes has been documenting the progress of the Xamarin Platform for some years now. We commended him as a Xamarin MVP, and his engagement with the developer community has led Microsoft to name him a Microsoft Regional Director (RD).

I now leave you in Dan's capable hands to explore and enjoy Xamarin.Forms using XAML.

—Miguel de Icaza
Distinguished Engineer, Microsoft
Former CTO and co-founder, Xamarin

About the Authors

Dan Hermes (@danhermes) is a Microsoft Regional Director (RD), Xamarin MVP, Microsoft MVP, IBM Champion, and founder of Lexicon Systems. Mr. Hermes helps developers create great mobile apps and, leveraging IoT and AI, helps businesses develop a winning mobile strategy. Dan's firm has advised dozens of successful businesses on their apps in healthcare, retail, government, education, finance, transportation, biotech, and others. Xamarin mobile projects include a cross-platform app for Thermo Fisher Scientific which won a W3 and a Davey award and was a finalist for a Xammy award as well as a medical app used by over 40,000 surgeons. Dan develops Azure and Xamarin course curriculum for Microsoft and edX. He speaks at conferences, universities, and user groups such as Microsoft Ignite, Boston Code Camp, IBM InterConnect, Xamarin Dev Days, Microsoft Azure Day, and his group: Boston Mobile C# Developers' Group. He has penned articles for publications such as IBM's *Mobile Business Insights* and Microsoft's *MSDN Magazine*. Dan wrote the best-selling Apress book *Xamarin Mobile Application Development*, recommended reading at the Harvard Extension School and the first book of its kind in the MIT online library. Dan travels coast to coast to speak with developers, technologists, and businesses who want to understand how to build cross-platform mobile apps in C# using Xamarin (when he's not busy building apps).

Read more about Dan at `https://lexicon.systems`

ABOUT THE AUTHORS

 **Nima Mazloumi** holds a doctoral degree in Business Administration and Information Systems at the University of Mannheim. He has been a full-stack engineer for more than 18 years and is passionate about people, processes, and technology. He has worked for commercial, public, and nonprofit organizations in Europe and the Middle East and has managed almost all divisions of an IT organization. Currently, Nima resides with his family in California and works as a Senior Director for One Planet Ops Inc., a company that creates and invests in successful Internet-based businesses and is dedicated to philanthropy. Nima is a singer-songwriter and involved in community building activities.

About the Technical Reviewer

 **Glenn Stephens** is a software developer working with mobile and cloud technologies. He writing software for over 30 years. Glenn has worn many hats over the years including Managing Director, Chief Executive Officer, Solution Architect, Software Development Manager, and Programmer and worked in a variety of industries, from High-End Security, e-health, to Finance and Education and has won awards for several of his projects. He has a Bachelor of Computer Science and a Master of Business Administration with a specialization in e-business.

An author, speaker, and app builder, he has been writing code since the late 1980s with musical taste to match. You can find him most days on the Sunshine Coast, Australia, where he is based. When he's not coding, he enjoys playing the piano, reading, and spending time with his family.

Acknowledgments

Hats off to the champions and guardians of the written word in an age when video prevails. Without the foresight of Apress editor Jim DeWolf and perseverance of Todd Green and director Welmoed Spahr, this book would not exist.

I am grateful for the contributions of Dr. Nima Mazloumi that lend a tremendous thoroughness and accuracy to this book.

Glenn Stephens, I thank you for your considerable insights as our technical reviewer.

Thanks Jill Balzano and Mark Powers for your patience and consistency in the management of this project.

Mathieu Clerici of Los Xamarinos, thank you for helping to hammer our Xamarin solutions into shape. Thank you for all your development over the years. I couldn't ask for a better Xamarin architect/coder.

Many thanks to XAML code contributors: Jason Awbrey, Jim Bennett, Mark Allan, and Alex Blount.

David Ortinau, Senior Program Manager of Mobile Developer Tools and Xamarin. Forms team lead at Microsoft and James Montemagno, Principal Program Manager of Mobile Developer Tools at Microsoft and the greatest Xamarin evangelist the world will ever see, thank you for your reviews and direction.

Thanks to everyone here at Lexicon Systems!

Lastly, thanks to all of you not listed here who had a hand in this book.

Introduction

The hardest decision I made in writing this book was not including XAML examples in the book proper. ... I chose to adhere to my mission for this book: cross-platform C# code-first coverage of the foundations of the Xamarin platform.

—Dan Hermes, Xamarin Mobile Application Development, Apress, 2015

That quote is from the introduction to my last Xamarin book written in 2015 about C#. Now is the time for XAML.

The book you hold in your hand is a natural evolution of my previous book entitled *Xamarin Mobile Application Development.* That book covered UI development with Xamarin.Forms using C#. With all the same key topics plus new features, like FlexLayouts, Styles, CSS, Commands, and Behaviors, this book covers Xamarin.Forms using *XAML.* Whether you're coming from Windows Presentation Foundation (WPF) or C#, or you're just going deeper with Xamarin, this guide covers the most oft-used topics and techniques for Xamarin.Forms using XAML.

This book is a XAML version of my previous C# book, *Xamarin Mobile Application Development*, plus some new and updated topics. It's neither a new edition nor a completely different book. It's just XAMLized.

What's Inside

This book is a hands-on Xamarin.Forms primer and a cross-platform reference for building native Android and iOS using XAML. This book explores the important concepts, elements, and recipes using Xamarin.Forms layouts, controls, and lists with visual formatting techniques including styles, themes, and CSS as well as coding approaches including behaviors and commands.

Widen your XAML foundation with a solid review of XAML object creation and syntax. Explore constructors and factory methods and how to configure objects using XAML's many syntaxes including property element syntax, content property syntax, and event handler syntax.

When you've reached the limits of what Xamarin.Forms can do out of the box, you'll want to customize your Xamarin.Forms controls by using effects and custom renderers to leverage platform-specific features.

You'll also learn all the key Xamarin UI navigation patterns: hierarchical and modal, drill-down lists, tabs, navigation drawer, and others. You can use the provided navigation code to build out the skeleton of just about any business app.

This book is a guide to SQLite data access. We'll cover the most common ways to access a SQLite database in a Xamarin app and how to build a data access layer (DAL). Once you have a database set up, you'll want to bind your data to your UI. You can do this by hand or use Xamarin.Forms data binding to bind UI elements to data sources. We'll cover many techniques for read and write data binding to both data models and to view models for a Model-View-ViewModel (MVVM) architecture.

Who This Book Is For

If you're a developer, architect, or technical manager who can read XAML and C# examples to learn about cross-platform mobile development using the Xamarin platform, then this book is for you.

How to Download Code Examples

All of the code for this book, the C# and Extensible Application Markup Language (XAML) solutions, can be found in two places online:

- GitHub via the book's product page, located at `www.apress.com/9781484240298`. For more detailed information, please visit `http://www.apress.com/source-code`.

- GitHub at `https://github.com/danhermes/xamarin-xaml-book-examples`.

Get Started with Xamarin.Forms Right Now!

No time for reading? Browse Chapter 1 for ten minutes, and then download the navigation code for Chapter 7. Rip off some of my Chapter 7 navigation patterns to use immediately in your app and get started coding right now. Leave the book open to Chapter 3 so you can build some layouts inside your navigation pages. Good luck!

Chapter Contents

The book begins with Xamarin.Forms and XAML, laying a solid foundation there before delving into how to use XAML to wield Xamarin.Forms. This book is laid out progressively from the most straightforward and foundational topics in Xamarin.Forms to the progressively more intricate and challenging. Each chapter is also laid out that way, beginning with the basics and proceeding into the more interesting concepts. Here are the chapters:

Chapter 1—Building Apps Using Xamarin

A Xamarin.Forms primer and a comparison of XAML vs. C# and Xamarin.Forms vs. platform-specific approaches, such as Xamarin.iOS and Xamarin.Android. Covers Xamarin.Forms solutions, pages, layouts, and views.

Chapter 2—Building Xamarin.Forms Apps Using XAML

Explore XAML syntax and features, such as namespaces and markup extensions, and how these are used in Xamarin.Forms. Use constructors and factory methods to instantiate your XAML classes. Learn all the ways that XAML elements are set and used including property element syntax, content property syntax, and event handler syntax.

Chapter 3—UI Design Using Layouts

Layouts help us organize the positioning and formatting of controls, allowing us to structure and design the screens of our mobile app.

Chapter 4—Styles, Themes, and CSS

Using Resource libraries to centralize UI properties. Styles leverage this approach to provide an app-wide UI architecture for consistency, reusability, and maintainability. Themes further this approach with pre-fab but customizable styles. Follow the next iteration in Cascading Style Sheets (CSS) with XAML.

Chapter 5—User Interaction Using Controls (Views)

Review Xamarin's basic UI interactions: pickers, sliders, switches, and other controls. Create custom controls and control templates for reusable UI elements. Commands, triggers, and behaviors facilitate deeper connections between your UI and your code handlers.

Chapter 6—Making a Scrollable List

Lists are one of the simplest and most powerful methods of data display and selection in mobile apps. Explore the power of the ListView and how to data bind, group list items with headers and footers, create user interaction with taps and context actions, and customize your rows.

Chapter 7—Navigation

Navigation lets a user traverse an app, move from screen to screen, and access features. Hierarchical, modal, navigation drawers, drill-down lists, and other key patterns make up the core of mobile UI navigation. State management is the handling of data passed between screens as the user navigates through the app.

Chapter 8—Custom Renderers, Effects, and Native Controls

Extend the capability of Xamarin.Forms views beyond their out-of-the-box functionality by customizing them using custom renderers, effects, and native views. Xamarin.iOS and Xamarin.Android have scores of features inaccessible using only the Xamarin.Forms abstraction reachable using effects, custom renderers, and native views.

Chapter 9—Local Data Access with SQLite and Data Binding

SQLite is a popular choice with many Xamarin developers and a great place to start learning mobile database access. Store and retrieve data locally by using SQLite-NET. Using Xamarin.Forms data binding, fuse UI elements to your data models. Use the MVVM pattern by binding to a view model.

CODE COMPLETE

There is a "Cliff's Notes" navigation path through this book. If you just want the bottom line on a topic, find the section you're interested in and jump right to the CODE COMPLETE section. This is a complete code listing at the end of many (but not all) major topics. Many times all we want is a quick code recipe on a topic and that's how to get it here in this book. If you need explanation about the code, turn back to the beginning of the section and step through the detailed construction of that code.

Prerequisites

You'll need a very basic understanding of what Xamarin and Xamarin.Forms are. Preferably you've downloaded a solution or two, built them, and run them on your simulator or device. Even more preferable, you've coded a few lines of XAML and C# and built a solution or two. If you've done none of those things, then I'll recommend that you pair this volume with the Xamarin online docs to keep you moving. If you've done all or most of those things, then proceed without fear.

System Requirements

Xamarin is installed with Visual Studio and is subject to the Visual Studio license structure. Xamarin is a VS install option, whether you use VS Professional, VS Enterprise, or VS for Mac or prefer a more casual route, Visual Studio Community or Visual Studio Community for Mac, which are both free. As of this writing, here are the OS and software requirements for Xamarin development:

Mac

Visual Studio 2017 for Mac will install and run on the following operating systems:

- macOS Sierra 10.12: Community, Professional, and Enterprise

- Mac OS X El Capitan 10.11: Community, Professional, and Enterprise

---

Note The latest version of Xcode 8.3 requires macOS Sierra 10.12; therefore, Xamarin.iOS and Xamarin.Mac projects also require that minimum version.

Windows

Visual Studio 2017 will install and run on the following operating systems:

- Windows 10 version 1507 or higher: Home, Professional, Education, and Enterprise (LTSC and S are not supported)

- Windows Server 2016: Standard and Datacenter

- Windows 8.1 (with Update 2919355): Core, Professional, and Enterprise

- Windows Server 2012 R2 (with Update 2919355): Essentials, Standard, Datacenter

- Windows 7 SP1 (with latest Windows Updates): Home Premium, Professional, Enterprise, Ultimate

Errata

The authors, the technical reviewers, and many Apress staff have made every effort to find and eliminate all errors from this book's text and code. Even so, there are bound to be one or two glitches left. To keep you informed, there's an Errata tab on the Apress book page (`www.apress.com/9781484240298`). If you find any errors that haven't already been reported, such as misspellings or faulty code, please let us know by e-mailing support@ apress.com.

Customer Support

Apress wants to hear what you think—what you liked, what you didn't like, and what you think could be done better next time. You can send comments to feedback@apress.com. Be sure to mention the book title in your message.

Contacting the Authors

You can follow Dan Hermes on Twitter at @danhermes, read his latest news at `https:// lexicon.systems`, or e-mail him at `dan@lexiconsystemsinc.com`. You can e-mail Nima at `nima@mazloumi.de`.

If you are seeking general Xamarin product support, please use the Xamarin documentation page at `https://docs.microsoft.com/en-us/xamarin/xamarin-forms/` or the Xamarin forums at `https://forums.xamarin.com/`

Summary

Whether you're new to Xamarin or a seasoned vet, there are new ideas and tricks for you in here. Enjoy getting your XAML on!

CHAPTER 1

Building Apps Using Xamarin

Xamarin has become so cross-platform that it now includes iOS, Android, Windows, macOS, Tizen, WPF, Hololens, GTK, and others. That's a lot of platforms. How does Xamarin do it?

Descended from the open-source Mono Project that brought .NET to Linux, the Xamarin platform is a port of .NET to the iOS and Android operating systems. Underlying Xamarin.Android is Mono for Android, and beneath Xamarin.iOS is MonoTouch. These are C# bindings to the native Android and iOS APIs for development on mobile and tablet devices. This gives us the power of the Android and iOS user interface, notifications, graphics, animation, and phone features such as location and camera—all using C# and XAML. Each new release of the Android and iOS operating systems is matched by a new Xamarin release that includes bindings to their new APIs. Xamarin.Forms is a layer on top of the other UI bindings, which provides a fully cross-platform UI library.

This chapter provides a refresher of the two ways to build an app using Xamarin:

- *Xamarin.Forms* is a cross-platform UI library for Android, iOS, and many others.

- *A platform-specific (or native) UI* approach uses Xamarin.Android, Xamarin.iOS.

We will talk about when Xamarin.Forms is useful and when a more platform-specific approach might be better. Then we'll delve into building a Xamarin.Forms UI using pages, layouts, and views. We will create a Xamarin.Forms solution containing shared projects and platform-specific ones. While adding Xamarin.Forms controls to a project, we will touch upon basic UI concepts such as image handling and formatting controls in a layout.

Let's start by discussing **Xamarin.Forms**.

© Dan Hermes 2019
D. Hermes and N. Mazloumi, *Building Xamarin.Forms Mobile Apps Using XAML*,
https://doi.org/10.1007/978-1-4842-4030-4_1

Understanding Xamarin.Forms

Xamarin.Forms is a toolkit of cross-platform UI classes built atop the more foundational platform-specific UI classes: Xamarin.Android and Xamarin.iOS. Xamarin.Android and Xamarin.iOS provide mapped classes to their respective native UI SDKs: iOS UIKit and Android SDK. Xamarin.Forms also binds directly many other platforms. This provides a cross-platform set of UI components that render in each of these three native operating systems (see Figure 1-1).

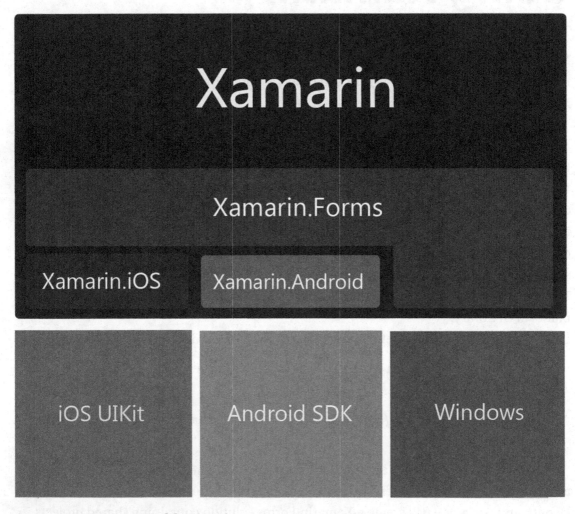

Figure 1-1. *Xamarin libraries bind to native OS libraries*

XAML vs. C#

Xamarin.Forms provides a cross-platform toolkit of pages, layouts, and controls and is a great place to start to begin building an app quickly. There are two ways to create user interfaces in Xamarin.Forms, either in C# using the rich Xamarin.Forms API or using Extensible Markup Language (XAML), a declarative markup language created by Microsoft used to define user interfaces. My previous book, *Xamarin Mobile Application Development*, covered the C# approach, but this book is all about XAML. You can create exactly the same kind of UI in both C# and XAML, so the choice is largely subjective and personal, although there are architectural considerations. XAML forces separation of the View code, while the C# approach does not. Jason Smith, the principal software engineer on the Xamarin.Forms team at Microsoft, explained it this way, "We build Xamarin. Forms code first. That means that all features are first created to work using C#, then we implement them for XAML."

Xamarin.Forms elements are built using `Page`, `Layout`, and `View` classes. This API provides a broad range of built-in cross-platform mobile UI patterns. Beginning with the highest-level `Page` objects, it provides familiar menu pages such as `NavigationPage` for hierarchical drilldown menus, `TabbedPage` for tab menus, a `MasterDetailPage` for making navigation drawers, a `CarouselPage` for scrolling image pages, and a `ContentPage,` a base class for creating custom pages. Layouts span the standard formats we use on various platforms including `StackLayout`, `AbsoluteLayout`, `RelativeLayout`, `Grid`, `ScrollView`, and `ContentView,` the base layout class. Used within those layouts are dozens of familiar controls, or views, such as `ListView`, `Button`, `DatePicker`, and `TableView`. Many of these views have built-in data binding options.

Tip Various synonyms for mobile UI *screens* exist, such as *views* and *pages*, and these are used interchangeably. A *view* can mean a *screen* but can also refer to a *control* in certain contexts.

Xamarin.Forms comprises platform-independent classes that are bound to their native platform-specific counterparts. This means we can develop basic, native UIs for all three platforms with almost no knowledge of iOS and Android UIs. Rejoice but beware! Purists warn that trying to build apps for these platforms without an understanding of the native APIs is a reckless undertaking. Let's heed the spirit of their concerns. We must take a keen interest in Android and iOS platforms, their evolution, features, idiosyncrasies, and releases. We can also wallow in the convenience and genius of the amazing cross-platform abstraction that is Xamarin.Forms!

Xamarin.Forms Solution Architecture

One of the greatest benefits of Xamarin.Forms is that it gives us the ability to develop native mobile apps for several platforms simultaneously. Figure 1-2 shows the solution architecture for a cross-platform Xamarin.Forms app developed for iOS, Android, and any of the other supported platforms. In the spirit of good architecture and reusability, a Xamarin.Forms cross-platform solution often uses shared C# application code containing the business logic and data access layer, shown as the bottom level of the diagram. This is frequently referred to as the Core Library. The cross-platform Xamarin.Forms UI layer is also C# and is depicted as the middle layer in the figure. The thin, broken layer at the top is a tiny amount of platform-specific C# UI code in platform-specific projects required to initialize and run the app in each native OS.

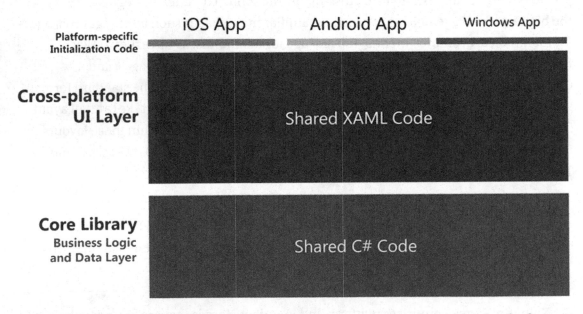

Figure 1-2. *Xamarin.Forms solution architecture: one app for multiple platforms*

Figure 1-2 is simplified to communicate the fundamentals of Xamarin.Forms. The reality is that hybridization between Xamarin.Forms and platform-specific code is possible, useful, and encouraged. It can happen at a number of levels. First, within the Xamarin.Forms customization options, which include custom renderers, effects, and native views. Customization gives us platform-specific classes for rendering platform-specific features on a Xamarin.Forms page. Hybridization can also happen within platform-specific Android activities and iOS view controllers that run alongside Xamarin.Forms pages or within platform-specific classes that are called as needed to handle native functionality such as location, camera, graphics, or animation. This sophisticated approach (which is now commonplace) leads to a more complex architecture, shown in Figure 1-3, and must be handled carefully. Note the addition of the platform-specific UI layer.

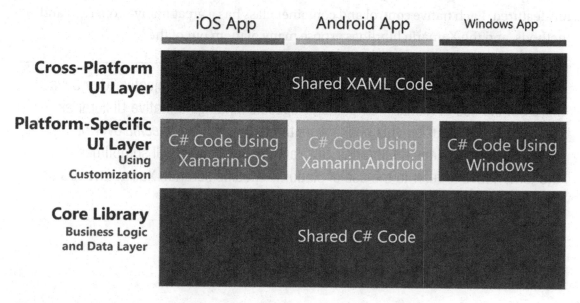

Figure 1-3. Xamarin.Forms architecture with customization

Note   Chapter 8 provides more on the use of customization and platform-specific code in Xamarin.Forms solutions.

When are Xamarin.Forms appropriate to use and when do we consider other Xamarin options? I'll address this key question a bit later in the chapter, but first let's define Xamarin's platform-specific UI options.

Understanding the Platform-Specific UI Approach

Before Xamarin.Forms, there were the platform-specific (or native) UI options, which include the Xamarin.Android, Xamarin.iOS, and Windows Phone SDK libraries. Building screens using platform-specific UIs requires some understanding of the native UIs exposed by these libraries. We don't need to code directly in iOS UIKit or Android SDK, as we're one layer removed when using Xamarin bindings in C#. Using the Windows SDK, of course, we're coding natively in C# against the Windows OS. The advantage of using Xamarin's platform-specific UIs is that these libraries are established and full-featured. Each native control and container class has a great many properties and methods, and the Xamarin bindings expose many of them out of the box.

Note   We're not talking about native UI development using Objective-C or Java here but the use of Xamarin C# platform-specific bindings to native UI libraries. To avoid such confusion, this book favors the term *platform-specific* over *native* when referring to Xamarin libraries, but Xamarin developers will sometimes use the term *native* to refer to the use of platform-specific libraries Xamarin.iOS and Xamarin.Android.

Platform-Specific UI Solution Architecture

Figure 1-4 shows how a platform-specific solution designed to be cross-platform shares C# application code containing the business logic and data access layer, just like a Xamarin.Forms solution. The UI layer is another story: it's all platform-specific. UI C# code in these projects uses classes that are bound directly to the native API: iOS, Android, or Windows sans binding.

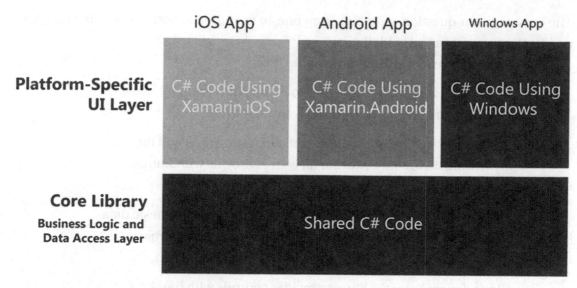

Figure 1-4. *Platform-specific UI solution architecture*

If you compare this diagram to the Xamarin.Forms diagram in Figure 1-2, you'll see that there's a lot more coding to be done here: a UI for every platform as opposed to one for all. Why would anyone bother to do it this way? There are quite a few good reasons why some or even all of the code might be done better this way. So how do we know when to use Forms?

Choosing Xamarin.Forms or a Platform-Specific UI

Most Xamarin projects are faced with this decision:

Which do I use, Xamarin.Forms or a Xamarin platform-specific UI?

The comparison is ease and portability of Xamarin.Forms versus the full-featured functionality of Xamarin's platform-specific UIs, namely, Xamarin.Android and Xamarin.iOS. The platform-specific Xamarin APIs have considerably more features than Xamarin.Forms out of the box, although customization closes the gap with some work.

The answer to our question will range from one, to the other, to both, depending on your needs. Here are suggested guidelines:

Use Xamarin.Forms for the following:

Learning Xamarin: If you're new to mobile development using C#, then Xamarin.Forms is a great way to get started!

Sharing UI code: Save development and testing time and money by writing the UI only once for all your platforms with Xamarin. Forms (e.g., Android, iOS).

Business apps: Xamarin.Forms does these things well—basic data display, navigation, and data entry. This is a good fit for many business apps.

Basic design: Xamarin.Forms provides controls with baseline design features, facilitating basic visual formatting.

Simple cross-platform screens: Xamarin.Forms is great for creating fully functional basic screens. For more complex screens, leverage Xamarin.Forms custom renderers for platform-specific details.

Use a platform-specific UI (Xamarin.iOS or Xamarin.Android) for

Complex screens: When an entire screen (or an entire app) requires a nuanced and complex design and UI approach, and Xamarin.Forms isn't quite up to the task, go with a platform-specific UI using Xamarin.Android and Xamarin.iOS.

Consumer apps: Platform-specific UI has everything a developer needs to create a consumer app with complex visual design, nuanced gesture sensitivity, and high-end graphics and animation.

High design: This approach provides complete native UI APIs with low-level access to design properties on each control, allowing for a high visual standard of design. Native animation and graphics are also available with this approach.

Single-platform apps: If you're building for only one platform, and a cross-platform approach for your app is not important in the foreseeable future (a rare case even if you're starting with one platform), consider using a platform-specific UI.

However, clever developers are creating more and more advanced Forms apps. Also, the Xamarin development team at Microsoft moves quickly. With each new release of Xamarin.Forms, more properties and methods are included in the bindings, bringing this library closer to the platform-specific ones and giving us increased control over our cross-platform UI. Also, open-source projects and third-party tools such as Telerik's UI for Xamarin and Syncfusion Xamarin UI controls are swiftly extending the options available with added controls, charts, and data grids.

When complex tasks or high design are required by Xamarin.Forms, virtually anything is possible using customization.

Using Custom Renderers, Effects, and Native Views

You'll eventually need more from Xamarin.Forms than it gives you out of the box. When complex tasks or designs are required by Xamarin.Forms, virtually anything is possible using Xamarin.Forms customization. Custom renderers provide access to the lower-level, platform-specific, screen-rendering classes called renderers, which use platform-specific controls to create all Xamarin.Forms screens. Any Xamarin.Forms screen can be broken into platform-specific screens and classes using this approach. This means we can write a Xamarin.Forms page or app and customize it by platform whenever necessary. More about this in Chapter 8.

Custom renderers are powerful and thorough in their implementation as platform-specific enablers of Xamarin.Forms UI elements. Custom renderers are, however, heavy artillery. If you want something more tactical, like merely customizing a property on a Xamarin.Forms control, consider an "effect." In addition to exposing properties, effects also have the capacity to pass parameters to those properties and define events on Xamarin.Forms controls. You pass parameters to the effect using attached properties or the Common Language Runtime (CLR).

Sometimes you just want a real native control. You'll settle for nothing less than absolute power. Thankfully there's now a way to get this in Xamarin.Forms via native view declaration. They're easiest to use in XAML, secondarily in C#.

All of this means that you can write a Xamarin.Forms page or app and customize it by platform, which is raw power in your hands as you work with a cross-platform toolset.

Use customization mindfully or risk a fragmented UI code base that probably should have been written entirely as a platform-specific UI. Used judiciously, customization can turn your basic, lackluster product into a versatile, unique, popular app. Let's do a quick refresher of the mobile user interface.

Exploring the Elements of Mobile UIs

Xamarin is a unifying tool serving several platforms, many of which can have different names for the same things. Here are some unifying terms, weighted heavily in the direction of Xamarin.Forms:

> *Screens, views, and pages* in mobile apps are made up of several basic groups of components: pages, layouts, and controls. Pages can be full or partial screens or groups of controls. In Xamarin. Forms, these are called pages because they derive from the `Page` class. In iOS, they are views; and in Android, they're screens, layouts, or sometimes loosely referred to as activities.

> *Controls* are the individual UI elements we use to display information or provide selection or navigation. Xamarin.Forms calls these views, because a `View` is the class that controls inherit from. Certain controls are called widgets in Android. More on these shortly in Chapter 5.

> *Layouts* are containers for controls that determine their size, placement, and relationship to one another. Xamarin.Forms and Android use this term, while in iOS everything is a view. More on these in Chapter 3.

> *Lists*, typically scrollable and selectable, are one of the most important data display and selection tools in the mobile UI. More on these in Chapter 6.

> *Navigation* provides the user with a way to traverse the app by using menus, tabs, toolbars, lists, tappable icons, and the up and back buttons. More on this in Chapter 7.

> *Modals, dialog boxes, and alerts* are usually pop-up screens that provide information and require some response from the user. More on these in Chapter 7.

Now that we have context and some terminology to work with, let's get started with Xamarin.Forms!

Using the Xamarin.Forms UI

Pages, layouts, and views make up the core of the Xamarin.Forms UI (Figure 1-5). Pages are the primary container, and each screen is populated by a single Page class. A page may contain variations of the Layout class, which may then hold other layouts, used for placing and sizing their contents. The purpose of pages and layouts is to contain and present views, which are controls inherited from class View.

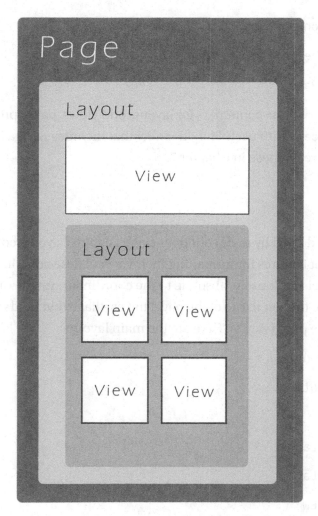

Figure 1-5. *Page, layouts, and views on a Xamarin.Forms screen*

Page

The Page class is the primary container of each main screen in the app. Derived from Xamarin.Forms.VisualElement, Page is a base class for the creation of other top-level UI classes. Here are the primary pages:

- ContentPage
- MasterDetailPage
- NavigationPage
- TabbedPage
- CarouselPage

In addition to serving as containers for layouts and views, pages provide a rich menu of prefabricated screens with useful functionality that includes navigation and gesture responsiveness. More on these in Chapter 7.

Layout

Views are placed and sized by their container class, Layout. Layouts come in a variety of flavors with different features for formatting their views. These containers allow views to be formatted precisely, loosely, absolute to the coordinate system, or relative to one another. Layouts are the soft tissue of the page, the cartilage that holds together the solid, visible aspects of the page (views). Here are the main layouts:

- StackLayout
- FlexLayout
- Grid
- AbsoluteLayout
- RelativeLayout
- ScrollView
- Frame
- ContentView

The layout's `Content` and/or `Children` properties contain other layouts and views. Horizontal and vertical alignment is set by the properties `HorizontalOptions` and `VerticalOptions`. Rows, columns, and cells within a layout can be padded with space, sized to expand to fill available space, or shrunk to fit their content. More on layouts in chapter 3.

Tip   Xamarin.Forms layouts are derived from the `View` class, so everything contained in a page is actually some form of a view.

View

Views are controls, the visible and interactive elements on a page. These range from the basic views like buttons, labels, and text boxes to the more advanced views like lists and navigation. Views contain properties that determine their content, font, color, and alignment. Horizontal and vertical alignment is set by properties `HorizontalOptions` and `VerticalOptions`. Like layouts, views can be padded with space, sized to expand to fill available space, or shrunk to fit their content. Later in this chapter, we'll code some views, then visit them again in Chapter 5 and throughout the book. These are the primary views grouped by function:

- Basic—fundamental views

  - `Label`

  - `Image`

  - `Button`

  - `BoxView`

- List—make a scrollable, selectable list

  - `ListView`

  - `SearchBar`

- Text entry—user entry of text strings using a keyboard

  - `Entry`

  - `Editor`

- Selection—user choice of a wide range of fields

  - `Picker`

  - `DatePicker`

  - `TimePicker`

  - `Stepper`

  - `Slider`

  - `Switch`

- User feedback—notify the user of app processing status

  - `ActivityIndicator`

  - `ProgressBar`

- Others

  - `Map`

  - `WebView`

Tip   Be careful not to confuse the Xamarin.Forms View class with a view meaning screen or presentation layer.

Creating a Xamarin.Forms Solution

Xamarin provides templates that contain the necessary projects to create a Xamarin. Forms app. A cross-platform solution usually contains these projects:

Xamarin.Forms: Cross-platform UI code called by one of the platform-specific projects. This can be accomplished using .NET Standard, though for backward compatibility, Portable Class Library (PCL) and shared project are also available. The example we'll be creating in this chapter uses .NET Standard.

Xamarin.Android: Android-specific code, including Android project startup.

Xamarin.iOS: iOS-specific code, including iOS project startup.

Core Library: Shared app logic such as business logic and data access layer using .NET Standard, a PCL, or a shared project.

Figure 1-6 shows the main projects usually found in a Xamarin.Forms solution.

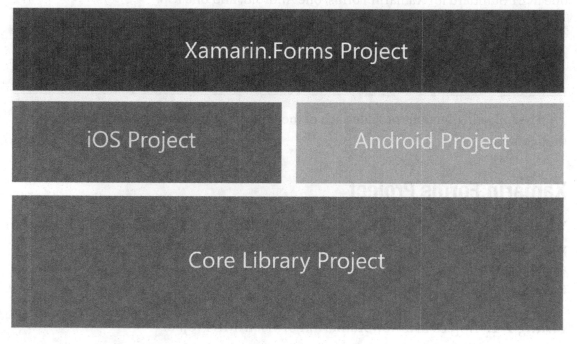

Figure 1-6. *Xamarin.Forms solution*

Tip   The Core Library project is not added by solution templates and must be created manually, either as a .NET Standard project or a shared project. If you are just getting started with Xamarin.Forms, you can skip the Core Library for now and put all your shared files in the Xamarin.Forms project.

Let's create a simple demo app to help us explore the foundations of Xamarin.Forms and many of its commonly used features.

Create a Xamarin.Forms solution. In Visual Studio, create a New Project and select project type Visual C# ➤ Cross-Platform ➤ Mobile App (Xamarin.Forms). In Visual Studio for Mac, create a New Solution and select project type Multi-platform ➤ App ➤ Xamarin.Forms ➤ Blank Forms App. Name it FormsExample.

This will create multiple projects: one for Xamarin.Forms code and then platform-specific projects including Android and iOS. The platform-specific projects available depend on whether you're on a PC or a Mac, whether you're in Visual Studio or Visual Studio for Mac, and the licenses you own. Visual Studio for Mac will give you an iOS project and an Android project. A PC with Visual Studio will create three projects: one .NET Standard for Xamarin.Forms, one Android, and one iOS.

Tip   Xamarin is free with a Visual Studio license, and Visual Studio Community edition is free.

The following sections provide each of the projects in the solution and the code they contain.

Xamarin.Forms Project

When using Visual Studio, the Xamarin.Forms project contains `App.cs` (Listing 1-1), which defines and returns the main page of the app. The `Application` object serves as the base class of `App` and provides the `MainPage` property as well as lifecycle events `OnStart`, `OnSleep`, and `OnResume`.

Listing 1-1. App.cs in a New Xamarin.Forms XAML Project

```
public partial class App : Application
{
    public App ()
    {
        InitializeComponent();

        MainPage = new MainPage();
    }

    protected override void OnStart ()
    {
        // Handle when your app starts
    }
```

```
    protected override void OnSleep ()
    {
        // Handle when your app sleeps
    }

    protected override void OnResume ()
    {
        // Handle when your app resumes
    }
}
```

Each platform has a wrapper class that takes the shared App class and renders it as its native implementation. The default code sets the MainPage property in its constructor to this case a `ContentPage` object called MainPage. Soon we will replace `MainPage` with our own `ContentPage` class and place controls on it using XAML.

Tip   A static `Application.Current` property references the current application object anywhere in your app.

The `OnStart`, `OnSleep`, and `OnResume` method overrides created for us are used to manage our app when it is moved to and from the background.

Application Lifecycle Methods: OnStart, OnSleep, and OnResume

When the user clicks the Back or Home (or App Switcher) buttons on their device, an app moves into the background. When they reselect the app again, it resumes and moves back into the foreground. The starting of an app, the progression of the app from the foreground into a background state then back into the foreground again, until termination, is called the application *lifecycle*. The `Application` class includes three virtual methods to handle lifecycle events:

- **OnStart**—Called when the app is first started. Useful for loading values into memory that are needed by the app.

- **OnSleep**—Called each time the app is moved into the background. Useful for cleanup and initiating background calls.

- **OnResume**—Called when the app is resumed after being in the background. Useful for reloading values into memory and returning from background threads.

OnSleep is also used for normal application termination (not a crash). Any time an app moves into a background state, it must be assumed that it may never return from that state.

Tip Use the Properties dictionary for disk persistence in these methods when an app is backgrounded. See Chapter 7 for more on state management.

Building Pages Using ContentPage

The MainPage property in App.cs (Listing 1-1) is assigned the default page in Xamarin. Forms: MainPage. The XAML for MainPage is shown in Listing 1-2. It contains one layout called StackLayout and one view or control called Label.

Listing 1-2. MainPage.xaml in a New Xamarin.Forms XAML Project

```xml
<?xml version="1.0" encoding="utf-8" ?>
<ContentPage xmlns="http://xamarin.com/schemas/2014/forms"
             xmlns:x="http://schemas.microsoft.com/winfx/2009/xaml"
             xmlns:local="clr-namespace:MyApp"
             x:Class=" MyApp.MainPage">
    <StackLayout>
        <!-- Place new controls here -->
        <Label Text="Welcome to Xamarin.Forms!"
            HorizontalOptions="Center"
            VerticalOptions="CenterAndExpand" />
    </StackLayout>
</ContentPage>
```

MainPage's C# code behind is simple, as you can see in Listing 1-3. The class derives from ContentPage and has an InitializeComponent method in its constructor to render its accompanying XAML.

Listing 1-3. `MainPage.xaml.cs` in a New Xamarin.Forms XAML Project

```
public partial class MainPage : ContentPage
    {
        public MainPage()
        {
            InitializeComponent();
        }
    }
```

`ContentPage` has properties that affect the appearance of the page. The `Padding` property creates space around the margins of the page to improve readability and design. `BackgroundImage` can contain an image that is displayed on the background of the page.

Several of `ContentPage`'s members are useful for navigation and state management. The `Title` property contains text, and the `Icon` property contains an image that is displayed at the top of the page when `NavigationPage` is implemented. Lifecycle methods `OnAppearing` and `OnDisappearing` can be overridden to handle initialization and finalization of a `ContentPage`. The `ToolBarItems` property is useful for creating a drop-down menu. All of these navigation-related members are covered in Chapter 7.

Xamarin.Android

The Android project contains a startup file called `MainActivity.cs`, which defines an activity class inherited from `Xamarin.Forms.Platform.Android.FormsApplicationActivity` as seen in Listing 1-4.

Listing 1-4. `MainActivity.cs` in the FormsExample.Droid Project

```
namespace FormsExample.Droid
{
    [Activity(Label = "FormsExample", Icon = "@drawable/icon",
    MainLauncher = true, ConfigurationChanges = ConfigChanges.
    ScreenSize | ConfigChanges.Orientation)]
    public class MainActivity : global::Xamarin.Forms.Platform.
    Android.FormsApplicationActivity
    {
```

```
protected override void OnCreate(Bundle bundle)
{
    base.OnCreate(bundle);
    global::Xamarin.Forms.Forms.Init(this, bundle);
    LoadApplication(new App());
}
    }
}
```

In the OnCreate method, Xamarin.Forms is initialized and LoadApplication sets App as the current Application.

Xamarin.iOS

The iOS project contains a startup file called AppDelegate (Listing 1-5) which inherits from Xamarin.Forms.Platform.iOS.FormsApplicationDelegate.

Listing 1-5. AppDelegate.cs in the FormsExample.iOS Project

```
namespace FormsExample.iOS
{
    [Register("AppDelegate")]
    public partial class AppDelegate : global::Xamarin.Forms.
    Platform.iOS.FormsApplicationDelegate
    {
        public override bool FinishedLaunching(UIApplication app,
        NSDictionary options)
        {
            global::Xamarin.Forms.Forms.Init();
            LoadApplication(new App());
            return base.FinishedLaunching(app, options);
        }
    }
}
```

Xamarin.Forms is initialized in the Init() method and LoadApplication sets App as the current page.

All of our platform-specific initializers, the Android MainActivity and the iOS AppDelegate, get the starting page from the Xamarin.Forms App class, which, by default, returns a stubbed demo page.

Core Library

The Core Library is a project in a Xamarin.Forms solution for the business and/or data access layer of an app which should be largely platform independent. Although *not explicitly created* as part of the Xamarin.Forms solution templates, a Core Library project is standard practice. Create one yourself and add it to your solution. This can contain data models, shared files or resources, data access, business logic, or references to PCLs. This is the place for platform-independent middle-tier or back-end non-UI code. It is referenced by any or all of the other projects in the solution. Use it to optimize code reuse and to decouple the UI projects from the data access layer and business logic. Note Core Library is an advanced solution architecture. If you're just starting out with Xamarin.Forms, consider putting your data access, business logic, and shared code in the Xamarin.Forms project, and hold off on using a Core Library for now.

Now we need to build out the pages of our app. Time to code!

Setting the App's Main Page

First we create a custom page in the Xamarin.Forms project and set it to be the app's main page. Add a new file to your project and select the Content Page. This will create a class inherited from ContentPage. Call it ContentPageExample. Both a XAML and a C# code behind file will be created. Here's the XAML file, ContentPageExample.xaml:

```
<ContentPage xmlns="http://xamarin.com/schemas/2014/forms"
        xmlns:x="http://schemas.microsoft.com/winfx/2009/xaml"
        x:Class="FormsExample.ContentPageExample">
    <ContentPage.Content>
        <StackLayout>
            <Label Text="Welcome to Xamarin.Forms!"
                VerticalOptions="CenterAndExpand"
                HorizontalOptions="CenterAndExpand" />
```

```
        </StackLayout>
    </ContentPage.Content>
</ContentPage>
```

Here is the C# code behind called ContentPageExample.cs:

```
namespace FormsExample
{
    public partial class ContentPageExample : ContentPage
    {
        public ContentPageExample ()
        {
            InitializeComponent ();
        }
    }
}
```

Then back in the Xamarin.Forms App.cs, we update the App constructor to set an instance of our new ContentPageExample class as the MainPage:

```
namespace FormsExample
{
    public class App : Application
    {
        public App()
        {
            MainPage = new ContentPageExample();
        }
```

Now we have the custom page class ready and can load up our ContentPageExample XAML file with controls.

Adding Xamarin.Forms Views

View is the term for *control* in Xamarin.Forms, the smallest unit of UI construction. Most views inherit from the View class and provide basic UI functions, such as a label or a button. From this point on, we will use the terms *view* and *control* interchangeably.

Tip   All example code solutions can be found under the title of this book on `https://www.apress.com/us/book/9781484240298` in the Source Code/ Downloads tab, or on GitHub at `https://github.com/danhermes/xamarin-xaml-book-examples`.

Let's start simply and put some views into ContentPageExample.xaml.

Label View

Labels display single or multiline text. Here are some examples:

```
<Label Text="Label" FontSize="40" HorizontalOptions="Center" />
<Label FontSize="20" HorizontalOptions="CenterAndExpand">
    <Label.Text>
        This control is great for
        displaying one or more
        lines of text.
    </Label.Text>
</Label>
```

Multiline text happens *implicitly* when enough text is used that it wraps, or *explicitly* with line breaks.

A Label view has two types of alignment, view-justification and text-justification. The entire view is justified within a layout using the HorizonalOptions and VerticalOptions properties assigned using LayoutOptions. Label text is justified within a Label using Label's HorizontalTextAlignment and VerticallTextAlignment properties.

```
HorizontalTextAlignment = "End"
```

The TextAlignment enumeration assigned to these alignment properties has three values: Start, Center, and End.

Next, the labels must be assigned to a layout for placement on the page. In this example we use the text alignment defaults and don't explicitly declare text alignment.

Placing Views Using StackLayout

A Layout view acts as a container for other views. Since a ContentPage can have only one layout or view, all the views on our page must be placed in a single container that is assigned to the ContentPage's Content property. Here we employ StackLayout, a subclass of Layout that can "stack" child views vertically in ContentPageExample.xaml:

```
<StackLayout HeightRequest="1500">
    <Label Text = "Label" FontSize="40" HorizontalOptions="Center" />
    <Label FontSize="20" HorizontalOptions="CenterAndExpand">
        <Label.Text>
            This control is great for
            displaying one or more
            lines of text.
        </Label.Text>
    </Label>
</StackLayout>
```

We place all the child views onto the StackLayout parent view and set the requested height with HeightRequest. HeightRequest has been set larger than the visible page so later we can make it scroll.

Note   StackLayout child views are laid vertically unless horizontal order is specified using Orientation = "Horizontal".

Compile and run the code. Figure 1-7 shows our labels on the StackLayout for iOS and Android, respectively.

Figure 1-7. *Xamarin.Forms Labels on a StackLayout*

If you're using iOS and want your Xamarin.Forms projects to look more like examples in this book that have a black background and white text, or you're using another platform and want more of an iOS look, setting background color and font color can help you.

Background Color and Font Color

Page background color and view font color can be changed using the `ContentPage`'s `BackgroundColor` property and the `TextColor` property found on text-based `Views`.

If you are working on an iOS project and want your work to look more like the book examples with black backgrounds, add this line to your page:

```
<ContentPage BackgroundColor= "Black"
```

If you want it to look more classically iOS, then set it to `Color.White`. Text color will then be set automatically to a lighter color. However, you can control text color manually on text controls with the `TextColor` property.

```
<Label TextColor= "White"
```

We use fonts in many controls, so let's do a quick overview of those.

Using Fonts

Format text on controls by using these properties:

> *FontFamily*: Set the name of the font in the `FontFamily` property;
> otherwise, the platform's default font will be used, for example,
> `FontFamily = "Courier"`.

> *FontSize*: The font size and weight are specified in the `FontSize`
> property using a double value or a `NamedSize` enumeration. Here
> is an example using a double: `FontSize = "40"`. Set a relative
> size by using `NamedSize` values such as `NamedSize.Large`, using
> `NamedSize` members `Large`, `Medium`, `Small`, and `Micro`, for
> example, `FontSize ="Large"`.

FontAttributes: Font styles such as bold and italics are specified using the FontAttributes property. Single attributes are set like this: FontAttributes = "Bold" options are None, Bold, and Italic.

Multiple attributes are specified using an attribute string formatted as "[font-face],[attributes],[size]".

Tip   These text formatting properties can be also set up app-wide using Styles, which is covered in Chapter 4.

Using Platform-Specific Fonts

Make sure your font name will work for all your target platforms, or your page may fail mysteriously. If you need different font names per platform, use the OnPlatform tag, which sets the value according to the platform, like this:

```
<Label.FontFamily>
    <OnPlatform x:TypeArguments="x:String">
            <On Platform="iOS">Courier</On>
            <On Platform="Android">Droid Sans Mono</On>
    </OnPlatform>
</Label.FontFamily>
```

Tip   Another way to declare the On tags in OnPlatform involves the Value parameter.

```
<On Platform="Android" Value="Droid Sans Mono"/>
```

Button View

Xamarin.Forms buttons are rectangular and clickable.

Let's add a plain ole button:

```
<Button Text = "Make It So" FontSize="Large" HorizontalOptions="Center"
    VerticalOptions="Fill" Clicked="ButtonClicked" />
```

The Text property contains the text visible on the button. HorizontalOptions and VerticalOptions (discussed in the next section) determine the control's alignment and size. This NamedSize font setting makes the font Large.

Tip   Buttons can be customized using the BorderColor, BorderWidth, BorderRadius, and TextColor properties. The BorderWidth is defaulted to zero on iOS.

Add the button to our StackLayout.

```
<StackLayout HeightRequest="1500">
    <Label Text = "Label" FontSize="40" HorizontalOptions="Center" />
    <Label FontSize="20" HorizontalOptions="CenterAndExpand">
        <Label.Text>
            This control is great for
            displaying one or more
            lines of text.
        </Label.Text>
    </Label>
    <Button Text = "Make It So" FontSize="Large" HorizontalOptions="Center"
        VerticalOptions="Fill" Clicked="ButtonClicked" />
</StackLayout>
```

Figure 1-8 shows the new button.

Figure 1-8. *Xamarin.Forms Button*

Now let's assign an event handler in `ContentPageExample.cs`, either inline:

```
button.Clicked += (sender, args) =>
{
  ((Button)sender) = "It is so!";
};
```

Or by assigning a method:

```
button.Clicked += OnButtonClicked;
```

...which is called outside the page constructor:

```
void OnButtonClicked(object sender, EventArgs e)
    {
        ((Button)sender) = "It is so!";
    };
```

When you click the button, the button text changes, as in Figure 1-9.

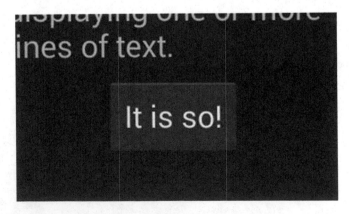

Figure 1-9. `button.Clicked` *event fired*

Tip   BorderWidth assigns the weight of the line that draws the button.

Setting View Alignment and Size: HorizontalOptions and VerticalOptions

Horizontal and vertical alignment and, to a certain degree, the size of controls are managed by setting the HorizontalOptions and/or VerticalOptions properties to a value of the LayoutOptions class, for example:

```
<Button HorizontalOptions="Center" VerticalOptions="Fill" />
```

Considerations in view layout are the *space provided* to the view by the layout and surrounding elements, the *padding* space around the view, and the *size* of the view itself. These types of formatting are accomplished using LayoutOptions and AndExpand.

Justification with LayoutOptions

Individual control layout is defined along a single axis by setting the HorizontalOptions or VerticalOptions property to one of the LayoutOptions classes:

- Start left or top—justifies the control (depending upon layout Orientation).

- Center centers the control.

- End right or bottom—justifies the control.

- Fill expands the size of the control to fill the space provided.

For example:

```
<Button HorizontalOptions = "Start" />
```

AndExpand Pads with Space

Setting HorizontalOptions or VerticalOptions to these LayoutOptions classes provides padding space around the view:

- StartAndExpand left or top-justifies the control and pads around the control with space.

- CenterAndExpand centers the control and pads around the control with space.

- EndAndExpand right or bottom-justifies the control and pads around the control with space.

- FillAndExpand expands the size of the control and pads around the control with space.

For example:

```
<Button HorizontalOptions = "StartAndExpand" />
```

Tip HorizontalOptions set to Fill and FillandExpand look the same with a single control in a column.

VerticalOptions set to Center or Fill is useful only if vertical space has been explicitly provided. Otherwise, these options can appear to do nothing. LayoutOptions.Fill won't make your control taller if there's no space to grow.

VerticalOptions set to Expand and CenterAndExpand imposes padding space around a control in a StackLayout.

There are more formatting examples later in this chapter and a lot more on the topic of control layout and alignment in Chapter 3. Next let's create some user input.

Entry View for Text Input

The following code creates a text box for user entry of a single line of text. Entry inherits from the InputView class, a derivative of the View class.

```
<Entry Placeholder="Username" VerticalOptions="Center" Keyboard="Text" />
```

User input goes into the Text property as a String.

Note the use of the Placeholder property, an inline label for the name of the field and a common technique in the mobile UI often preferable to space-consuming labels placed above or beside the entry control. The Keyboard property is a member of InputView and provides a range of options for the onscreen keyboard that appears for input, including Text, Numeric, Telephone, URL, and Email. Remember to add the entry to your StackLayout (see Listing 1-6 later in the chapter). Figure 1-10 shows the new entry control for username.

Figure 1-10. *Xamarin.Forms user entry view*

Tip   Set IsPassword = "True" to replace entered text letters with dots.
For multiline entry, use the Editor control.

BoxView

The BoxView control creates a colored graphical rectangle, useful as a placeholder that can be later replaced by an image or other more complex control or group of controls. This control is useful when you're waiting on the designer to get his/her act together.

```
<BoxView Color="Silver" WidthRequest="150" HeightRequest="150"
    HorizontalOptions="StartAndExpand" VerticalOptions="Fill" />
```

The Color property can be set to any Color member value. The default dimensions are 40×40 pixels, which can be changed using the WidthRequest and HeightRequest properties.

Tip   Be careful when setting `HorizontalOptions` and `VerticalOptions` to `Fill` and `FillAndExpand`, as this can override your `HeightRequest` and `WidthRequest` dimensions.

Add the BoxView to your StackLayout (see Listing 1-6 later in the chapter) and see the result here in Figure 1-11.

Figure 1-11. *Xamarin.Forms BoxView*

Eventually your designer will give you those promised icons and you can replace your BoxViews with real images.

Image View

The Image view holds an image for display on your page from a local or online file:

```
<Image Source="monkey.png" Aspect="AspectFit" HorizontalOptions="End"
VerticalOptions="Fill" />
```

Figure 1-12 shows the monkey image at the bottom right.

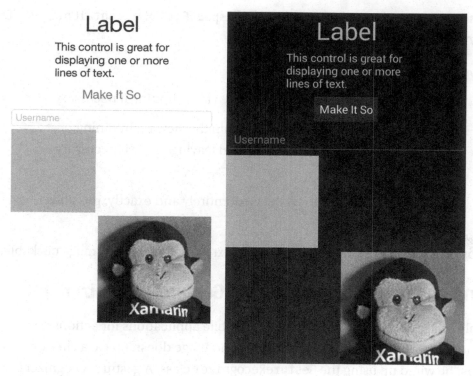

Figure 1-12. *Image view*

Let's look at how an image is handled.

Local Images

Local image files have platform-specific image folders in their respective projects:

> ***Android*** uses the Resources/drawable folder. Don't use special characters in the filename. The Build Action must be set to Android Resource.

> **iOS** 9 and later uses Asset Lists and Image Sets which can be set up in Visual Studio on the iOS project. Apple has deprecated the /Resources folder approach where we would create images for Retina displays with an @2x or @3x suffix on the filename.

Image Sizing: Aspect Property

The Image.Aspect property determines image sizing and is set by using the Aspect enumerator—for example:

```
<Image Source="monkey.png" Aspect="AspectFit" HorizontalOptions="End"
VerticalOptions="Fill" />
```

These are the Aspect members:

AspectFill: Scale the image to fill the view, clipping if necessary.

AspectFit: Scale the image to fit within the view maintaining
the aspect ratio with no distortion and leaving space if necessary
(letterboxing).

Fill: Scale the image to fill the view entirely and exactly, possibly
distorting the image.

Those are the image formatting options. Next we will make our image clickable.

Making an Image Clickable with a GestureRecognizer

Tappable images and icons are common in mobile applications for actions and
navigation. Like many Xamarin.Forms views, the Image doesn't have a click or tap event
and must be wired up using the GestureRecognizer class. A gesture recognizer is a class
that can be added to many views to respond to user interaction. It currently supports
just the tap gesture. The terms *click* and *tap* are used interchangeably in mobile UI
development.

Add the standard gesture recognizer to the image.

```
<Image Source="monkey.png" Aspect="AspectFit" HorizontalOptions="End"
VerticalOptions="Fill" >
    <Image.GestureRecognizers>
        <TapGestureRecognizer Tapped="ImageTapped"/>
    </Image.GestureRecognizers>
</Image>
```

Create a handler to manage the Tapped event. Change the image's Opacity to .5 in
the handler, which will fade the image slightly when tapped.

```
protected void ImageTapped(object sender, EventArgs e) {
    Image image = ((Image)sender);
    image.Opacity = .5;
    image.Opacity = 1;
}
```

Give that a try and make your monkey fade so you can see that the gesture recognizer works.

Tip   An alternative implementation of `GestureRecognizer` uses the `Command` property:

```
<Image.GestureRecognizers>
<TapGestureRecognizer Command="{Binding ImageTappedCommand}"/>
</Image.GestureRecognizers>
```

User feedback is a crucial concept in mobile UI development. Any time a user does something in the UI there should be some subtle acknowledgment by the app. A tap, for instance, should respond to the user with visible feedback. Usually an image will gray out or have a white background for a sec when touched. Let's do that professionally using the image's `Opacity` property but adding `async/await` to create a slight delay in our fade without affecting the app's performance.

Add an `async/await` with a delay that will cause the image to fade slightly for a fraction of a second. Remember to add `using System.Threading.Tasks;` to the top of your .cs file.

```
async protected void ImageTapped(object sender, EventArgs e) {
      Image image = ((Image)sender);
      image.Opacity = .5;
      await Task.Delay(200);
      image.Opacity = 1;
  }
```

Tapping on the image will now fade the image slightly, then back to normal, providing a responsive user experience.

Tip   For more subtle animation, instead of Opacity, use the FadeTo method:

```
await image.FadeTo(0.5, 450);
await Task.Delay(1000);
await image.FadeTo(1, 450);
```

In your own projects, you'll use gesture recognizers (and `async/await`) to actually *do* something when an image is tapped. If you want to see `async/await` in action in this example, bump up the `Delay` to 2000, then click the "Make It So" button while it's `awaiting` and you'll see that the app is still responsive. You could do many things in this `Tapped` handler without interrupting the flow of the app! Often when a button or image is pressed, the result should be backgrounded using `async/await` for an optimal user experience.

Tip   `Async/await` is a standard C# technique for queuing up activities in the background for simultaneous activity using the Task Parallel Library (TPL). Many Xamarin methods and functions are provisioned for background processing using `async/await`.

We have one more view to add, a container class to permit scrolling of our views.

ScrollView

The `ScrollView` layout contains a single child and imparts scrollability to its contents:

```
<ScrollView VerticalOptions="FillAndExpand">
```

Here we nest the `StackLayout` within this `ScrollView,` so our entire layout of views will now be scrollable.

```
<ScrollView VerticalOptions="FillAndExpand">
    <StackLayout HeightRequest="1500">
    <Label Text = "Label" FontSize="40" HorizontalOptions="Center" />
        ...
    </StackLayout>
</ScrollView>
```

Tip   `ScrollView` scrolls vertically by default but can also scroll sideways using the Orientation property. For example, `Orientation = "Horizontal"`.

That's it for the views on this page. The final touch will be padding around the entire page, so views won't be mashed up against the sides of the screen.

Padding Around the Entire Page

The ContentPage's Padding property creates space around the entire page. Here's the property assignment:

```
<ContentPage.Padding> [left], [top], [right], [bottom]
</ContentPage.Padding>
```

This example will place padding left, right, and bottom, but not top:

```
<ContentPage.Padding> 10, 0, 10, 5 </ContentPage.Padding>
```

This code will pad horizontal sides, left and right, and vertical sides, top and bottom:

```
<ContentPage.Padding> 10, 5 </ContentPage.Padding>
```

This will place equal space on all four sides:

```
<ContentPage.Padding> 10 </ContentPage.Padding>
```

If you're using an iPhone or iPad, then your app may extend onto the top of the screen, obscuring the status bar. The following example will slide a page just below the iOS status bar while keeping the page flush to the top of the screen for other OSes. The OnPlatform method supplies different values or actions depending on the native OS (iOS, Android). In this case, the Padding property is platform-dependent.

```
<ContentPage.Padding>
  <OnPlatform x:TypeArguments="Thickness">
    <On Platform="iOS" Value="10, 20, 10, 5"/>
    <On Platform="Android" Value="10, 0, 10, 5"/>
  </OnPlatform>    </ContentPage.Padding>
```

This last Padding expression is what we use in this project and in most projects in this book, padding around the edges of the page with a bit more room at the top on iOS for the status bar.

Figure 1-13 shows a final build and run on both platforms.

Figure 1-13. *Final build and run of the FormsExample solution*

CODE COMPLETE: Adding Xamarin.Forms Views

Listings 1-6 and 1-7 provide the complete code for the added Xamarin.Forms views in the FormsExample solution. This listing contains the more recent form of OnPlatform.

Listing 1-6. ContentPageExample.xaml in the FormsExample Project

```
<?xml version="1.0" encoding="UTF-8"?>
<ContentPage xmlns="http://xamarin.com/schemas/2014/forms" xmlns:x="http://
schemas.microsoft.com/winfx/2009/xaml" x:Class="FormsExample.
ContentPageExample">
    <ContentPage.Padding>
        <OnPlatform x:TypeArguments="Thickness">
          <OnPlatform.iOS>
            10, 20, 10, 5
```

```xml
        </OnPlatform.iOS>
        <OnPlatform.Android>
          10, 0, 10, 5
        </OnPlatform.Android>
        <OnPlatform.WinPhone>
          10, 0, 10, 5
        </OnPlatform.WinPhone>
      </OnPlatform>
  </ContentPage.Padding>
  <ContentPage.Content>
      <ScrollView VerticalOptions="FillAndExpand">
          <StackLayout HeightRequest="1500">
              <Label Text = "Label" FontSize="40"
              HorizontalOptions="Center" />
              <Label FontSize="20" HorizontalOptions="CenterAndExpand">
                  <Label.Text>
                      This control is great for
                      displaying one or more
                      lines of text.
                  </Label.Text>
              </Label>
              <Button Text = "Make It So" FontSize="Large"
              HorizontalOptions="Center" VerticalOptions="Fill"
              Clicked="ButtonClicked" />
              <Entry Placeholder="Username" VerticalOptions="Center"
              Keyboard="Text" />
              <BoxView Color="Silver" WidthRequest="150"
              HeightRequest="150" HorizontalOptions="StartAndExpand"
              VerticalOptions="Fill" />
              <Image Source="monkey.png" Aspect="AspectFit"
              HorizontalOptions="End" VerticalOptions="Fill" >
                  <Image.GestureRecognizers>
                      <TapGestureRecognizer Tapped="ImageTapped"/>
                  </Image.GestureRecognizers>
              </Image>
```

```
            </StackLayout>
        </ScrollView>
    </ContentPage.Content>
</ContentPage>
```

Listing 1-7. ContentPageExample.xaml.cs *in the FormsExample Project*

```csharp
using System;
using System.Collections.Generic;
using System.Threading.Tasks;
using Xamarin.Forms;

namespace FormsExample
{
    public partial class ContentPageExample : ContentPage
    {
        public ContentPageExample ()
        {
            InitializeComponent ();
        }

        protected void ButtonClicked(object sender, EventArgs e) {

            ((Button)sender).Text = "It is so!";
        }

        async protected void ImageTapped(object sender, EventArgs e) {

            Image image = ((Image)sender);

            image.Opacity = .5;
            await Task.Delay(200);
            image.Opacity = 1;
        }
    }
}
```

Summary

Xamarin.Forms provides a jumping-off point for cross-platform mobile app UI development, fully loaded with stock and customizable pages, layouts, and views. This book tackles Xamarin development using XAML for UI declaration with C# code behinds.

A Xamarin.Forms solution typically has a separate project for each of these platforms: Android and iOS. A Xamarin.Forms project is useful for housing cross-platform UIs, and a Core Library project contains the business logic and data access layer.

Developers are faced with a decision of Xamarin.Forms vs. a platform-specific UI approach with Xamarin.Android and Xamarin.iOS. The more Xamarin.Forms releases that come out, the less of a decision this is, as Xamarin.Forms approaches the functionality of native UI APIs. Xamarin.Forms custom renderers, effects, and native views help us combine the two approaches.

View is the Xamarin.Forms term for *control*, and we delved into a few of the most frequently used views: `Label`, `Entry`, `BoxView`, `Image`, `StackLayout`, and `ScrollView`.

Xamarin.Forms XAML, like all markup languages, comes with its own set of considerations, grammars, rules, and techniques to help us build our apps UI. Let's dive into XAML!

CHAPTER 2

Building Xamarin.Forms Apps Using XAML

The eXtensible Application Markup Language (XAML, pronounced "zammel") is used to define user interfaces (UI) for frameworks such as the Windows Presentation Foundation (WPF), the Universal Windows Platform (UWP), and Xamarin.Forms. These XAML dialects share the same syntax based on the 2009 XAML specification but differ in their vocabularies, which may eventually be aligned under one XAML Standard.

Every XAML document is an XML document with one root element and nested child elements. In XAML, an element represents a corresponding C# class such as an application, a visual element, or control defined in Xamarin.Forms. The attributes of the elements represent the properties or events supported by the class. XAML provides two ways to assign values to properties and events—as an attribute of the element or as a child element. Either way, the attribute assigns the value of a property or wires an event to an event handler you write in C# in the code behind file.

As I mentioned in the intro, my other book, *Xamarin Mobile Application Development,* focused on creating UI for Xamarin.Forms using C#. This book is about creating UI using XAML. XAML helps you separate the visual design from the underlying business logic. XAML and accompanying code behind files are written using Visual Studio or Visual Studio for Mac.

In this chapter, we will focus primarily on XAML syntax to help you read and write XAML. We'll begin with basic XAML syntax: tags can form elements which can be decorated with attributes which are property/value pairs, all of which are nested into a hierarchy. XAML elements can represent real classes and their members. We'll use namespaces to extend the vocabulary available in an XML document. XAML syntax employs a number of approaches for the definition of elements and attributes ranging

© Dan Hermes 2019
D. Hermes and N. Mazloumi, *Building Xamarin.Forms Mobile Apps Using XAML,*
https://doi.org/10.1007/978-1-4842-4030-4_2

from the property element syntax to the collection syntax. Each XAML file has a C# code behind. The XAML Standard is the holy grail of XAML development so we'll touch on it.

Since XAML is based upon XML, let us first delve into basic XML syntax.

Basic Syntax

Xamarin.Forms XAML is based on XML and the 2009 XAML specification. A basic understanding of these two languages is essential to be able to read and write XAML effectively.

The XML syntax determines the basic structure of XAML files comprised of elements, attributes, and namespaces. The 2009 XAML specification applies XML to the realm of programming languages where elements represent classes and attributes class members. XAML adds basic data types, vocabulary to name and reference elements, and approaches to construct objects using constructors and factory methods of classes.

For some of you, the next few paragraphs may be a review, but if you're not up on your XML skills, then read carefully. Let's start with the basic structure of a XAML document based on XML.

XML Syntax

At the core of XAML is the eXtensible Markup Language (XML). The main building blocks of an XML document are elements, attributes, hierarchy, and namespaces. Elements are entities declared using begin and end tags and defined using tag-encased data or other tags. Attributes are properties assigned to an element. A hierarchy is the structure created using nested elements. Next we'll look at each in turn.

Element

The declaration of an element uses the *element syntax*, so it has a begin and end tag surrounding the element values. Use the element syntax to declare a Label view and to assign "Some Text":

```
<Label>Some Text</Label>
```

In an empty `Label`, the end tag can be omitted by adding a forward slash at the end of the begin tag, like this:

```
<Label/>
```

Attribute

Ascribe metadata to elements using *attributes*, which can be assigned a value. The *attribute syntax* is used to assign primitive values to an attribute by placing the attribute name inside the begin tag of an element, and its value is stored in double or single quotes following an equal sign. Use the attribute syntax to assign a value to the `Text` property of `Label`:

```
<Label Text="Some Text"/>
```

Hierarchy

A typical XML document is comprised of many nested elements, referred to as a *hierarchy*. In Chapter 1, Listing 1-7, a sample page is defined, comprised of a `ContentPage` element, which includes a `StackLayout` element with several child views such as `Label` and `Button`. This makes XML particularly interesting for user interface design, where pages contain layouts and views. Use a `ContentPage` with a `StackLayout` that includes a `Label` and a `Button` to define the hierarchy of a page, as outlined in Listing 2-1.

Listing 2-1. Hierarchy of XML Elements

```
<ContentPage>
    <StackLayout>
        <Label Text="This control is great ..."/>
        <Button Text="Make It So"/>
    </StackLayout>
</ContentPage>
```

Tip   In XAML, element and attribute names correspond to class and member names in C#.

XML Namespaces

Namespaces extend the vocabulary available in an XML document, allowing the use of more uniquely defined elements and attributes. Each namespace is given a prefix to avoid ambiguity within an XML document in case multiple namespaces are used that may have elements or attributes with identical names. Add a namespace to an XML document using the XML `xmlns` attribute with the syntax `xmlns:prefix="URI"`. An element can have unlimited `xmlns` attributes for as long as the prefix is unique. For one `xmlns` declaration in the XML document, the prefix can be omitted, which makes the vocabulary of that namespace the default. All elements in the XML without a prefix belong to that namespace. Listing 1-7, in Chapter 1, adds the XAML and the Xamarin. Forms namespaces to the `ContentPage` element using

```
xmlns="http://xamarin.com/schemas/2014/forms"
xmlns:x="http://schemas.microsoft.com/winfx/2009/xaml"
```

In Xamarin the default namespace is reserved for the Xamarin.Forms namespace, which is why `ContentPage`, `StackLayout`, `Label`, and `Button` have no prefix. For XAML terms the prefix x needs to be added, e.g., `x:TypeArguments`, which is used in Chapter 1, Listing 1-6, to specify the platform-specific `Thickness`. Both XAML and Xamarin.Forms use as the Uniform Resource Identifier (URI) simply a Uniform Resource Locator (URL) for that matter, which is not further evaluated other than being unique.

Tip   XML namespaces can be declared on any element. However, in Xamarin. Forms all namespaces must be defined in the root element, e.g., `ContentPage`.

Those are the key syntaxes in XML, so now let's move on to XAML.

XAML Syntax

The 2009 XAML specification gives us a way to describe classes and class members in a declarative way using XML elements and attributes. Namespaces behave similarly to the `using` keyword in C#, allowing class libraries to extend the vocabulary available in XAML. XAML already comes with its own vocabulary including basic data types, markup extensions to extend the basic syntax with classes backed by code, and approaches to name and reference elements and to specify to the runtime how to construct objects.

Tip   XAML does not allow code or conditional expressions such as `for`, `while`, do, and `loop` inside the XML document.

At the end of this topic, the list of all XAML terms used in Xamarin.Forms is provided as a reference.

Classes and Members

In XAML, XML elements represent actual C# *classes* that are instantiated to objects at runtime. The *members* of a class are represented as XML attributes. At runtime, the assigned attribute value is used to set the value of the property of an object. The attribute name corresponds with the member name of a class. The `Label` element with the attribute Text in Listing 2-1 `<Label Text="This control is great ..."/>` represents a class `Label` that has a `public` member called Text. At runtime, an object of type `Label` will be instantiated and the value of its Text property will be set to `"This control is great ..."`. Use the attribute syntax to assign values of primitive types as `string`, `bool`, `double`, and `int` to an attribute. At runtime, these are projected to `String`, `Boolean`, `Double`, and `Int32` objects.

XAML Namespaces

Adding a namespace in XAML is equivalent to the `using` directive in C# and makes a C# namespace available to the XAML document, allowing any of the classes in that namespace to be used as elements in the XAML. XAML itself is added as a namespace to a `ContentPage` like this:

```
<ContentPage xmlns:x="http://schemas.microsoft.com/winfx/2009/xaml"
x:Class="FormsExample.ContentPageExample"/>
```

The URI points to Microsoft's web site, and the x prefix means that XAML elements and attributes have to use this prefix inside the document. Use `x:Class` to specify the C# name of a `ContentPage`, like this:

```
x:Class="FormsExample.ContentPageExample"
```

This defines that the class `ContentPageExample` in the namespace `FormsExample` is a subclass of `ContentPage`. This also means that there is an associated code behind file that contains your class definition for `ContentPageExample`, as demonstrated in Chapter 1, Listing 1-7.

In XAML the `xmlns` attribute in combination with the *Common Language Runtime* namespace (`clr-namespace`) and the `assembly` name can be used to load namespaces and libraries to the XAML document that are available within a project. For the sake of simplicity, we'll reference a system library, though typically we reference our local namespaces in the project. Listing 2-2 demonstrates how to use the .NET `System` library in the assembly `mscorlib.dll` in XAML in order to use `System.String` to assign a string literal to a `Label`.

Listing 2-2. Adding External Class Libraries

```
<ContentPage xmlns:sys="clr-namespace:System;assembly=mscorlib" ...>
    <Label><sys:String>Hello System.String</sys:String></Label>
</ContentPage>
```

The colon sign is used when specifying the namespace and the equal sign when specifying the assembly. The assembly name must correspond to the actual library that is referenced in your Xamarin project without the `.dll` file extension, which is the case for the majority of NuGet package names.

Markup Extensions

Markup extensions extend the basic XML syntax, are backed by code, and can perform specific tasks. You can use the attribute or element syntax to specify a markup extension. To distinguish a markup extension from a string literal, use curly braces when using the attribute syntax such as `{x:Static Color.Maroon}`.

Tip   In Xamarin.Forms any class that implements the `IMarkupExtension` interface and its method `ProvideValue` is a markup extension. All XAML markup extensions are implemented through this mechanism.

The intrinsic XAML markup extensions also supported by Xamarin.Forms include

- `Static`

- `Array`

- `Type`

- `Reference`

Let's look at each of them in detail.

Static

The *Static* markup extension is used to access static fields, properties, and constant fields as well as enumeration members. These do not need to be `public` as long as they are in the same assembly. In Chapter 1, the declaration `<BoxView Color="Maroon"/>` uses the `Color Maroon`, which is a `static` member of the class `Color`. With `Static` we can achieve the same result:

```
<BoxView Color="{x:Static Color.Maroon}" WidthRequest="150"
HeightRequest="150"/>
```

Alternatively, to the attribute syntax, the element syntax can be used when working with markup extensions, as shown in Listing 2-3.

Listing 2-3. Markup Extensions Using Element Syntax

```
<BoxView WidthRequest="150" HeightRequest="150">
    <BoxView.Color>
        <x:Static>Color.Lime</x:Static>
    </BoxView.Color>
</BoxView>
```

Figure 2-1 shows the `Maroon` and `Lime` boxes on iOS and Android platforms.

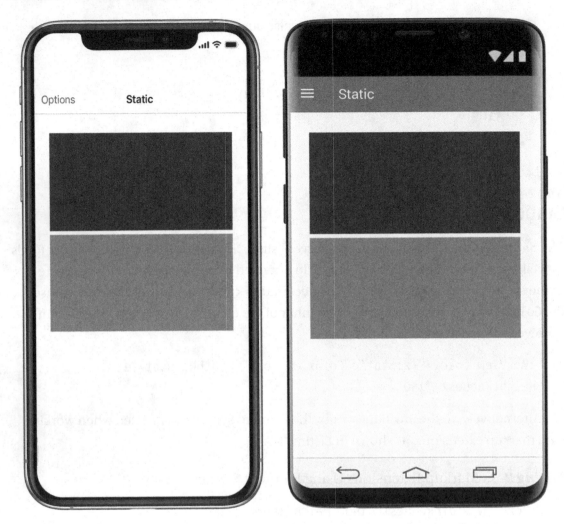

Figure 2-1. *Maroon and Lime BoxViews using Static to assign a value*

Array

Use the *Array* markup extension to define arrays with objects of a specific Type as shown in Listing 2-4 to create an Array of Strings.

Listing 2-4. Using Array

```
<x:Array Type="{x:Type x:String}">
    <x:String>A</x:String>
    <x:String>B</x:String>
</x:Array>
```

Use a `Picker` view to create a drop-down list, by assigning an `Array` to the `Picker`'s `ItemsSource`, like this:

```
<Picker><Picker.ItemsSource><x:Array>...</x:Array></Picker.ItemsSource>
</Picker>
```

Figure 2-2 shows the result on both platforms.

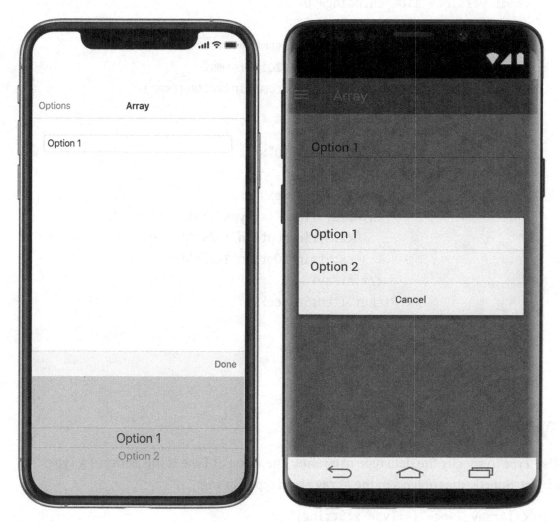

Figure 2-2. *Using Array as the ItemsSource of a Picker view*

CODE COMPLETE: Array Markup Extension

Listing 2-5 provides the complete code for creating a `Picker` that uses an `Array` as the `ItemsSource`.

Listing 2-5. Using Array

```xml
<?xml version="1.0" encoding="UTF-8"?>
<ContentPage Title="Array"
xmlns:sys="clr-namespace:System;assembly=mscorlib"
xmlns="http://xamarin.com/schemas/2014/forms"
xmlns:x="http://schemas.microsoft.com/winfx/2009/xaml"
x:Class="XamlExamples.ArrayPage">
    <ContentPage.Content>
        <StackLayout Padding="30,30">
            <Picker>
                <Picker.ItemsSource>
                    <x:Array Type="{x:Type x:String}">
                        <x:String>Option 1</x:String>
                        <x:String>Option 2</x:String>
                    </x:Array>
                </Picker.ItemsSource>
            </Picker>
        </StackLayout>
    </ContentPage.Content>
</ContentPage>
```

Type

Use *Type* to specify the data type of a value. The value of Type is the name of a Type object. Specify that objects in the `Array` are of type `String`:

```xml
<x:Array Type="{x:Type x:String}">
```

Reference

The *Reference* markup extension is used in combination with the Name directive to reference an object previously declared in the XAML. Use Name to assign a unique name to a Label view and Reference in an Entry control to reference the Label by its name in order to link the two Text properties, as shown in Listing 2-6.

Listing 2-6. Using x:Reference

```
<Label x:Name="MyLabel" Text="Hello Entry" />
<Entry Text="{Binding Path=Text, Source={x:Reference MyLabel}}" />
```

The example demonstrates the use of the Xamarin.Forms markup extension Binding, which is covered more in depth in Chapter 9. However, in the preceding example, we first use Binding to assign the Label view as the Source of the Entry control, that is, Source={x:Reference MyLabel}, and then link the Text property of Label to the Text attribute of the Entry through Text="{Binding Text, ...}".

The Binding markup extension demonstrates two other concepts related to markup extensions:

1. *Multiple properties*: Markup extensions are essentially C# classes with public members. Use a comma to assign values to multiple members, e.g., {Binding Path="", Source=""}.

2. *Nesting*: The values assigned to the properties of a markup extension can be objects. Use nested curly braces to assign complex values to a property, e.g., Source={x:Reference MyLabel}. The Reference markup extension is nested inside the Binding markup extension. At runtime, the innermost markup extension is evaluated first.

Figure 2-3 shows the result on both platforms.

Figure 2-3. *Binding Label as the Source to Entry and linking the two Text properties*

CODE COMPLETE: Reference Markup Extension

Listing 2-7 provides the complete code for creating a Label that is referenced by an Entry as the Source.

Listing 2-7. Using Reference

```xml
<?xml version="1.0" encoding="UTF-8"?>
<ContentPage Title="Reference"
xmlns="http://xamarin.com/schemas/2014/forms"
xmlns:x="http://schemas.microsoft.com/winfx/2009/xaml"
x:Class="XamlExamples.ReferencePage">
    <ContentPage.Content>
        <StackLayout Padding="30,30">
            <Label x:Name="MyLabel" Text="Hello Entry" />
            <Entry Text="{Binding Path=Text, Source={x:Reference
            MyLabel}}" />
        </StackLayout>
    </ContentPage.Content>
</ContentPage>
```

Tip   If the default value of a property is not `null`, use the XAML `Null` markup extension to set the value of a property to null, e.g., `<Label Text="{x:Null}"/>`.

Constructors

Each Xamarin.Forms XAML element provides a built-in *default constructor* to allow the runtime to instantiate an object without depending on any particular property. Values specified to attributes are assigned to the object properties after the object is instantiated. Some classes also have constructors that expect arguments or even *factory methods,* which are `public static` methods that may accept arguments and return an object. Let's discuss each of these approaches.

Default Constructor

All views in Xamarin.Forms have a built-in default constructor. The empty element tag can be used without any attributes to create an instance of the class it represents. Use the empty element DatePicker to instruct the runtime to create an instance of the view to select a date, like this:

```
<DatePicker/>
```

Non-default Constructor

Some Xamarin.Forms classes have additional constructors that require passing in arguments, referred to as *non-default constructors*. The Color class in Xamarin.Forms has several non-default constructors. Use the Arguments element to pass arguments to a constructor. The number of arguments must match one of the Color constructors. A single Double argument is used for grayscale colors; three Double parameters are used to construct a Color from red, green, and blue values; and four Double values are used to create a Color also passing in the alpha channel, as shown in Listing 2-8, to set the Color for a BoxView.

Listing 2-8. Utilizing Constructors and Passing in Parameters Using x:Arguments

```
<BoxView>
    <BoxView.Color>
        <Color>
            <x:Arguments>
                <x:Double>0.25</x:Double>
                <x:Double>0.75</x:Double>
                <x:Double>0.2</x:Double>
                <x:Double>0.9</x:Double>
            </x:Arguments>
        </Color>
    </BoxView.Color>
</BoxView>
```

Factory Method

Some Xamarin.Forms classes provide publicly accessible static methods, also known as *factory methods,* to construct an object. XAML provides the FactoryMethod attribute to specify the factory method an element should use in order to construct an object. The Color class has several factory methods, that is, FromRgb, FromRgba, FromHsla, and FromHex, to create a Color instance. Use FactoryMethod attribute inside the Color element begin tag to specify the factory method followed by the Arguments element to provide the parameters, as shown in Listing 2-9.

Listing 2-9. Constructing Objects Using Factory Methods

```
<BoxView>
    <BoxView.Color>
        <Color x:FactoryMethod="FromHex">
            <x:Arguments>
                <x:String>#02dd52</x:String>
            </x:Arguments>
        </Color>
    </BoxView.Color>
</BoxView>
```

Figure 2-4 shows the result on both platforms.

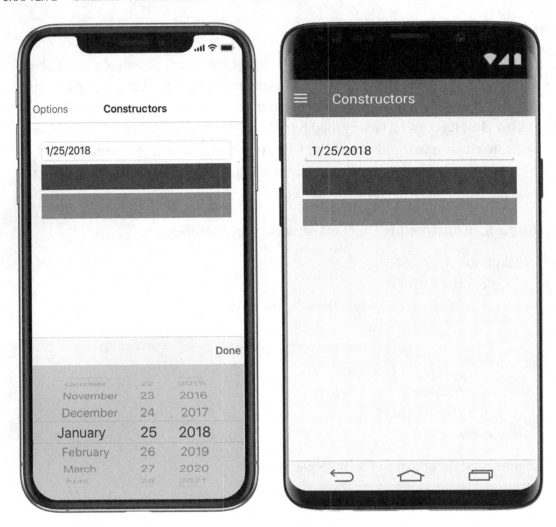

Figure 2-4. *Constructing views using the default constructors, non-default constructors, and factory methods*

CODE COMPLETE: XAML Constructors

Listing 2-10 provides the complete code for constructing objects using the default constructors, non-default constructors, and factory methods.

Listing 2-10. Default and Non-default Constructors and Factory Methods in XAML

```
<?xml version="1.0" encoding="UTF-8"?>
<ContentPage xmlns="http://xamarin.com/schemas/2014/forms"
xmlns:x="http://schemas.microsoft.com/winfx/2009/xaml"
```

```xml
      x:Class="XamlExamples.ConstructorsPage">
    <ContentPage.Content>
        <StackLayout Padding="30,30">
            <DatePicker />
            <BoxView>
                <BoxView.Color>
                    <Color>
                        <x:Arguments>
                            <x:Double>0.5</x:Double>
                            <x:Double>0.0</x:Double>
                            <x:Double>0.0</x:Double>
                            <x:Double>0.9</x:Double>
                        </x:Arguments>
                    </Color>
                </BoxView.Color>
            </BoxView>
            <BoxView>
                <BoxView.Color>
                    <Color x:FactoryMethod="FromHex">
                        <x:Arguments>
                            <x:String>#CDDC39</x:String>
                        </x:Arguments>
                    </Color>
                </BoxView.Color>
            </BoxView>
        </StackLayout>
    </ContentPage.Content>
</ContentPage>
```

Let's complete the XAML syntax topic with an overview of all XAML terms available in Xamarin.Forms.

XAML Terms

Xamarin.Forms supports a subset of the terms defined in the 2009 XAML specification, the majority of which we have discussed in this chapter. The purpose of this section is to provide a summary as a reference. The terms can be grouped into basic types that represent the respective C# type defined in the System namespace, keywords used to identify and reference elements, and terms used to construct objects:

- *Simple data types*: The following XAML basic types are supported by Xamarin.Forms. Use these terms to represent their corresponding types defined in the System namespace.

  - *Null*: Use the XAML Null markup extension to set the value of a property to null.

  - *Array*: Use Array to define arrays with objects of a specific Type.

  - *Type*: Use Type to specify the data type of a value.

  - *Object*: Represents System.Object and is useful if you want to create an array that can expect any type, e.g.: <x:Array Type="{x:Type x:Object}">...</x:Array>

  - *Boolean*, *Byte*, *Int16*, *Int32*, *Int64*, *Single*, *Double*, *Decimal*, *Char*, *String*, and *TimeSpan*: These are mapped to the corresponding simple type in C#.

  - *DateTime*: This type does not exist in the 2009 XAML specification and was added by Xamarin.Forms. Use DateTime to specify a date and time of day.

- *Classes, Identifiers, and References*: Use terms in this category to identify classes, name elements and reference them:

  - *Class*: Use Class in the root element of a XAML document to wire the element with its underlying C# class.

  - *Key*: Use Key register and uniquely identify a resource in a dictionary.

- *Name*: Use Name to assign a unique name to an element and have Xamarin.Forms create a local variable with this name created for you in the code behind.

- *Reference*: Use Reference in XAML to reference a previously named element.

- *Static*: Use Static to access static properties, fields, constants, or enumeration values.

- *Constructing objects*: Use the following terms to instantiate objects.

  - *Arguments*: Use this term to pass arguments to a non-default constructor or a factory method.

  - *TypeArguments*: Use TypeArguments to instantiate classes that use generics such as List<T> or Dictionary<T,T>. Using the System namespace, you can define your own dictionary in XAML <sys:Dictionary x:TypeArguments="sys:String,sys:Object"> that instantiates a Dictionary object at runtime with string as the key type and object as the value type.

  - *FactoryMethod*: Use FactoryMethod for elements that have a static method defined in the C# class and return an instance of the element.

Now that we've covered the important aspects of XAML syntax, let's move on to Xamarin.Forms syntax.

Xamarin.Forms Syntax

Xamarin.Forms syntax uses the element and attribute syntax introduced in XML to extend the functionality available in XAML. Six approaches are made available:

- *Property element syntax*: Use the property element syntax if the value that is being assigned is a complex object and cannot be represented by a string literal. Property elements can also specify platform-specific values using the OnPlatform tag.

- *Content property syntax*: Classes can have one of their members defined as a content property, which serves as a default property for the view. For brevity, this property name can then be omitted in the XAML, and the property value can be declared between the element's begin and end tag.

- *Enumeration value syntax*: Use this syntax to pass or assign a constant name of an enumeration to a property.

- *Event handler syntax*: Use the event handler syntax to wire a property that represents an event to the event handler defined in the code behind.

- *Collection syntax*: Some properties represent collections. Use the collection syntax to assign elements as children of the collections.

- *Attached property syntax*: Extend the functionality of elements using attached properties to define new properties for an element that elements have not defined themselves.

Let's examine each approach.

Property Element Syntax

A common approach to assign values to object properties is to use XML element tags instead of an attribute using the class.member notation for the element name. This is referred to as *property element syntax*. Use Label.Text to assign to the Text attribute of the Label element, e.g.:

```
<Label>
    <Label.Text>Hello</Label.Text>
</Label>
```

Content Property Syntax

In Xamarin.Forms, each element can have a default property where its value is assigned between the element's begin and end tags. Views can declare one of their properties as a content property using the C# attribute ContentProperty, e.g.:

```
[ContentProperty("Text")]
public class Label : View {}
```

ContentProperty indicates that the property can be omitted when using the property element syntax, which is referred to as *content property syntax*. In the following example, <Label.Text> can be omitted entirely, that is:

```
<Label>Hello</Label>
```

The content property syntax reduces the verbosity of the XAML document. Most of the Xamarin.Forms views, layouts, and pages specify a content property, such as the Content property of ContentPage. This means that the start and end tags <ContentPage.Content> and </ContentPage.Content> can also be omitted entirely in Listing 2-10.

Enumeration Value Syntax

Many classes in Xamarin.Forms use enumerations to restrict the values a member can be assigned to. The *enumeration value syntax* is based on the attribute syntax where the string literal assigned represents the constant name in an enumeration. Use the NamedSize enumeration to assign a platform-specific size to the FontSize attribute of Button, e.g.:

```
<Button FontSize="Medium" Text="Medium Size Button" />
```

In the example, Medium is assigned as the size to the FontSize property. Xamarin. Forms uses the built-in value converter class FontSizeConverter to evaluate the string literal, first trying to convert it to a Double and if that fails calling the Device. GetNamedSize method to convert the constant name Medium to the device-specific double value.

Some attributes allow a combination of enumeration values. These are referred to as *flags attributes*, which indicates that the enumeration is treated as a bit field. Use a comma to assign multiple flags to the FontAttributes property of Button, that is:

```
<Button FontAttributes="Italic,Bold" Text="Italic Bold Button" />
```

Event Handler Syntax

The *event handler* syntax is based on the attribute syntax and provides the foundation of XAML behaviors, commands, and triggers. Write an event handler in the code behind and wire them to Xamarin.Forms views to respond to user interactions. Specify the name of the event supported by a particular Xamarin.Forms view as attribute name and the name of the C# event handler as the attribute value, e.g.:

```
<Button Text="Make It So" Clicked="ButtonClicked" />
```

In Listing 1-7 Clicked="ButtonClicked" registers the event handler ButtonClicked with the event Clicked defined in the Button class. The runtime takes care of registering the handler to the event, and the garbage collection removes the handler when the Button view is destroyed. In the code behind, define the event handler to change the Text of the Button to "It is so!" once the user clicks the Button, as shown in Listing 2-11.

Listing 2-11. Code Behind Event Handler

```
protected void ButtonClicked(object sender, EventArgs e) {
    ((Button)sender).Text = "It is so!";
}
```

It is recommended to declare an event handler as protected or even private. The sender argument of type object refers to the Button view in the XAML that is wired to this event handler. You can cast it to Button object, e.g., (Button)sender or sender as Button. The second argument represents the event object.

Call an asynchronous event using the async/await syntax, as demonstrated in Listing 2-12.

Listing 2-12. Asynchronous Event Handler Using async/await

```
private async Task<bool> ButtonClicked(object sender, EventArgs e) {
    var b = sender as Button;
    b.Text = "It is so!";
    return await Task.FromResult(true);
}
```

The asynchronous method ButtonClicked returns true after the Task.FromResult method completes.

Collection Syntax

Xamarin.Forms Layout subclasses such as StackLayout or Grid act as containers and have a Children property that is declared as content property and is omitted in XAML. The *collection syntax* uses the content element syntax to add a Label, Button, and Grid to StackLayout, as shown in Listing 2-13.

Listing 2-13. Using Collection Syntax to Add Child Elements to a Container

```
<StackLayout Padding="30,30">
    <Label/>
    <Button/>
    <Grid/>
</StackLayout>
```

The Children collection is read-only. Xamarin.Forms uses the Add method internally for each object that is instantiated at runtime to add the object to the Children collection.

Attached Property Syntax

Some classes in Xamarin.Forms need to assign values to an element without the element even having that property. This is achieved using the *attached property syntax*, which is based on the property element syntax. The Layout Grid requires its Children to be positioned in rows and columns. Create Grid.Row and Grid.Column as new attributes of Label to place the view inside a cell, e.g.:

```
<Grid>
    <Label Grid.Row="1" Grid.Column="1" Text="Cell (1,1)" />
</Grid>
```

This positions the Label in the first row and column of the Grid. Attached properties can be simple or complex objects that encapsulate business logic.

Figure 2-5 shows the result on both platforms.

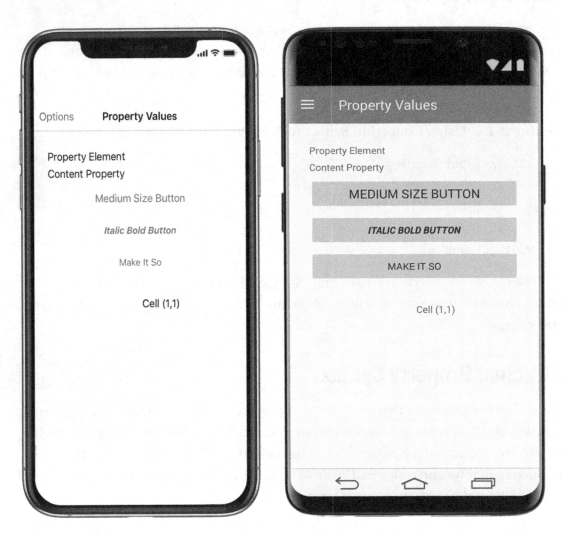

Figure 2-5. *Approaches for setting property values in Xamarin.Forms*

CODE COMPLETE: Setting Property Values

Listing 2-14 demonstrates the different approaches to assign values to properties.

Listing 2-14. Setting Property Values in XAML

```
<?xml version="1.0" encoding="UTF-8"?>
<ContentPage xmlns="http://xamarin.com/schemas/2014/forms"
xmlns:x="http://schemas.microsoft.com/winfx/2009/xaml"
```

```
x:Class="XamlExamples.PropertyValuesPage">
    <ContentPage.Content>
        <StackLayout Padding="30,30">
            <Label>
                <Label.Text>Property Element</Label.Text>
            </Label>
            <Label>Content Property</Label>
            <Button FontSize="Medium" Text="Medium Size Button" />
            <Button FontAttributes="Italic,Bold" Text="Italic Bold
            Button" />
            <Button Text="Make It So" Clicked="ButtonClicked" />
            <Grid>
                <Label Grid.Row="1" Grid.Column="1" Text="Cell (1,1)" />
            </Grid>
        </StackLayout>
    </ContentPage.Content>
</ContentPage>
```

This completes the overview of the XAML syntax. Let's move on to the anatomy of XAML documents itself.

Anatomy of XAML Files

A XAML document is comprised of three files: the platform-independent XAML, the associated code behind file, and the generated file, which is used internally, as shown in Figure 2-6.

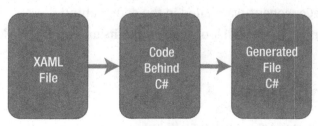

Figure 2-6. *XAML, code behind, and generated files*

The main file you interact with is the *XAML file* (`.xaml`). It contains the user interface definition.

The associated C# file (`.xaml.cs`) that has the corresponding business logic is called a *code behind*, functioning very much like its equivalent in web and desktop application development. The code behind contains a partial class definition with the same name specified in the `x:Class` attribute of the root element in the XAML. When starting an application, the platform-specific iOS or Droid project executes the `LoadApplication` method passing in an instance of the `App` class, which instantiates the XAML page using its default constructor. The constructor calls the `InitializeComponent` method to load the XAML into the application.

The XAML parser generates for each platform a *generated file* (`.xaml.g.cs`), which contains the constructors, classes, and properties to implement the XAML. It contains another partial class, now with the implementation of the `InitializeComponent` method. This method calls the `LoadFromXaml` method at runtime to load the actual user interface as an object graph when you run the application. The XAML parser uses, unless specified differently, the default constructor of the elements in the XAML to instantiate the objects and then set the values of the object properties if provided in the XAML.

The names of the event handlers specified in XAML must be instance methods that exist in the code behind. They cannot be `static`. Event handlers need to be used wisely, ideally only to enhance the controls they are serving and not to access services and business layer. Instead consider using other techniques such as behaviors, commands, and triggers (see Chapter 5) or data binding (see Chapter 9) for more reusable code.

The XAML parser generates for each named element in the XAML using the `x:Name` directive a local variable with the same name inside the generated file that can be accessed only from within the code behind. The local variable in the generated file is instantiated using the `FindByName` method. Local variables can be accessed only after the method `InitializeComponent` was called in the code behind.

That's XAML syntax. Next we'll look at the benefits and uses of XAML compilation.

XAML Compilation

XAML can be compiled in Visual Studio using the Xamarin compiler (XAMLC), which provides a performance improvement, compile-time error checking, and a smaller executable since the XAML files aren't needed at runtime. For backward compatibility, this feature is turned off by default. When XAML is set not to compile, then it is interpreted upon execution and the execution takes longer, and runtime errors that could have been picked up at compile time will increase. Turn on compilation at both the assembly and the class level by adding the XamlCompilation attribute. Here is the usage at the assembly level:

```
[assembly: XamlCompilation (XamlCompilationOptions.Compile)]
namespace PhotoApp
{
   ...
}
```

The class level implementation is almost identical.

```
[XamlCompilation (XamlCompilationOptions.Compile)]
public class MyPage : ContentPage
{
   ...
}
```

Before moving on to Xamarin.Forms, here is an overview of how Xamarin.Forms XAML relates to other XAML dialects.

XAML Standard

Microsoft has initiated a process of aligning XAML dialects across multiple products such as Xamarin.Forms and non-Xamarin.Forms XAML like WPF. This could possibly result in name changes of Xamarin.Forms core classes, controls, layouts, and property enumerations. So far they've provided a mapping from XAML Standard elements to Xamarin.Forms equivalent in the form of aliases.

Developers can preview this by adding the Xamarin.Forms.Alias NuGet package to the Forms and platform projects and adding the namespace Xamarin.Forms.Alias to the XAML page, e.g.:

```
xmlns:a="clr-namespace:Xamarin.Forms.Alias;assembly=Xamarin.Forms.Alias"
```

Instead of <Label Text="Xamarin.Forms"/>, use the alias <a:TextBlock Text="WPF"/>.

Tables 2-1 and 2-2 list the aliases for Xamarin.Forms controls, properties, and enumerations available as a preview.

Table 2-1. *Xamarin.Forms Controls and Equivalent XAML Standard*

Xamarin.Forms Control	XAML Standard Alias
Frame	Border
Picker	ComboBox
ActivityIndicator	ProgressRing
StackLayout	StackPanel
Label	TextBlock
Entry	TextBox
Switch	ToggleSwitch
ContentView	UserControl

Table 2-2. *Xamarin.Forms Properties, Enumeration, and Equivalent XAML Standard*

Xamarin.Forms Control	Xamarin.Forms Property or Enum	XAML Standard
Button, Entry, Label, DatePicker, Editor, SearchBar, TimePicker	TextColor	Foreground
VisualElement	BackgroundColor	Background*
Picker, Button	BorderColor, OutlineColor	BorderBrush
Button	BorderWidth	BorderThickness
ProgressBar	Progress	Value
Button, Entry, Label, Editor, SearchBar, Span, Font	FontAttributes Bold, Italic, None	FontStyle Italic, Normal
		FontWeights* Bold, Normal
InputView	Keyboard Default, Url, Number, Telephone, Text, Chat, Email	InputScopeNameValue Default, Url, Number, TelephoneNumber, Text, Chat, EmailNameOrAddress
StackPanel	StackOrientation	Orientation*

Items marked with * are currently incomplete.

The future of XAML Standard is unclear. Such standardization is, as ever, desirable but problematic. Someday we may see an exodus to the XAML Standard syntax, but in the meantime use the XAML format provided in Xamarin.Forms and be aware of the `Xamarin.Forms.Alias` NuGet package.

That's XAML syntax in relation to the larger XAML universe and XAML Standard.

Summary

Xamarin.Forms XAML is based on XML and 2009 XAML syntax and is used to define cross-platform user interfaces. Pages, layouts, and controls provided by the Xamarin. Forms class library and the intrinsic 2009 XAML terms are made available to the XAML document through the `xmlns` namespace directive.

In this chapter, we have discussed how to declare elements, assign values to properties, use markup extensions to reference static members, create arrays, reference other elements inside the XAML, and use non-default constructors and factory methods to instantiate classes. We covered approaches Xamarin.Forms provides to assign values that can be simple data types, enumeration values, collections, event handlers, and even values to properties not defined in the element itself.

Using XAML offers an alternative to the C# approach of writing platform-specific iOS and Android user interfaces. This layer of abstraction allows creating truly cross-platform applications. The XAML files are stored inside the platform-independent .NET Standard project. You can increase the reusability and maintainability of the mobile application by following design patterns, such as MVVM, instead of allowing the code behind file to define your pattern for you.

Let's now move on to the Xamarin.Forms XAML vocabulary to build rich user interfaces.

CHAPTER 3

UI Design Using Layouts

A *layout* is a container for controls, images, text, and other layouts. Central to the creation of mobile UIs, layouts help us to design our pages by facilitating the placement of views and nested layouts (for more views). If you've worked with HTML `<div>`, `<table>`, or `<form>` elements, then layouts should feel familiar to you. The purpose of a layout is to indicate the location and size of each of its child elements. This is typically done in three ways: relative to the individual controls in the layout, relative to the origin of the layout, or using an overlaid structure such as a grid. Each layout type has a mechanism for placing child views within it, specifying the size and location of each view, and creating space between and around the views.

In this chapter, you will build small projects to work with each of the layout types and their features. First you'll learn about the various types of layouts and explore custom controls. Here is an overview of these types.

Xamarin.Forms Layouts

Xamarin.Forms layouts inherit from the `View` class and can contain views or other layouts. Xamarin.Forms layouts include the following:

- `StackLayout`: Stacks child views vertically or horizontally

- `FlexLayout`: Wraps or stacks child views with justification, alignment, proportional growth, and ordering

- `Grid`: Creates a table-like container with rows and columns to hold views

- `RelativeLayout`: Uses constraints that create relationships between the elements to define the location and size of child views

© Dan Hermes 2019
D. Hermes and N. Mazloumi, *Building Xamarin.Forms Mobile Apps Using XAML*,
https://doi.org/10.1007/978-1-4842-4030-4_3

- AbsoluteLayout: Sets the child view's location and size by using bounding rectangles or proportions to the overall layout

- Frame: Draws a frame-like border around the container

Using Xamarin.Forms Layouts

Layouts in Xamarin.Forms are containers that hold and format views. Each layout has its own set of constraints and behaviors to suit a range of design needs. You can format simple pages with a few controls quickly and easily by using StackLayout. Try FlexLayout when you need a fluid layout with control over wrapping, order, and the expansion and alignment of views. RelativeLayout is useful when you know the coordinate relationships between controls. Use AbsoluteLayout when you know only in which quadrants and areas of the page your controls should appear, and when you need layering. Grid provides a table-like container. ContentView is a base class for building custom layout views, such as custom controls, which can contain multiple layouts and other views, useful as a reusable component. A Frame layout provides a visible, rectangular frame around its contents.

The simplest Xamarin.Forms layout is the StackLayout.

StackLayout

Views in a StackLayout are stacked vertically unless horizontal placement is specified. StackLayout is a quick, loose layout useful for prototyping and simple screens. You add views as children to the parent view and arrange them by using HorizontalOptions and VerticalOptions, which can also be used to expand views and provide spacing between views. Useful for all Xamarin.Forms layouts, the Padding property creates space around the edges of the entire layout.

Add a StackLayout tag pair to your ContentPage like this:

```
<ContentPage>
    <ContentPage.Content>
        <StackLayout >
            <!-- Add Views Here -->
        </StackLayout>
    </ContentPage.Content>
</ContentPage>
```

Tip   All example code solutions can be found on Apress.com (from the Source Code/Downloads tab, access the title of this book) or on GitHub at `https://github.com/danhermes/xamarin-xaml-book-examples`.

Listing 3-1 is a declaration of child views in the StackLayout with no spacing between views. The default orientation is Vertical, meaning that views stack beneath one another. The Spacing property creates padding of the specified size between each view.

Listing 3-1. *StackLayoutHorizontal.xaml in LayoutExample.Xaml Project*

```
<StackLayout Spacing="0">
    <Label Text="Start is flush left" HorizontalOptions="Start" />
    <Label Text="Center" HorizontalOptions="Center" />
    <Label Text="End is flush right" HorizontalOptions="End" />
</StackLayout>
```

In Figure 3-1, note the HorizontalOptions placement for LayoutOptions.Start, Center, and End.

Figure 3-1. *StackLayout HorizontalOptions*

Padding Around the Entire Layout

Much like page padding, the ContentPage's Padding property creates space around the entire layout:

```
<ContentPage xmlns="http://xamarin.com/schemas/2014/forms"
    xmlns:x="http://schemas.microsoft.com/winfx/2009/xaml"
    x:Class="LayoutExample.Xaml.Views.StackLayoutHorizontal"
    Padding="10,10,10,5">
```

Here are the Padding parameter names:

```
Padding="left, top, right, bottom"
```

The following example places padding to the left, right, and bottom, but not on top:

Padding="10,0,10,5"

This places equal space on all four sides:

Padding="10"

Pad left/right sides or top/bottom with equal spacing ("horizontal, vertical"):

Padding="10,5"

Stacking with Vertical Orientation

Vertical stacking, the default orientation, places each view beneath the previous one. The VerticalOptions declaration using FillAndExpand pads the end of the layout with space, pushing other views to the bottom of the page. Also, there are four horizontal positions: Start, Center, End, and Fill. These are fields of the LayoutOptions class.

Let's make the default vertical orientation explicit, so you can see it, and add a few views to the first example (Listing 3-2).

Listing 3-2. StackLayoutVertical.xaml

```
<StackLayout Spacing="0" Orientation="Vertical" VerticalOptions="
FillAndExpand">
    <Label Text="Start is flush left" HorizontalOptions="Start" />
    <Label Text="Start 2" HorizontalOptions="Start" />
    <Label Text="Center" HorizontalOptions="Center" />
    <Label Text="Center 2" HorizontalOptions="Center" />
    <Label Text="End 1" HorizontalOptions="End" />
    <Label Text="End is flush right" HorizontalOptions="End" />
</StackLayout>
```

Figure 3-2 shows how each view is placed lower than its sibling with vertical orientation and how each view is justified horizontally using HorizontalOptions.

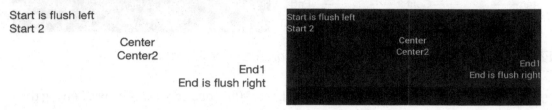

Figure 3-2. *Top-to-bottom stacking with vertical orientation*

There's a fourth horizontal position: Fill. This causes the view to consume the available area left to right, start to end:

```
HorizontalOptions = "Fill"
```

Later in this section we'll cover the Expand layout options (such as FillAndExpand), which cause views to expand and pad the available area around the view with space.

Tip   Make sure you have enough space in your layout or these alignments won't be visible.

If you have more than three views to be positioned horizontally, the horizontal orientation is preferable.

Stacking with Horizontal Orientation

Views can be stacked horizontally by setting the Orientation property to Horizontal, as shown in Listing 3-3. All views are on the same horizontal axis.

Listing 3-3. StackLayoutHorizontal.xaml Continued

```
<StackLayout Spacing="0" Orientation="Horizontal">
    <Label Text="Start------" />
    <Label Text="------Center------" HorizontalOptions="CenterAndExpand" />
    <Label Text="------End" />
</StackLayout>
```

Because the orientation is horizontal, the first and last view didn't require a HorizontalOptions param.

Figure 3-3 shows how each view is placed to the right of its sibling.

Figure 3-3. *Left-to-right stacking with horizontal orientation*

Horizontal padding from the expanded LayoutOptions separates views. Setting the center view's HorizontalOptions to CenterAndExpand, the full parameter being LayoutOptions.CenterAndExpand, provides space to the left and right of a centered view.

You can order views horizontally by setting Orientation to Horizontal, though exact placement is impossible. Views are stacked left to right in the order added to the layout, with cues from HorizontalOptions.

Figure 3-4 shows what the StackLayout looks like if we were to add a few more views to the right of the previous views.

Figure 3-4. *Six views stacked left to right*

Listing 3-4 is the code with those extra views. In the online code examples, I'm moving back and forth between StackLayoutHorizontal.xaml, which contains the simpler examples, and StackLayoutVertical.xaml, which adds extra views.

Listing 3-4. StackLayoutVertical.xaml with Views Using HorizontalOptions

```
<StackLayout Spacing="0" Orientation="Horizontal">
    <Label Text="Start 1 ---" />
    <Label Text="Start 2 ---" />
    <Label Text="---Center 1 ---" HorizontalOptions="CenterAndExpand" />
    <Label Text="---Center 2 ---" HorizontalOptions="CenterAndExpand" />
    <Label Text="---End 1 " />
    <Label Text="---End 2 " />
</StackLayout>
```

If you want to combine your child layouts into a parent layout, consider nesting layouts.

Nesting Layouts

Layouts can contain other layouts within the Children property.

A complex page with multiple rows of horizontally oriented views is accomplished with nested StackLayouts:

```
<StackLayout>
    <StackLayout>
        <!-- Your Views -->
    </StackLayout>
    <StackLayout>
        <!—More of Your Views -->
    </StackLayout>
</StackLayout>
```

Tip   If more than one nested StackLayout is used, other layouts should be considered, such as FlexLayout or Grid, which lend themselves better to complexity.

Controlling the size of views in a layout and the spacing between them is important to formatting.

Expanding and Padding Views by Using LayoutOptions

Use the Expand layout option to cause views to expand or to pad the available area with space. FillAndExpand causes views to grow without creating padding space around them. All other expand options pad around the view with space.

Tip   These features are easier to see if you set a background color for the view by using the BackgroundColor property.

The following are HorizontalOptions left-to-right formatting options:

- **FillAndExpand** expands the view to the right:

  HorizontalOptions = "FillAndExpand"

- **StartAndExpand** pads to the right with space:

  HorizontalOptions = "StartAndExpand"

- **EndAndExpand** pads to the left with space:

  HorizontalOptions = "EndAndExpand"

- **CenterAndExpand** pads to the left and right with space:

  HorizontalOptions = "CenterAndExpand"

The following top-to-bottom formatting options are available for VerticalOptions:

- **FillAndExpand** expands the view to the bottom:

  VerticalOptions = "FillAndExpand"

- **StartAndExpand** pads to the bottom with space:

  VerticalOptions = "StartAndExpand"

- **EndAndExpand** pads to the top with space:

  VerticalOptions = "EndAndExpand"

- **CenterAndExpand** pads to the top and bottom with space:

  VerticalOptions = "CenterAndExpand"

Note   Expand layout options are only useful only if there are sibling views in the layout.

CODE COMPLETE: StackLayout

Listing 3-5 shows our full StackLayout example with a vertical and horizontal layout, the use of HorizontalOptions, and the Expand layout option, as shown in Figure 3-5.

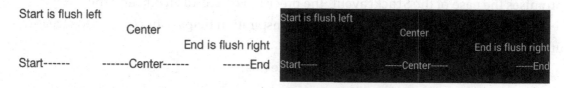

Figure 3-5. *Two StackLayouts: one vertical and one horizontal*

Listing 3-5. StackLayoutHorizontal.xaml Code Complete

```
<?xml version="1.0" encoding="UTF-8"?>
<ContentPage xmlns="http://xamarin.com/schemas/2014/    forms"
xmlns:x="http://schemas.microsoft.com/winfx/2009/xaml"
x:Class="LayoutExample.Xaml.Views.StackLayoutHorizontal"
Padding="10,10,10,5">
    <StackLayout>
        <StackLayout Spacing="0" Orientation="Vertical" VerticalOptions=
        "FillAndExpand">
            <Label Text="Start is flush left" HorizontalOptions="Start" />
            <Label Text="Center" HorizontalOptions="Center" />
            <Label Text="End is flush right" HorizontalOptions="End" />
        </StackLayout>
        <StackLayout Spacing="0" Orientation="Horizontal">
            <Label Text="Start------" />
            <Label Text="------Center------" HorizontalOptions=
            "CenterAndExpand" />
            <Label Text="------End" />
        </StackLayout>
    </StackLayout>
</ContentPage>
```

Now that we're oriented, let's move on to a more powerful and versatile layout: FlexLayout.

FlexLayout

One of the latest additions to Xamarin's layout toolbox, FlexLayout is the swiss army knife of layouts. Derived from the CSS Flexible Box Layout Module, the FlexLayout promises the ease of the StackLayout, the precision of a Grid layout, and the responsiveness of a RelativeLayout. Its CSS inspiration helps your controls to elegantly utilize the entire screen of a device.

Add a FlexLayout to your ContentPage like this:

```
<ContentPage>
<ContentPage.Content>
    <FlexLayout Direction="Column"
            AlignItems="Center"
            JustifyContent="SpaceEvenly">
        <!-- Add Views Here -->
    </FlexLayout>
</ContentPage>
```

Positioning views in a FlexLayout begins with the axis.

Position Views Using Axes

There are two axes that help define the behavior of views on a FlexLayout: the main axis and the cross axis. *You set the main axis using the Direction property,* horizontally (Row) by default unless horizontal placement is specified (Column). Once your main axis is set, you can position your views using JustifyContent and AlignItems:

- **JustifyContent** uses the *main axis* to set where views should begin, like Start, Center, and End, or simply provide spacing between views.

- **AlignItems** uses the *cross axis* to line up the tops, bottoms, or all sides of your views.

Create a new XAML page and name it FlexLayoutExample. Add a FlexLayout with Direction set to Column, or vertical. Set AlignItems to Center so views will be centered left to right, and for JustifyContent use SpaceEvenly, which works much like FillAndExpand to distribute your views along the main axis (vertical right now) with equal size and spacing. Add a few buttons, as in Listing 3-6.

Listing 3-6. Basic FlexLayout in FlexLayoutExample.xaml

```
<FlexLayout Direction="Column"
        AlignItems="Center"
        JustifyContent="SpaceEvenly">
    <Button Text="First" />
    < Button Text="Second" />
    < Button Text="Third" />
</FlexLayout>
```

Run and you should see our good ol' First, Second, and Third top to bottom (Figure 3-6).

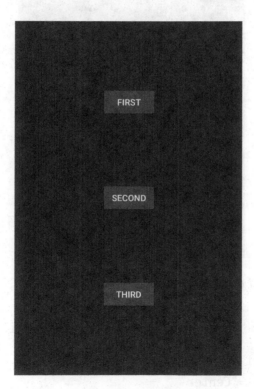

Figure 3-6. *FlexLayout with Direction set to Column*

Horizontal view flow is achieved by changing Direction to Row:

```
<FlexLayout Direction="Row"
        AlignItems="Center"
        JustifyContent="SpaceEvenly">
```

Left to right views along the main axis are shown in Figure 3-7.

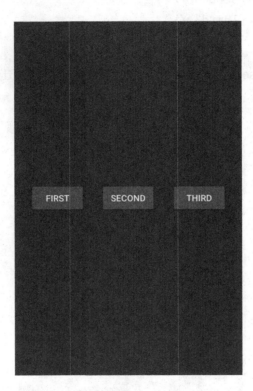

Figure 3-7. *FlexLayout with Direction set to Row*

Push your views to the beginning of the row by setting JustifyContent to Start:

```
<FlexLayout Direction="Row"
        AlignItems="Center"
        JustifyContent="Start">
```

With Direction set to Row, the JustifyContent setting of Start slides all your views to the left, as shown in Figure 3-8.

Figure 3-8. *FlexLayout with JustifyContent set to Start*

Slide them to the left with JustifyContent set to End, or center them with Center.

Since AlignItems works with the cross axis, which is currently vertical, you can set it to Start to top-align your views within the space allotted to them (Figure 3-9):

```
<FlexLayout Direction="Row"
        AlignItems="Start"
        JustifyContent="Start">
```

Figure 3-9. *FlexLayout with AlignItems set to Start*

Tip   Override `AlignItems` for a single View using `FlexLayout.AlignSelf`.

FlexLayout Patterns

`FlexLayout` is flexible. Here are some ways you might use it:

- **Stack**: Make a basic stack, vertical or horizontal, like a `StackLayout`. In Listing 3-6 we set `Direction` to `Column` and stacked some controls vertically. Setting `Direction` to `Row` stacks controls horizontally.

- **Wrap**: Format many items such as images by wrapping them when they reach the edge of the screen. Use the `FlexLayout's Wrap` property, setting it to `Wrap` (`NoWrap` is the default). Put the `FlexLayout` in a `ScrollView` so the user may scroll through the wrapped items.

- **Catalog**: Create static data-packed panels to scroll through and select. Place a `FlexLayout` in a `ScrollView` and fill it with `Frames` (see later in this chapter) containing details and possibly an image. This static list of `Frames` will scroll in whatever `Direction` you set but is not bindable like a `ListView`.

- **Page**: Nest two FlexLayouts to create a page with a header, footer, content, and side margins. Expand the content section vertically using the `FlexLayout.Grow` property (set it to 1) on your content view, which works like the star specification in a `Grid` layout. Within your side margin views, set the `FlexLayout.Basis` to the desired pixel width (e.g., 20). Note that `Grow` and `Basis` are set on views, not on FlexLayout (e.g., `<Label Text="Content" FlexLayout.Grow="1" />`).

Tip   Order or reorder your `FlexLayout` views using the `Order` property. Add `FlexLayout.Order` to views, assigning them an integer (e.g., `<Button Text="First" FlexLayout.Order="1" />`).

Grid

Grid is a table-like container of views. It is organized into rows and columns, each with a height and width, placed at specific row/column coordinates called *cells*. `GridUnitType` provides options for sizing rows and columns, while the `grid.Children.Add` method allows both single-cell and multicell views. `ColumnSpacing` and `RowSpacing` provide padding between cells.

Tip   `TableView` is another cell-based view but is not technically a layout. It is useful for building simple groups of items such as settings dialog boxes and grouped menus. Chapter 7 has a `TableView` example.

Create a `Grid` object and define a single row and column, as shown in Listing 3-7.

Listing 3-7. Starting GridExample1.xaml

```
<Grid>
    <Grid.RowDefinitions>
        <RowDefinition Height="Auto" />
    </Grid.RowDefinitions>
    <Grid.ColumnDefinitions>
        <ColumnDefinition Width="Auto" />
    </Grid.ColumnDefinitions>
</Grid>
```

Specify `Height` in each `RowDefinition`, and `Width` in each `ColumnDefinition`. Auto autosizes cells for either `Height` or `Width`.

Tip   The default `GridLength` setting for `Height` and `Width`, `Star`, expands the dimension of a row or column as much as possible.

Add a view at column and row 0, the only cell in our table:

```
<Label Text="I'm at 0,0" FontSize="30" FontAttributes="Bold" />
```

Now let's crank this table up to four rows by three columns:

```
<Grid>
    <Grid.RowDefinitions>
        <RowDefinition Height="Auto" />
        <RowDefinition Height="Auto" />
        <RowDefinition Height="Auto" />
        <RowDefinition Height="Auto" />
    </Grid.RowDefinitions>
    <Grid.ColumnDefinitions>
        <ColumnDefinition Width="Auto" />
        <ColumnDefinition Width="Auto" />
        <ColumnDefinition Width="Auto" />
    </Grid.ColumnDefinitions>
</Grid>
```

Then add three more views at (1,1), (2,2), and (0,3). Add a little label formatting to make things more exciting:

```
<Label Text="I'm at 0,0" FontSize="30" FontAttributes="Bold" />
<Label Text="Me? 1,1" FontSize="30" FontAttributes="Bold"
TextColor="Black" BackgroundColor="Lime" Grid.Row="1" Grid.Column="1" />
<Label Text="2,2 here" FontSize="30" FontAttributes="Bold"
TextColor="White" BackgroundColor="Red" Grid.Row="2" Grid.Column="2" />
<Label Text="I'm at 0,3" FontSize="30" FontAttributes="Bold" Grid.
Row="3" Grid.Column="0" />
```

Figure 3-10 shows our Grid with four labels, completing the code in GridExample1.cs.

Figure 3-10. *Grid containing four views*

Auto took care of column widths and row heights for us, expanding to accommodate view content.

Tip   Empty cells can impact your grid. A row set to Height ="Auto" that contains no views will have a height of zero. A column set to Width = "Auto" that contains no views will have zero width.

Here's a row and column definition shortcut. RowDefinition and ColumnDefinition set Height and Width to Star by default, so <RowDefinition Height="*" /> can be accomplished by <RowDefinition />.

<RowDefinition Width="*" /> can be accomplished by <ColumnDefinition />.

We'll discuss the "*" in the next section, Sizing Rows and Columns.

To follow along with the online examples, save your current example, `GridExample1.cs`, and then create a XAML page class called `GridExample2`. Copy your entire `Grid` from `GridExample1.xaml` into `GridExample2.xaml` (taking care not to copy the first line of the `ContentPage` declaration) and continue working with `GridExample2`. Remember to update your application class (such as `App.cs`) with the new `MainPage` reference to `GridExample2`.

Sizing Rows and Columns

The size of rows and columns is determined by `GridLength`. You can autosize, expand, or set specific heights and widths on rows or columns. `GridLength` is defined by its `GridUnitType`, of which there are three:

- **Auto** sizes the dimension of a row or column to its content.

- **Absolute** indicates a numeric dimension of the row or column. Using XAML the `GridUnitType.Absolute` is implied by the use of a numeric value.

- **Star** ("*") is the default setting, which expands the dimension of a row or column into the space that remains after Absolutes and Autos have been allocated.

Assign an `Absolute` `GridLength` object to `Height` in `RowDefinitions`:

```
<RowDefinition Height="200" />
```

or a `Star` to `Width` in `ColumnDefinition`:

```
<ColumnDefinition Width="1*" />
```

Sizing to Fit Views

The `Auto` value of `GridUnitType` sizes the row or column to the size of the contained views. Our `Grid` example is made up entirely of `Auto` sized rows:

```
<RowDefinition Height="Auto" />
```

Now let's add `Absolute` and `Star`.

Tip   Small views used with `Auto` can make it seem like rows or columns are missing. `Star` is used to expand the grid to its proper proportions. See "Expanding Views Proportionally" later in this chapter.

Setting Exact Size

The `Absolute` value of `GridUnitType` sets the exact height or width of a row or column. Change the second `RowDefinition Height` to an absolute size of 200 units:

```
<Grid.RowDefinitions>
    <RowDefinition Height="Auto" />
    <RowDefinition Height="200" />
    <RowDefinition Height="Auto" />
    <RowDefinition Height="Auto" />
</Grid.RowDefinitions>
```

The second row is set to an absolute height of units, stretching it vertically, as shown in Figure 3-11. This code is found in `GridExample2.xaml`.

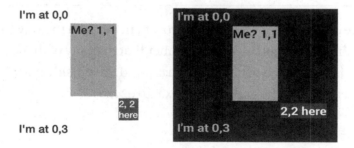

Figure 3-11.   *Using GridUnitType.Absolute to set a tall row height at 1,1*

`Width` assigned using `GridUnitType.Absolute` works in a manner similar to the `Height` assignment:

```
<ColumnDefinition Width="200" />
```

Expanding Views to Fit Available Space

GridUnitType.Star, or "*", the default setting for both Height and Width, expands a view within rows or columns to fill the remaining space. This is useful for filling the screen horizontally with columns or vertically with rows to the edge of the screen, especially when views are small. It behaves similarly to the FillAndExpand layout option, inserting padding space into the specified row or column.

Expand vertically by setting the Height of a RowDefinition. Change the third RowDefinition to use Star.

```
<Grid.RowDefinitions>
    <RowDefinition Height="Auto" />
    <RowDefinition Height="200" />
    <RowDefinition Height="1*" />
    <RowDefinition Height="Auto" />
</Grid.RowDefinitions>
```

Note   What's the "1" in the Height assignment to "1*"? Read on to the next section on expanding views proportionally.

GridUnitType.Star expands to push the row beneath it all the way to the bottom of the screen, as shown in Figure 3-12. Remember that in many of these examples, the Padding property is being used to create space around the outside edges of the page (see Listing 3-8). This completes the code in GridExample2.xaml.

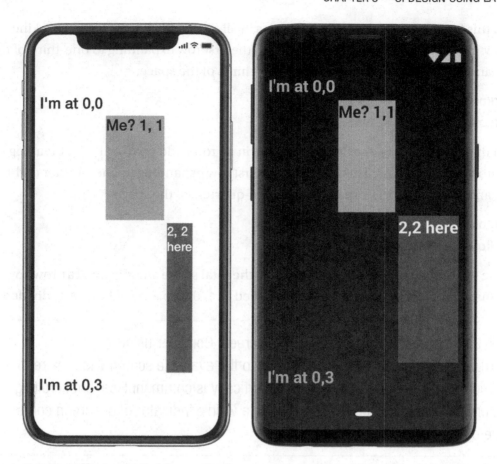

Figure 3-12. *Filling available vertical space by using GridUnitType.Star in the Height*

Expand horizontally by setting the width of `ColumnDefinition`. `Width` assigned using `GridUnitType.Star` works in a manner similar to the `Height` assignment, expanding the column to the right to consume the remaining space on right edge of the screen:

```
<ColumnDefinition Width="1*" />
```

Expanding Views Proportionally

You can control the proportions of cell sizes to one another in `GridUnitType.Star` cells by using the first parameter in `GridLength`. This technique is particularly useful with small views.

In this first example, the first parameters in all rows add up to 3 (1 + 2), breaking the row into three equal parts. This results in the first row expanding to one-third of the space and the second row expanding to two-thirds of the space:

```
<RowDefinition Height="1*" />
<RowDefinition Height="2*" />
```

In this next example, the first parameters in all rows add up to 4 (1 + 3), breaking the row into four equal parts. This results in the first row expanding to one-quarter of the space and the second row expanding to three-quarters of the space:

```
<RowDefinition Height="1*" />
<RowDefinition Height="3*" />
```

The first parameter represents a share of the total space among the Star rows or columns. If all of these parameters are specified as 1, the space will be evenly divided.

Tip   Large grids can run off the visible screen. Consider using GridLengthType.Star to expand only to the available screen width paired with a vertical ScrollView. Scrolling grids vertically is commonplace, but scrolling horizontally is rare in mobile apps without a visible indicator of offscreen content (page dots, arrows, etc.).

Creating Multicell Views

Single views can be sized to span multiple cells in the grid by using the RowSpan and ColumnSpan properties. These properties set the number of cells that a single view can occupy.

Spanning Columns

Expand a view from left to right across multiple columns by using the second and third parameters of the Add method, indexLeftColumn and indexRightColumn, to specify the columns to span.

To follow along with the online examples, save your current example, GridExample2, and then create a new XAML page called GridExample3. Copy the XAML from GridExample2.xaml into GridExample3.xaml and continue with GridExample3.xaml. Remember to update App.cs with the new MainPage reference to GridExample3.

Let's expand our (1,1) view into the column to the right. Add a `Star`-typed `Width` to the second column so it will expand horizontally:

```
<Grid.ColumnDefinitions>
    <ColumnDefinition Width="Auto" />
    <ColumnDefinition Width="1*" />
    <ColumnDefinition Width="Auto" />
</Grid.ColumnDefinitions>
```

Start with the view at (1,1). Change this `Label` view to use RowSpan and ColumnSpan, which you will set to occupy two columns:

```
<Label Text="Me? 1,1" FontSize="30" FontAttributes="Bold"
TextColor="Black" BackgroundColor="Lime" Grid.Row="1" Grid.Column="1"
Grid.RowSpan="1" Grid.ColumnSpan="2" />
```

From left to right, this view spans the left side of column 1 to the left side of column 3—a distance of two columns. (Yes, it's a little strange that there is no visible column 3, but the notation requires an endpoint, and that happens to be the beginning of the column or row we are expanding to.) See the result in Figure 3-13.

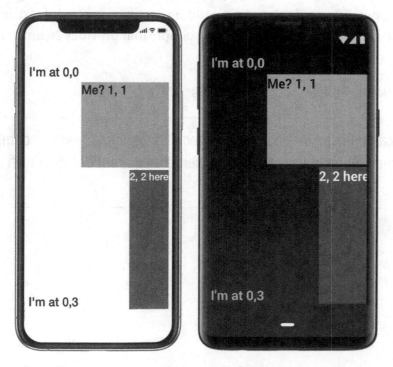

Figure 3-13. *The cell at 1,1 spans columns, and 2,2 spans rows*

From top to bottom, this view spans from the top of row 1 to the top of row 2 (a distance of only one row).

Spanning Rows

Expand a view from a cell down through multiple rows by specifying rows to span in the `Grid.RowSpan` property on the view. Now change the view at (2,2) to occupy two rows:

```
<Label Text="2,2 here" FontSize="30" FontAttributes="Bold"
TextColor="White" BackgroundColor="Red" Grid.Row="2" Grid.Column="2"
Grid.RowSpan="2" Grid.ColumnSpan="1" />
```

From left to right, this view spans the left side of column 2 to the left side of column 3. From top to bottom, this view spans from the top of row 2 to the top of row 4 (a distance of two rows) and yields what you see in Figure 3-13. (There's no visible row 4; it's just an endpoint.) This completes the code in `GridExample3.cs`.

Padding Between Cells

You can add space between cells by using `RowSpacing` and `ColumnSpacing` properties of your `Grid` layout. `RowSpacing` provides padding between rows, while `ColumnSpacing` provides space between columns. Here's an example that provides 20 units of padding for each:

```
<Grid ColumnSpacing="20" RowSpacing="20">
```

Tip   Cells can be used for good visual effect. For example, you can combine grid cells containing an image overlaid with a semitransparent BoxView with labels overtop.

CODE COMPLETE: Grid

Listing 3-8 is our Grid example shown previously in Figure 3-12 sporting four labels, two of which span multiple rows or columns.

Listing 3-8. GridExample2.xaml Code Complete

```xml
<?xml version="1.0" encoding="UTF-8"?>
<ContentPage xmlns="http://xamarin.com/schemas/2014/forms" xmlns:x="http://
schemas.microsoft.com/winfx/2009/xaml" x:Class="LayoutExample.Xaml.Views.
GridExample2" Padding="10,10,10,5">
    <Grid>
        <Grid.RowDefinitions>
            <RowDefinition Height="Auto" />
            <RowDefinition Height="200" />
            <RowDefinition Height="Auto" />
            <RowDefinition Height="Auto" />
        </Grid.RowDefinitions>
        <Grid.ColumnDefinitions>
            <ColumnDefinition Width="Auto" />
            <ColumnDefinition Width="Auto" />
            <ColumnDefinition Width="Auto" />
        </Grid.ColumnDefinitions>
        <Label Text="I'm at 0,0" FontSize="30" FontAttributes="Bold" />
        <Label Text="Me? 1,1" FontSize="30" FontAttributes="Bold"
        TextColor="Black" BackgroundColor="Lime" Grid.Row="1" Grid.
        Column="1" />
        <Label Text="2,2 here" FontSize="30" FontAttributes="Bold"
        TextColor="White" BackgroundColor="Red" Grid.Row="2" Grid.
        Column="2" />
        <Label Text="I'm at 0,3" FontSize="30" FontAttributes="Bold" Grid.
        Row="3" Grid.Column="0" />
    </Grid>
</ContentPage>
```

RelativeLayout

RelativeLayout auto-scales its elements to different screen sizes. Made up of the parent layout view and its child views, this layout is defined by the relationships between views. Each child view is tied to its sibling views or to the parent layout view by using constraints. A constraint can bind view locations and sizes: x/y coordinates and width/height dimensions. RelativeLayout allows us to create an interconnected web of views that stretch like rubber bands to fit the screen, providing built-in responsive design or auto-layout.

Tip   RelativeLayout is useful for apps that must present well on widely varying resolutions, such as on phones and tablets.

Let's start with a fresh XAML page, create a RelativeLayout instance, and place a label at 0,0 in the upper-left corner of the layout, as shown in Listing 3-9.

Listing 3-9. Starting RelativeLayoutExample.xaml

```
<ContentPage xmlns="http://xamarin.com/schemas/2014/forms"
    xmlns:x="http://schemas.microsoft.com/winfx/2009/xaml"
    x:Class="LayoutExample.Xaml.Views.RelativeLayoutExample"
    x:Name="Self" Padding="10,10,10,5">
    <RelativeLayout x:Name="LayoutContainer">
        <Label x:Name="UpperLeft" Text="Upper Left" FontSize="20"
            RelativeLayout.XConstraint="{ConstraintExpression
            Type=Constant, Constant=0}"
            RelativeLayout.YConstraint="{ConstraintExpression
            Type=Constant, Constant=0}"/>
    </RelativeLayout>
</ContentPage>
```

The UpperLeft label is added with a location constraint to the parent layout; using Constant = 0 for both x and y places the label in the upper-left corner, at the origin: 0,0. Next we want to add more views in relation to the existing parent and child views.

Tip   RelativeLayout is not optimized for speed. Consider alternatives such as Grid or FlexLayout, particularly when building ViewCells (see Chapter 6 on the use of ViewCells in building lists). In these cases, try Grid instead.

Setting View Location and Size

Each time we add a view to RelativeLayout, we ask: Do we want to set the *location* of the view, the *size* of the view, or both?

Specify *location* with XConstraint and YConstraint:

```
RelativeLayout.XConstraint="{ConstraintExpression Type=Constant,
Constant=10}"
RelativeLayout.YConstraint="{ConstraintExpression Type=Constant,
Constant=25}"
```

Specify *size* with WidthConstraint and HeightConstraint:

```
RelativeLayout.WidthConstraint="{ConstraintExpression Type=Constant,
Constant=50}"
RelativeLayout.HeightConstraint="{ConstraintExpression Type=Constant,
Constant=200}"
```

All these x/y coordinates, widths, and heights ultimately become absolute values. Data typing, however, restricts us to the use of Constraint classes. This encourages calculations based on the values of sibling and parent views, keeping things relative.

Using Constraints

Size and location are specified by using constraints. The Constraint object has three enumerations:

- **Constant**, for absolute x/y assignments of location and/or size
- **RelativeToParent**, for relative x/y calculations of location and/or size to the parent layout
- **RelativeToView**, for relative x/y calculations of location and/or size between child(sibling) views

The following sections discuss each in more detail.

Absolute Location and Size

Constant is used for absolute location or size.

Here is a *location* example, which places the UpperLeft label at coordinates 0,0 within the layout:

```
<Label x:Name="UpperLeft" Text="Upper Left" FontSize="20"
    RelativeLayout.XConstraint="{ConstraintExpression Type=Constant,
    Constant=0}"
    RelativeLayout.YConstraint="{ConstraintExpression Type=Constant,
    Constant=0}" />
```

This is a *size* example, creating a view at 100,100 with dimensions 50 units wide and 200 units high:

```
<Label Text="Constants are Absolute" FontSize="20" RelativeLayout.
XConstraint="{ConstraintExpression Type=Constant, Constant=100}"
RelativeLayout.YConstraint="{ConstraintExpression Type=Constant,
Constant=100}" RelativeLayout.WidthConstraint="{ConstraintExpression
Type=Constant, Constant=50}" RelativeLayout.HeightConstraint=
"{ConstraintExpression Type=Constant, Constant=200}" />
```

Tip   The numeric screen units used in many Xamarin.Forms views are relative units of measure that do not represent pixels, and their results vary according to screen size.

This new label is shown in Figure 3-14, with the text wrapping at 50 units wide.

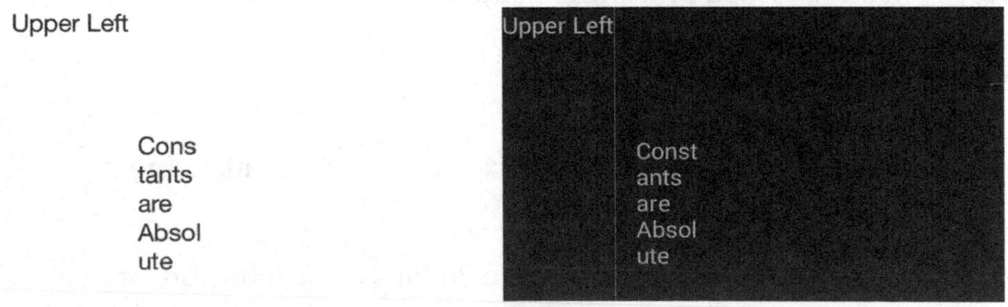

Figure 3-14. *Label with a Constant constraint*

RelativeToParent Constraint

The RelativeToParent constraint ties a view's location/size to the parent
RelativeLayout. This is useful for placing and sizing views in relation to the entire page
or section.

Instantiate another child view, such as Label, and add that to the child collection by
using a RelativeToParent constraint. This example places the location of the new child
view halfway down the length and width of the parent layout by setting Factor to 0.5:

```
<Label Text="Halfway down and across" FontSize="15"
 RelativeLayout.XConstraint="{ConstraintExpression Type=RelativeToParent,
 Property=Width, Factor=0.5}"
 RelativeLayout.YConstraint="{ConstraintExpression Type=RelativeToParent,
 Property=Height, Factor=0.5}" />
```

These assignments of Type to RelativeToParent use the parent view,
RelativeLayout, to return an x coordinate equal to half the width of the parent layout
and a y coordinate equal to half of the height of the parent layout (see Figure 3-15).

Figure 3-15. *RelativeToParent with a Height and Width calculation*

Create a BoxView halfway down the page that is half the height and half the width of the parent view by passing RelativeToParent calculations into the Add parameters:

```
<BoxView Color="Accent" HorizontalOptions="Start" VerticalOptions="Start
AndExpand"
RelativeLayout.XConstraint="{ConstraintExpression Type=RelativeToParent,
Property=Width, Factor=0}"
RelativeLayout.YConstraint="{ConstraintExpression Type=RelativeToParent,
Property=Height, Factor=0.5}"
RelativeLayout.HeightConstraint="{ConstraintExpression
Type=RelativeToParent, Property=Height, Factor=0.5}"
RelativeLayout.WidthConstraint="{ConstraintExpression
Type=RelativeToParent, Property=Width, Factor=0.5}" />
```

The result looks like Figure 3-16.

Figure 3-16. *A BoxView placed using RelativeToParent*

Tip   XAML constraints are versatile and easy to use, but C# constraints offer more complex layout options.

RelativeToView Constraint

RelativeToView constrains a view's location/size to that of another view. This is typically used to offset views by a few pixels using the Constant property. More complex juxtapositions are often required, however, such as setting controls below or beside another. Although some complex constraints can be achieved using XAML, it's often easier to use C#, and that is the case here. (Listing 3-10 can be executed using XAML's {x:Reference} markup extension.) Instantiate another child view, such as a Label, and add that to the child collection by using a RelativeToView constraint. This example places the location of the new child view beneath the sibling view, but we're working in the C# code behind.

Listing 3-10. RelativeToView Constraint in RelativeLayoutExample.cs

```
Label below = new Label
{
    Text = "Below Upper Left",
    FontSize = 15
};

LayoutContainer.Children.Add(below,
    Constraint.Constant(0),
    Constraint.RelativeToView(UpperLeft, (parent, sibling) =>
        {
            return sibling.Y + sibling.Height;
        })
);
```

Note   The Constant property can be used to offset views by pixel counts and can have a positive value, such as Constant = 20, or a negative one, like Constant = -20.

The BelowUpperLeft view is placed below the UpperLeft view, as shown in Figure 3-17 (for Android).

Figure 3-17. *Place one label below another by using* `RelativeToView`

CODE COMPLETE: RelativeLayout

Listing 3-11 is our full XAML example for `RelativeLayout` using `Constraints: Constant`, `RelativeToParent`, and `RelativeToView` (see Figure 3-18).

Figure 3-18. *RelativeLayoutExample.cs using all the constraint types*

Listing 3-11. RelativeLayoutExample.xaml Code Complete

```
<?xml version="1.0" encoding="UTF-8"?>
<ContentPage xmlns="http://xamarin.com/schemas/2014/forms"
xmlns:x="http://schemas.microsoft.com/winfx/2009/xaml"
x:Class="LayoutExample.Xaml.Views.RelativeLayoutExample" x:Name="Self"
Padding="10,10,10,5">
    <RelativeLayout x:Name="LayoutContainer">
        <Label x:Name="UpperLeft" Text="Upper Left" FontSize="20"
        RelativeLayout.XConstraint="{ConstraintExpression Type=Constant,
        Constant=0}"
RelativeLayout.YConstraint="{ConstraintExpression Type=Constant,
Constant=0}" />
        <Label Text="Constants are Absolute" FontSize="20"
        RelativeLayout.XConstraint="{ConstraintExpression Type=Constant,
        Constant=100}"
        RelativeLayout.YConstraint="{ConstraintExpression
        Type=Constant, Constant=100}"
        RelativeLayout.WidthConstraint="{ConstraintExpression
        Type=Constant, Constant=50}"
        RelativeLayout.HeightConstraint="{ConstraintExpression
        Type=Constant, Constant=200}" />
      <Label Text="Halfway down and across" FontSize="15"
      RelativeLayout.XConstraint="{ConstraintExpression
      Type=RelativeToParent, Property=Width, Factor=0.5}"
      RelativeLayout.YConstraint="{ConstraintExpression
      Type=RelativeToParent, Property=Height, Factor=0.5}" />
      <BoxView Color="Accent" HorizontalOptions="Start" Vertical
      Options="StartAndExpand"
      RelativeLayout.XConstraint="{ConstraintExpression
      Type=RelativeToParent, Property=Width, Factor=0}"
      RelativeLayout.YConstraint="{ConstraintExpression
      Type=RelativeToParent, Property=Height, Factor=0.5}"
      RelativeLayout.HeightConstraint="{ConstraintExpression
      Type=RelativeToParent, Property=Height, Factor=0.5}"
```

```
        RelativeLayout.WidthConstraint="{ConstraintExpression
        Type=RelativeToParent, Property=Width, Factor=0.5}" />
        </RelativeLayout>
    </ContentPage>
```

Tip   See the downloadable code example for the complete C# files.

AbsoluteLayout

AbsoluteLayout is a collection of views placed at x/y coordinates ranging from 0 to 1 and bounded in size. View positions are not typically absolute, because we seldom use device-dependent x or y coordinates. Positions are usually relative to 0 being at the origin and 1 at the furthest point along a single axis. The layout is absolute in that views will go exactly where you put them, even on top of other views, so this can be useful for layering.

Using SetLayoutBounds, views in AbsoluteLayout are each bound to a bounding object, which can be a point or a rectangle. Using SetLayoutFlags, bounding points can determine location, while bounding rectangles can determine location and size.

Listing 3-12 provides an example of AbsoluteLayout.

Listing 3-12. Starting AbsoluteLayoutExample.xaml

```
<AbsoluteLayout VerticalOptions="FillAndExpand">
    <!-- Add Views Here -->
</AbsoluteLayout>
```

Now we'll add some views. In order to assign a view to AbsoluteLayout, the control is added to the AbsoluteLayout collection, and then LayoutFlags and LayoutBounds are set to define the position and size of the view. LayoutBounds parameters are "x, y, width, height":

```
<AbsoluteLayout VerticalOptions="FillAndExpand">
    <Label Text="FirstLabel" AbsoluteLayout.LayoutBounds="0, 0, AutoSize,
    AutoSize" AbsoluteLayout.LayoutFlags="PositionProportional" />
</AbsoluteLayout>
```

Figure 3-19 shows the result (for Android).

Figure 3-19. *Add a label to AbsoluteLayout*

Tip   AutoSize adjusts the height or width to the content within the view.

Note   HorizontalOptions, VerticalOptions, and Expand layout options are overridden by absolute positioning.

Creating Bounding Objects with SetLayoutBounds

Views in AbsoluteLayout can be placed at points or bounded by rectangles (invisible ones). Points come in handy when only a location without a sized area is needed. Rectangles and points are the bounding objects specified in LayoutBounds.

Let's continue with another rectangle example. Create a second label, add it to the layout, and then set layout flags and bounds to place it at the bottom-left corner of the page:

```
<Label Text="SecondLabel" AbsoluteLayout.LayoutBounds="0, 1, AutoSize,
AutoSize"
    AbsoluteLayout.LayoutFlags="PositionProportional" />
```

Figure 3-20 shows the result.

Figure 3-20. *SecondLabel placed at the bottom of the screen with y set to 1*

Setting Location and Size by Using Rectangles

Rectangles provide AbsoluteLayout with the location and size of a bounded area in which to place a view. These are the LayoutBounds parameters of the Rectangle:

```
AbsoluteLayout.LayoutBounds="locationX, locationY, Width, Height"
```

All parameters are doubles ranging from 0 to 1. Here are a few examples of how the LayoutBounds parameters affect location:

- Located at the origin with maximum width and height: "0, 0, 1, 1"

- Horizontally centered in the space provided: ".5, 0, 1, 1"

- Vertically centered in the space provided: "0, .5, 1, 1"

- Horizontally and vertically centered in the space provided: ".5, .5, 1, 1"

The following are examples of parameters affecting size:

- Located at the origin with maximum width and height: `"0, 0, 1, 1"`

- Located at the origin at 20% width: `"0, 0, .2, 1"`

- Located at the origin at 20% height: `"0, 0, 1, .2"`

- Located at the origin at 20% width and height: `"0, 0, .2, .2"`

Tip   The `AbsoluteLayout` examples in this chapter show relative units because that is the generally recommended cross-platform approach. `AbsoluteLayout` can also use device-specific units. Be certain you know what you're doing, as device-specific units can cause inconsistent results across different platforms and devices. Specify `LayoutFlags` to `None` and then use device-specific units with float values greater than 1 such as `<Label Text="DeviceLabel" AbsoluteLayout.LayoutBounds="250f, 250f, 200f, 50f" AbsoluteLayout.LayoutFlags="None" />`.

Setting Location by Using Points

Points can specify the location of a view when the size is not needed. Views can be added to `AbsoluteLayout` very simply by using a point:

```
<Label Text="PointLabel" AbsoluteLayout.LayoutBounds="0, 1"
AbsoluteLayout.LayoutFlags="PositionProportional" />
```

Points work just like the location portion of a rectangle, defining the x and y position by using doubles ranging from 0 to 1. Here are the `LayoutBounds` parameters for a point:

```
AbsoluteLayout.LayoutBounds="locationX, locationY"
```

Points and rectangles are just geometric objects until they're bound to a view's location or size by using `SetLayoutFlags`.

Tip   The most commonly used layout flags are `PositionProportional` and `All` because we are usually either placing a view or both placing and sizing it.

Images size well this way:
```
<Image AbsoluteLayout.LayoutBounds="0, 0,1,1" AbsoluteLayout.
LayoutFlags="All" />
```

Binding Location

Bind the x/y location of the bounding object to the view by using these flags:

- **PositionProportional** associates a rectangle or a point's x/y location proportionally with the location of the view, while size values are absolute:

  `AbsoluteLayout.LayoutFlags="PositionProportional"`

If the rectangle or point is at 0,0, the view will be at 0,0.

- **XProportional** associates a rectangle or a point's x coordinate proportionally, while all other values are absolute:

  `AbsoluteLayout.LayoutFlags="XProportional"`

- **YProportional** associates a rectangle or point's y coordinate proportionally, while all other values are absolute:

  `AbsoluteLayout.LayoutFlags="YProportional"`

Binding Size

Bind the size of the bounding object to the view by using these flags:

- **SizeProportional** associates the rectangle size proportionally with the size of the view, while position values are absolute:

  `AbsoluteLayout.LayoutFlags="SizeProportional"`

If the rectangle is size .2,.5, the view will be sized to .2,.5.

- **WidthProportional** associates the rectangle width proportionally with the width of the view, while all other values are absolute:

  ```
  AbsoluteLayout.LayoutFlags="WidthProportional"
  ```

- **HeightProportional** associates the rectangle height proportionally with the height of the view, while all other values are absolute:

  ```
  AbsoluteLayout.LayoutFlags="HeightProportional"
  ```

Binding Both Location and Size

Set values proportionally or as absolute for both location and size with a rectangle or point by using All or None.

- **All** associates the rectangle or point's x/y location and size proportionally with the location and size of the view:

  ```
  AbsoluteLayout.LayoutFlags="All"
  ```

- **None** associates all values as absolute:

  ```
  AbsoluteLayout.LayoutFlags="None"
  ```

CODE COMPLETE: AbsoluteLayout

Listing 3-13 uses AbsoluteLayout to add labels to the top and bottom of the screen shown previously in Figure 3-20. This example uses bounding rectangles with a few different ways to add the first Label (such as using points instead of bounding rectangles).

Listing 3-13. AbsoluteLayoutExample.xaml Using Rectangles

```
<ContentPage xmlns="http://xamarin.com/schemas/2014/
forms" xmlns:x="http://schemas.microsoft.com/winfx/2009/
xaml" x:Class="LayoutExample.Xaml.Views.AbsoluteLayoutExample"
Padding="10,10,10,5">
    <AbsoluteLayout VerticalOptions="FillAndExpand">
```

```
        <Label Text="FirstLabel" AbsoluteLayout.LayoutBounds="0, 0,
        AutoSize, AutoSize" AbsoluteLayout.LayoutFlags="PositionProport
        ional" />
        <Label Text="SecondLabel" AbsoluteLayout.LayoutBounds="0, 1,
        AutoSize, AutoSize" AbsoluteLayout.LayoutFlags="PositionProport
        ional" />
        <Label Text="PointLabel" AbsoluteLayout.LayoutBounds="0, 1"
        AbsoluteLayout.LayoutFlags="PositionProportional" />
    </AbsoluteLayout>
</ContentPage>
```

With AbsoluteLayout in hand we've covered the core family of Xamarin.Forms layouts. Now let's look at some distant layout cousins that we use for specific purposes, beginning with ContentView.

ContentView

The ContentView layout can act as a visual or virtual container class, like a custom control. ContentView is designed for reuse throughout your app. It's also useful for providing quick padding or formatting around another view or layout.

As a visual rectangular container, ContentView provides the standard Layout class properties such as Padding, BackgroundColor, HorizontalOptions, and VerticalOptions, much like a .NET panel control. As a virtual container, it can house a child layout containing multiple views for swapping in and out of a page, and for use on different pages, a lot like a .NET custom control or an Android fragment.

This is a simple ContentView (from a class called SubContentView), a soothing teal rectangle with a white text label:

```
<ContentView xmlns="http://xamarin.com/schemas/2014/
forms" xmlns:x="http://schemas.microsoft.com/winfx/2009/
xaml" x:Class="LayoutExample.Xaml.Views.SubContentView"
BackgroundColor="Teal" Padding="40" HorizontalOptions="Fill">
    <Label Text="a view, such as a label, a layout, or a layout of
    layouts" FontSize="20" FontAttributes="Bold" TextColor="White" />
</ContentView>
```

ContentView can be used like any other view and placed onto a layout. Figure 3-21 shows the label tucked inside ContentView. This ContentView is then placed on a ContentPage:

```
<ContentPage xmlns="http://xamarin.com/schemas/2014/forms"
xmlns:x="http://schemas.microsoft.com/winfx/2009/xaml"
x:Class="LayoutExample.Xaml.Views.ContentViewExample" xmlns:Views="clr-
namespace:LayoutExample.Xaml.Views;assembly=LayoutExample.Xaml"
Padding="10,10,10,5">
    <StackLayout>
        <Views:SubContentView />
    </StackLayout>
</ContentPage>
```

Note how the ContentView padding creates colored space around the label in Figure 3-21.

Figure 3-21. *ContentView in action*

113

> **Note**   If your screenshot doesn't match Figure 3-21 and ContentView consumes the entire screen, add this property to ContentView:
>
> VerticalOptions = "StartAndExpand"

CODE COMPLETE: ContentView

Listings 3-14 and 3-15 show the complete ContentView code example shown in Figure 3-21. Two kinds of padding are used here: the colored padding inside ContentView and the space around the edge of ContentPage.

Listing 3-14. ContentViewExample.xaml

```
<?xml version="1.0" encoding="UTF-8"?>
<ContentPage xmlns="http://xamarin.com/schemas/2014/forms" xmlns:x="http://
schemas.microsoft.com/winfx/2009/xaml" x:Class="LayoutExample.Xaml.
Views.ContentViewExample" xmlns:Views="clr-namespace:LayoutExample.Xaml.
Views;assembly=LayoutExample.Xaml" Padding="10,10,10,5">
    <StackLayout>
        <Views:SubContentView />
    </StackLayout>
</ContentPage>
```

Listing 3-15. SubContentView.xaml

```
    <?xml version="1.0" encoding="UTF-8"?>
    <ContentView xmlns="http://xamarin.com/schemas/2014/
    forms" xmlns:x="http://schemas.microsoft.com/winfx/2009/
    xaml" x:Class="LayoutExample.Xaml.Views.SubContentView"
    BackgroundColor="Teal" Padding="40" HorizontalOptions="Fill">
        <Label Text="a view, such as a label, a layout, or a layout of
        layouts" FontSize="20" FontAttributes="Bold" TextColor="White" />
    </ContentView>
```

Tip   The `ControlTemplate` and `ContentPresenter` layouts are used together for theming.

Frame

The `Frame` layout places a visible frame around itself. The `OutlineColor` property specifies the color of the frame. See Listing 3-16.

Listing 3-16.   FrameExample.xaml

```
<ContentPage xmlns="http://xamarin.com/schemas/2014/forms" xmlns:x="http://
schemas.microsoft.com/winfx/2009/xaml" x:Class="LayoutExample.Xaml.Views.
FrameExample" Padding="10,10,10,5">
    <Frame OutlineColor="Red">
        <Label Text="Framed" FontSize="40" />
    </Frame>
</ContentPage>
```

`HasShadow` is a `Boolean` property specifying a shadow effect when the platform supports it. The default `Padding` value on a `Frame` layout is 20.

Figure 3-22 shows the `Frame` layout.

Figure 3-22. *Frame layout*

Tip The CornerRadius property permits the rounding of frame corners.

Those are the layouts in Xamarin.Forms!

When building layouts, a related topic that arises is the creation of custom controls, used as components for building layouts.

Understanding Custom Controls

Custom controls in Xamarin are partial layouts that can be included in larger layouts on an as-needed basis, that can be created on all platforms, and that can be made to function like user controls, custom controls, or panels in .NET. Custom controls are barely touched upon in this book, but the topic bears mentioning in the context of constructing professional-grade layouts.

In Xamarin.Forms, ContentView is a base class for creating custom views for nesting, padding, and reuse. Custom controls should not be confused with *customized controls*, which are usually individual Xamarin.Forms views with enhanced platform-specific functionality that are built using a custom renderer (see Chapter 8). Even so, developers will sometimes refer to a single customized control as a custom control. Also, a customized control has the capacity to contain multiple controls and might then actually become a custom control.

Note   This chapter explores a static, manual approach to layouts. Many of these layouts, such as the Xamarin.Forms ones, contain bindable properties and can be bound to data sources and constructed dynamically at runtime. You'll learn about data binding in later chapters (Chapter 6 and Chapter 9).

Summary

Layouts are a fine example of just how similar these different platforms can be. Names change, but concepts don't, and for added continuity, Xamarin strives to incorporate the most useful aspects of these various platforms into Xamarin.Forms. Here are some of the universal terms related to layouts:

- *FlexLayouts* are the newest and most easy-to-use while also being one of the most versatile layouts.

- *StackLayouts* are the simplest layouts in Xamarin.Forms, great for easy pages and quick prototyping and wireframing.

- *Rectangles* frame views and their size and coordinate location.

- *RelativeLayouts* are useful when the task is simple and precise coordinates are on hand.

- *Constraints* bind views together like elastic that contextually determines size and location. Complex constraints require C#.

- *Layout options* handle alignment and formatting with HorizontalOptions and VerticalOptions.

- The *custom control* persists as a concept in mobile development, achieved in Xamarin.Forms with a ContentView.

- Grid layouts are Xamarin.Forms' table layout offering, giving us relativity, precision, and versatility.

Those are some of the fundamentals of mobile screen layouts. Now it's time to make those layouts and controls more beautiful using styling.

CHAPTER 4

Styles, Themes, and CSS

User interface design challenges us to elegantly and functionally position layouts and controls while maintaining a coherent design and a consistent user experience across the entire application. This chapter is not about creating beautiful and visually appealing applications, which is an art in and of itself. This chapter explores beautiful and appealing ways to architect your UI code, separating the presentation from the content and structure using resources, styles, themes, and Cascading Style Sheets. Creating beautiful designs is a journey, and the purpose of this chapter is to take you on a journey from a simple but functional page to one that is also beautiful, dynamic, and maintainable. Reusability of UI code offers consistency of design, cleaner and more readable code, and the agility to change the look of the application over time.

We're going to cover the entire Xamarin UI formatting story: beginning with manual styling, resources and dictionaries, styles, themes, and then Cascading Style Sheets (CSS). First, we will create a page without styling and then style it manually. Then, instead of manually hardcoding the property settings, we will use resources stored centrally in a dictionary and look them up statically and dynamically. We'll examine styles and how to use them explicitly on a view or implicitly on all instances of a view. We'll explore style inheritance and overriding techniques. We will take a look at the Xamarin.Forms Light and Dark theme and how to use them as the basis of a custom theme and, finally, use CSS as an alternative to XAML to style a page.

Our demo app is a feedback page that allows users to share their experience using the app.

Creating a Page Without Style

We'll begin with a basic page without styling that allows a user to provide feedback. It will have Subject and Message fields and a Submit and Cancel buttons. Soon we'll style the page.

© Dan Hermes 2019
D. Hermes and N. Mazloumi, *Building Xamarin.Forms Mobile Apps Using XAML*,
https://doi.org/10.1007/978-1-4842-4030-4_4

Create a Forms XAML Page called FeedbackPage.xaml with an Entry view representing the subject line and an Editor view for the feedback. Finally, add a submit and cancel Button to the form to handle user interactions. To structure the content, use a Grid layout with one column and three rows, one for the subject line, one for the feedback, and the last for a StackLayout that vertically places the two buttons, as shown in Listing 4-1.

Listing 4-1. Simple Feedback Page

```
<ContentPage Title="Plain" xmlns="http://xamarin.com/schemas/2014/forms"
xmlns:x="http://schemas.microsoft.com/winfx/2009/xaml"
x:Class="StyleExamples.FeedbackPage">
    <Grid>
        <Grid.RowDefinitions>
            <RowDefinition Height="Auto" />
            <RowDefinition Height="*" />
            <RowDefinition Height="Auto" />
        </Grid.RowDefinitions>
        <Grid.ColumnDefinitions>
            <ColumnDefinition Width="*" />
        </Grid.ColumnDefinitions>
        <Entry Placeholder="Enter Subject" Grid.Row="0" />
        <Editor x:Name="Feedback" Grid.Row="1" Unfocused="HandleFeedback"
        Focused="HandleFeedback" />
        <StackLayout Orientation="Vertical" Grid.Row="2">
            <Button Text="Cancel" />
            <Button Text="Submit" />
        </StackLayout>
    </Grid>
</ContentPage>
```

The Grid and StackLayout provide structure to the page, and the content comprises the Entry, Editor, and Button views. StackLayout is used with a vertical orientation to ensure that the two buttons are aligned below one another. The Entry, the Editor, and the StackLayout are positioned in the Grid using the Grid.Row attached property. Grid.Column is not required here, given that the Grid has only one column. The Grid column uses Star to consume all space available, that is, ColumnDefinition Width="*".

The first and third grid rows only use as much space as needed by the subject line and the submit and cancel buttons, whereas the rest of the vertical space is allocated to the feedback area using and RowDefinition Height="*".

The Editor view does not have a Placeholder property like the Entry view does. Create placeholder text by hand by assigning a HandleFeedback method to both the Focused and Unfocused properties. Create the HandleFeedback event handler in the code behind that sets the Text of the Editor when it gains or loses focus, as shown in Listing 4-2.

Listing 4-2. Simple Feedback Page

```
public partial class FeedbackPage : ContentPage {
    const string placeHolderText = "Type your message here";
    void HandleFeedback(object sender, Xamarin.Forms.FocusEventArgs e) {
        var text = Feedback.Text;
        if (Feedback.Text == placeHolderText) {
            Feedback.Text = string.Empty;
            return;
        }
        if (Feedback.Text == string.Empty) {
            Feedback.Text = placeHolderText;
            return;
        }
    }
    public FeedbackPage() {
        InitializeComponent();
        Feedback.Text = placeHolderText;
    }
}
```

For every named XAML element, the XAML parser creates a local variable in the resulting generated file. When the page is initialized, the Text property of the Editor view, which is called Feedback in the XAML, is set to a placeHolderText. When the Editor gains or loses focus, the HandleFeedback method is called that checks whether the Editor Text is still the placeHolderText and empties it for the user to enter the feedback. If the Editor loses the focus and is still empty, it sets the Text back to the placeHolderText. This mimics the built-in functionality of the Entry view, which has this out of the box. In the App.cs project, wrap the FeedbackPage inside a NavigationPage and add it to the MainPage of the application. Figure 4-1 shows the result for both platforms.

Figure 4-1. *Simple feedback page*

The feedback page is functional and gray. Let's add some color.

Styling Manually Using View Formatting Properties

Improve the appearance of the FeedbackPage by providing colors for the text and backgrounds, using layout and view formatting properties.

1. Create a new XAML page called LocalDesignPage.xaml and copy the XAML over from FeedbackPage.xaml.

2. Use the BackgroundColor property of ContentPage and Grid to visually separate the form canvas represented by the Grid from the page background by making the Grid gray and the ContentPage background green.

    ```
    <ContentPage BackgroundColor="#4CAF50">
    <Grid BackgroundColor="#AAAAAA">
    ```

3. Use the Grid Padding and Margin properties to provide some space for the content away from the screen bezel.

    ```
    <Grid Padding="30" Margin="30">
    ```

4. Surround the feedback input field with a StackLayout that has a Silver BackgroundColor and is just one pixel bigger than the Editor control.

    ```
    <StackLayout Orientation="Vertical" Padding="1"
    BackgroundColor="Silver">
    ```

5. Give the feedback input field all the space it can get vertically.

    ```
    <Editor VerticalOptions="FillAndExpand">
    ```

6. Add TextColor and FontAttributes to the subject line and feedback input field.

    ```
    <Entry TextColor="Navy" FontAttributes="Italic" />
    <Editor TextColor="Navy" FontAttributes="Italic" />
    ```

7. Style the buttons to help the user make the right decision by making the submit button green and the cancel button orange with bold text using all the space they can get horizontally, as shown in Listing 4-3.

Listing 4-3. Simple Feedback Page

```
<Button Text="Submit" TextColor="White" FontAttributes="Bold"
BackgroundColor="#4CAF50" />
<Button Text="Cancel" HorizontalOptions="FillAndExpand"
TextColor="White"
FontAttributes="Bold" BackgroundColor="#f47442" />
```

Now we have a colorful feedback page, as shown in Figure 4-2 for both platforms.

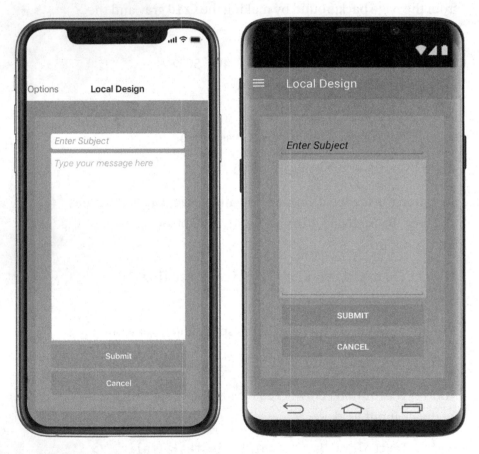

Figure 4-2. *Styled feedback page*

CODE COMPLETE: Feedback Page Using View Formatting Properties

Listing 4-4 provides the complete code for the LocalDesignPage.xaml.

Listing 4-4. Styled Feedback Page

```xml
<ContentPage BackgroundColor="#4CAF50" Title="Local Design"
xmlns="http://xamarin.com/schemas/2014/forms"
xmlns:x="http://schemas.microsoft.com/winfx/2009/xaml"
x:Class="StyleExamples.LocalDesignPage">
    <Grid Padding="30" Margin="30" BackgroundColor="#AAAAAA">
        <Grid.RowDefinitions>
            <RowDefinition Height="Auto" />
            <RowDefinition Height="*" />
            <RowDefinition Height="Auto" />
        </Grid.RowDefinitions>
        <Grid.ColumnDefinitions>
            <ColumnDefinition Width="*" />
        </Grid.ColumnDefinitions>
        <Entry Placeholder="Enter Subject" Grid.Row="0" TextColor="Navy"
        FontAttributes="Italic" />
        <StackLayout Orientation="Vertical" Grid.Row="1" Padding="1"
        BackgroundColor="Silver">
            <Editor x:Name="Feedback" VerticalOptions="FillAndExpand"
            TextColor="Navy" FontAttributes="Italic"
            Unfocused="HandleFeedback"
            Focused="HandleFeedback" />
        </StackLayout>
        <StackLayout Orientation="Vertical" Grid.Row="2">
            <Button Text="Submit" HorizontalOptions="FillAndExpand"
            TextColor="White" FontAttributes="Bold"
            BackgroundColor="#4CAF50" />
            <Button Text="Cancel" HorizontalOptions="FillAndExpand"
```

```
                TextColor="White" FontAttributes="Bold"
                BackgroundColor="#f47442" />
          </StackLayout>
       </Grid>
    </ContentPage>
```

The number of lines remained almost the same but the XAML is now cluttered with hardcoded values. Compared to this, the unstyled page in Listing 4-1 was short and elegant.

Resources can address the hardcoding issue. Let's see how.

Resources and Dictionaries

A *resource* is an object in a dictionary that can be retrieved by its string key. Any XAML element, in fact any C# class, can be defined as a resource. Common resources in XAML are templates, styles, frequently used values, and value converters.

A *resource dictionary* is a key value store. The keys are strings and the values any type of objects. Resource dictionaries play an important role within the styling system of Xamarin.Forms. They allow separation of the presentation from the content and structure of a page.

The lookup of a resource in a dictionary can be static or dynamic. Static lookup happens only once when the view is created. Subsequent changes to the resource are not applied to the view. Dynamic lookup allows a resource to change at runtime, and the change can be reflected in the view.

Resource dictionaries can be defined at the application, page, and view levels. Locally defined resources can override resources defined at the page or application level. Standard guidelines of scoping apply here: try and use view or page level resource dictionaries before defining them at the application level to create globals.

Tip   Resource dictionaries can be stored as separate, mergeable XAML files.

Pages, layouts, and controls, all views in Xamarin.Forms that subclass `VisualElement`, can contain resource definitions. `VisualElement` has a member called `Resources` of type `ResourceDictionary` for this purpose.

Defining Resources

Resources are objects stored in a resource dictionary that can be retrieved by their key. Define resources by adding a resource dictionary to a page, layout, or control and adding resources to that dictionary.

As an example, use the property element syntax ContentPage.Resources to define a ResourceDictionary with resources accessible to the FeedbackPage page and add a Color resource that represents the page BackgroundColor, as shown in Listing 4-5.

Listing 4-5. Defining Resources Inside a Resource Dictionary

```
<ContentPage.Resources>
    <ResourceDictionary>
        <Color x:Key="PageBgColor">#4CAF50</Color>
    </ResourceDictionary>
</ContentPage.Resources>
```

The Color with the key PageBgColor can now be referenced within the page.

Tip   Name resources based on what they are used for and not what they are, e.g., NukeButton instead of RedButton. This makes sure they are used for what they were intended for.

You could use other keyword variable names, such as XAML keyword Name, or whatever you choose, instead of Key, e.g.:

```
<Color x:Name="PageBgColor">#4CAF50</Color>
```

This will create the local variable PageBgColor in the C# code behind. It is recommended, however, to use the Key and to access the resource in the code behind through a dictionary lookup passing in the key and then casting the resulting object to the target type, e.g.:

```
var pageBgColor = (Color) Resources["PageBgColor"];
```

Create resources for all the colors, font styles, and even string literals used as placeholders, as shown in Listing 4-6.

Listing 4-6. Defining Resources Inside a Resource Dictionary

```
<ResourceDictionary>
    <x:String x:Key="SubjectPlaceholder">Enter Subject</x:String>
    <x:String x:Key="FeedbackPlaceholder">Enter your message here
    </x:String>
    <x:String x:Key="InputPlaceholder">Enter Subject</x:String>
    <Color x:Key="PageBgColor">#4CAF50</Color>
    <Color x:Key="FormBgColor">#AAAAAA</Color>
    <Color x:Key="InputTextColor">Navy</Color>
    <Color x:Key="InputPlaceholderColor">Silver</Color>
    <Color x:Key="FeedbackBorderColor">Silver</Color>
    <FontAttributes x:Key="InputFontStyle">Italic</FontAttributes>
    <Color x:Key="BtTextColor">White</Color>
    <Color x:Key="BtSubmitColor">#4CAF50</Color>
    <Color x:Key="BtCancelColor">#f47442</Color>
    <FontAttributes x:Key="BtFontStyle">Bold</FontAttributes>
</ResourceDictionary>
```

This resource dictionary is inline with `ContentPage.Resources`. Soon we'll break it out into its own XAML file so it can be used by different pages.

After defining your resources, you need to reference them. We'll begin by using the Xamarin.Forms `StaticResource` markup extensions.

Static Resource Lookup

The `StaticResource` markup extension assigns a value to a bindable property of an XAML element once, when the XAML object is created at runtime. Any subsequent changes to the resources are not reflected on the object, and so the lookup is static. Use the static lookup if a resource does not change during the lifetime of the application. This improves the performance of the application. Use the dynamic lookup instead if resources assigned to the view are intended to change, for example, to change the style of a view depending on the user interaction.

Caution   `StaticResource` throws an exception at runtime if the key does not exist.

Use the StaticResource markup extension to set the background color of the page with a lookup of the key PageBgColor in the resource dictionary. Use the Key property of StaticResource to pass in the key of the resource that should be used, e.g.:

```
<ContentPage BackgroundColor="{StaticResource Key=PageBgColor}" ...>
```

You learned in Chapter 2 that a property can be omitted if declared as a content property. The preceding declaration is therefore the same as

```
<ContentPage BackgroundColor="{StaticResource PageBgColor}" ...>
```

Create a new XAML page and call it StaticResourcesPage.xaml. Duplicate the LocalDesignPage.xaml page to begin with. Replace all the property assignments in the XAML with a lookup of the respective key you defined in the resource dictionary in Listing 4-6 using the StaticResource markup extension, as shown in Listing 4-7. The Grid column and row definitions are omitted for brevity.

Listing 4-7. Using StaticResource Inside XAML Instead of Hardcoded Values

```
<Grid Padding="30" Margin="30" BackgroundColor="{StaticResource
FormBgColor}">
....
    <Entry Placeholder="{StaticResource SubjectPlaceholder}"
    Grid.Row="0"
    TextColor="{StaticResource InputTextColor}" FontAttributes="
    {StaticResource
    InputFontStyle}" />
    <StackLayout Orientation="Vertical" Grid.Row="1" Padding="1"
    BackgroundColor="{StaticResource FeedbackBorderColor}">
        <Editor x:Name="Feedback" VerticalOptions="FillAndExpand"
        TextColor="{StaticResource InputTextColor}" FontAttributes="
        {StaticResource
        InputFontStyle}" Unfocused="HandleFeedback"
        Focused="HandleFeedback"
        />
    </StackLayout>
    <StackLayout Orientation="Vertical" Grid.Row="2">
        <Button Text="Submit" HorizontalOptions="FillAndExpand"
```

```
            TextColor="{StaticResource BtTextColor}" FontAttributes=
            "{StaticResource
            BtFontStyle}" BackgroundColor="{StaticResource BtSubmitColor}" />
            <Button Text="Cancel" HorizontalOptions="FillAndExpand"
            TextColor="{StaticResource BtTextColor}" FontAttributes="
            {StaticResource
            BtFontStyle}" BackgroundColor="{StaticResource BtCancelColor}" />
        </StackLayout>
    </Grid>
```

Replace in the code behind `StaticResourcesPage.xaml.cs` the hardcoded values for the feedback placeholder and the feedback text color with a lookup of the resource FeedbackPlaceholder and InputTextColor, as shown in Listing 4-8.

Listing 4-8. Using StaticResource Inside Code Behind Instead of Hardcoded Values

```csharp
public partial class StaticResourcesPage : ContentPage {
    void HandleFeedback(object sender, Xamarin.Forms.FocusEventArgs e){
        var placeHolderText = (string)Resources["FeedbackPlaceholder"];

        if (Feedback.Text == placeHolderText) {
            Feedback.Text = string.Empty;
            Feedback.TextColor = (Color)Resources["InputTextColor"];
            return;
        }

        if (Feedback.Text == string.Empty) {
            Feedback.Text = placeHolderText;
            Feedback.TextColor = (Color)Resources["InputPlaceholderColor"];
            return;
        }
    }

    public StaticResourcesPage() {
        InitializeComponent();
        Feedback.Text = (string)Resources["FeedbackPlaceholder"];
        Feedback.TextColor = (Color)Resources["InputPlaceholderColor"];
    }
}
```

The feedback page in Figure 4-3 looks exactly the same as Figure 4-2 with hardcoded styling. The improvement is in the coding technique.

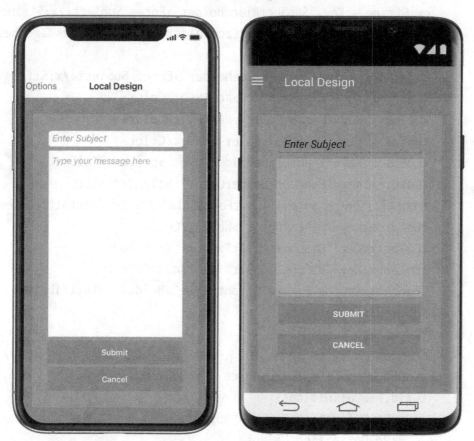

Figure 4-3. *Styled feedback page using resource and static lookup*

CODE COMPLETE: Feedback Page Using Static Resources

Listings 4-9 and Listing 4-10 provide the complete code for StaticResourcesPage.xaml and StaticResourcesPage.xaml.cs.

Listing 4-9. StaticResourcesPage.xaml in the Forms Project

```
<?xml version="1.0" encoding="UTF-8"?>
<ContentPage BackgroundColor="{StaticResource Key=PageBgColor}"
Title="StaticResource" xmlns="http://xamarin.com/schemas/2014/forms"
xmlns:x="http://schemas.microsoft.com/winfx/2009/xaml"
x:Class="StyleExamples.StaticResourcesPage">
```

```xml
<ContentPage.Resources>
    <ResourceDictionary>
        <x:String x:Key="SubjectPlaceholder">Enter Subject</x:String>
        <x:String x:Key="FeedbackPlaceholder">Type your message here</
        x:String>
        <x:String x:Key="InputPlaceholder">Enter Subject</x:String>
        <Color x:Key="PageBgColor">#4CAF50</Color>
        <Color x:Key="FormBgColor">#AAAAAA</Color>
        <Color x:Key="InputTextColor">Navy</Color>
        <Color x:Key="InputPlaceholderColor">Silver</Color>
        <Color x:Key="FeedbackBorderColor">Silver</Color>
        <FontAttributes x:Key="InputFontStyle">Italic</FontAttributes>
        <Color x:Key="BtTextColor">White</Color>
        <Color x:Key="BtSubmitColor">#4CAF50</Color>
        <Color x:Key="BtCancelColor">#f47442</Color>
        <FontAttributes x:Key="BtFontStyle">Bold</FontAttributes>
    </ResourceDictionary>
</ContentPage.Resources>
    <Grid Padding="30" Margin="30"
    BackgroundColor="{StaticResource FormBgColor}">
        <Grid.RowDefinitions>
            <RowDefinition Height="Auto"/>
            <RowDefinition Height="*"    />
            <RowDefinition Height="Auto"/>
        </Grid.RowDefinitions>
        <Grid.ColumnDefinitions>
            <ColumnDefinition Width="*" />
        </Grid.ColumnDefinitions>
        <Entry Placeholder="{StaticResource SubjectPlaceholder}"
        Grid.Row="0" TextColor="{StaticResource InputTextColor}"
        FontAttributes="{StaticResource InputFontStyle}" />
        <StackLayout Orientation="Vertical" Grid.Row="1" Padding="1"
        BackgroundColor="{StaticResource FeedbackBorderColor}">
            <Editor x:Name="Feedback" VerticalOptions="FillAndExpand"
            TextColor="{StaticResource InputTextColor}"
```

```
            FontAttributes="{StaticResource InputFontStyle}"
            Unfocused="HandleFeedback" Focused="HandleFeedback" />
        </StackLayout>
        <StackLayout Orientation="Vertical" Grid.Row="2">
            <Button Text="Submit" HorizontalOptions="FillAndExpand"
            TextColor="{StaticResource BtTextColor}"
            FontAttributes="{StaticResource BtFontStyle}"
            BackgroundColor="{StaticResource BtSubmitColor}" />
            <Button Text="Cancel" HorizontalOptions="FillAndExpand"
            TextColor="{StaticResource BtTextColor}"
            FontAttributes="{StaticResource BtFontStyle}"
            BackgroundColor="{StaticResource BtCancelColor}" />
        </StackLayout>
    </Grid>
</ContentPage>
```

Listing 4-10. StaticResourcesPage.xaml.cs in the Forms Project

```csharp
using Xamarin.Forms;

namespace StyleExamples {
    public partial class StaticResourcesPage : ContentPage {
        void HandleFeedback(object sender, Xamarin.Forms.FocusEventArgs e) {
            var placeHolderText = (string)Resources["FeedbackPlaceholder"];

            if (Feedback.Text == placeHolderText) {
                Feedback.Text = string.Empty;
                Feedback.TextColor = (Color)Resources["InputTextColor"];
                return;
            }

            if (Feedback.Text == string.Empty) {
                Feedback.Text = placeHolderText;
                Feedback.TextColor = (Color)Resources["InputPlaceholder
                Color"];
                return;
            }
        }
```

```
        public StaticResourcesPage() {
            InitializeComponent();
            Feedback.Text = (string)Resources["FeedbackPlaceholder"];
            Feedback.TextColor = (Color)Resources["InputPlaceholderColor"];
        }
    }
}
```

Static resources significantly improve the maintainability of the code because nothing is hardcoded, code is reused, and the styling is decoupled from the UI. However, the XAML is less readable compared to the previous two iterations where we had no styling or just hardcoded styles. Most importantly, the lookup of a resource is done once by StaticResource, and any subsequent changes to the resource cannot be applied to the page content.

Let's fix that using the DynamicResource markup extension.

Dynamic Resource Lookup

The DynamicResource markup extension assigns a value to a bindable property of an XAML element. Changes to the resource can be applied to the property at runtime; thus, the lookup is called dynamic. Use the dynamic lookup to ensure that a view is updated if its resources change in response to a user interaction. Dynamic lookup is resource intensive and can impact performance. The best practice is to use the static lookup until there is a need to change a resource at runtime.

Note   A DynamicResource does not need to exist when declaring the XAML. The application can add the key and object at runtime. XAML uses the default value of the bindable property if no resource can be found.

As with StaticResource you can omit the Key property of DynamicResource. Use the DynamicResource markup extension to replace the background color of the page with a lookup of the key PageBgColor in the resource dictionary, e.g.:

```
<ContentPage BackgroundColor="{DynamicResource PageBgColor}" ...>
```

Create a new XAML page and call the new page DynamicResourcePage.xaml. Copy the code from StaticResourcesPage.xaml into your new page. Replace all the StaticResource markup extensions with DynamicResource.

Our "Cancel" and "Submit" buttons are colorful and clickable. What if we guided the interaction a bit more by graying them out until the user at least enters a subject? Add a couple more Color resources to the resource dictionary for different background colors for the page and the button depending on whether the user entered a subject or not and to initialize the buttons when inactive, as shown in Listing 4-11.

Listing 4-11. Resources for Handling User Interactions

```
<Color x:Key="PageBgColorNoSubject">#85af87</Color>
<Color x:Key="PageBgColorWithSubject">#4CAF50</Color>
<Color x:Key="BtSubmitActiveColor">#4CAF50</Color>
<Color x:Key="BtCancelActiveColor">#f47442</Color>
<Color x:Key="BtInactiveColor">Gray</Color>
```

Next, assign PageBgColor, BtSubmitColor, and BtCancelColor dynamically depending on whether there is a subject line or not.

Changing a resource is done in the code behind, like this:

```
Resources["PageBgColor"] = Resources["PageBgColorNoSubject"];
```

Add the HandleSubject event handler to the Entry view to respond to gaining and losing focus in order to change the Color resources based on the user interaction, e.g.:

```
<Entry Unfocused="HandleSubject" Focused="HandleSubject" />
```

Both the Unfocused and Focused events are wired now to the HandleSubject handler. Create the HandleSubject method and check whether the subject line has any text. If no text is provided, change PageBgColor to PageBgColorNoSubject and both BtSubmitColor and BtCancelColor to BtInactiveColor and back to PageBgColorWithSubject and BtSubmitActiveColor and BtCancelActiveColor as soon as the user has changed the text and Entry view loses focus, as shown in Listing 4-12.

Listing 4-12. Changing Resource Objects Based on User Interaction

```
void HandleSubject(object sender, Xamarin.Forms.FocusEventArgs e) {
    if (Subject.Text == string.Empty) {
        Resources["PageBgColor"] = Resources["PageBgColorNoSubject"];
        Resources["BtSubmitColor"] = Resources["BtInactiveColor"];
    } else {
        Resources["PageBgColor"] = Resources["PageBgColorWithSubject"];
        Resources["BtSubmitColor"] = Resources["BtSubmitActiveColor"];
    }
}
```

Finally, initialize the page constructor to make sure the form is in an inactive state when it is visited for the first time, as shown in Listing 4-13.

Listing 4-13. DynamicResourcesPage Constructor

```
public DynamicResourcesPage() {
    InitializeComponent();
    Feedback.Text = (string)Resources["FeedbackPlaceholder"];
    Feedback.TextColor = (Color)Resources["InputPlaceholderColor"];
    Subject.Text = string.Empty;
    Resources["PageBgColor"] = Resources["PageBgColorNoSubject"];
    Resources["BtSubmitColor"] = Resources["BtInactiveColor"];
}
```

Figure 4-4 shows the result for both platforms.

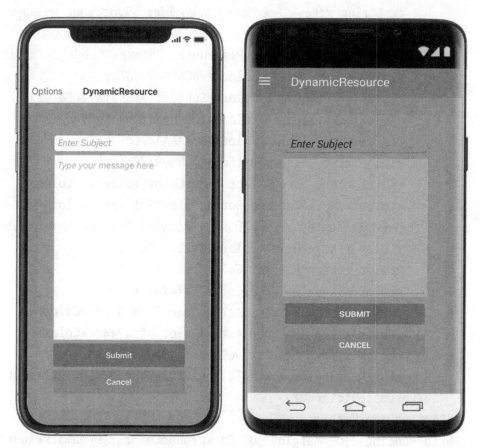

Figure 4-4. *Dynamic styling based on user interaction*

CODE COMPLETE: Feedback Page Using Dynamic Resources

Listings 4-14 and Listing 4-15 provide the complete code for the DynamicResourcePage.
xaml and DynamicResourcePage.xaml.cs.

Listing 4-14. Feedback Page XAML with Dynamic Resources

```
<ContentPage BackgroundColor="{DynamicResource PageBgColor}"
Title="DynamicResource" xmlns="http://xamarin.com/schemas/2014/forms"
xmlns:x="http://schemas.microsoft.com/winfx/2009/xaml"
x:Class="StyleExamples.DynamicResourcesPage">
    <ContentPage.Resources>
        <ResourceDictionary>
```

```
        <x:String x:Key="SubjectPlaceholder">Enter Subject</x:String>
        <x:String x:Key="FeedbackPlaceholder">Type your message here
        </x:String>
        <x:String x:Key="InputPlaceholder">Enter Subject</x:String>
        <Color x:Key="PageBgColor">#4CAF50</Color>
        <Color x:Key="PageBgColorNoSubject">#85af87</Color>
        <Color x:Key="PageBgColorWithSubject">#4CAF50</Color>
        <Color x:Key="FormBgColor">#AAAAAA</Color>
        <Color x:Key="InputTextColor">Navy</Color>
        <Color x:Key="InputPlaceholderColor">Silver</Color>
        <Color x:Key="FeedbackBorderColor">Silver</Color>
        <FontAttributes x:Key="InputFontStyle">Italic</FontAttributes>
        <Color x:Key="BtTextColor">White</Color>
        <Color x:Key="BtSubmitColor">#4CAF50</Color>
        <Color x:Key="BtCancelColor">#f47442</Color>
        <Color x:Key="BtSubmitActiveColor">#4CAF50</Color>
        <Color x:Key="BtCancelActiveColor">#f47442</Color>
        <Color x:Key="BtInactiveColor">Gray</Color>
        <FontAttributes x:Key="BtFontStyle">Bold</FontAttributes>
    </ResourceDictionary>
</ContentPage.Resources>
<Grid Padding="30" Margin="30" BackgroundColor="{DynamicResource
FormBgColor}">
    <Grid.RowDefinitions>
        <RowDefinition Height="Auto"/>
        <RowDefinition Height="*"    />
        <RowDefinition Height="Auto"/>
    </Grid.RowDefinitions>
    <Grid.ColumnDefinitions>
        <ColumnDefinition Width="*" />
    </Grid.ColumnDefinitions>
    <Entry x:Name="Subject" Placeholder="{DynamicResource
    SubjectPlaceholder}"
    Grid.Row="0" TextColor="{DynamicResource InputTextColor}"
    FontAttributes="{DynamicResource InputFontStyle}"
```

```
            Unfocused="HandleSubject"
            Focused="HandleSubject" />
            <StackLayout Orientation="Vertical" Grid.Row="1" Padding="1"
            BackgroundColor="{DynamicResource FeedbackBorderColor}">
                <Editor x:Name="Feedback" VerticalOptions="FillAndExpand"
                TextColor="{DynamicResource InputTextColor}"
                FontAttributes="{DynamicResource InputFontStyle}"
                Unfocused="HandleFeedback" Focused="HandleFeedback" />
            </StackLayout>
            <StackLayout Orientation="Vertical" Grid.Row="2">
                <Button Text="Submit" HorizontalOptions="FillAndExpand"
                TextColor="{DynamicResource BtTextColor}"
                FontAttributes="{DynamicResource
                BtFontStyle}" BackgroundColor="{DynamicResource
                BtSubmitColor}" />
                <Button Text="Cancel" HorizontalOptions="FillAndExpand"
                TextColor="{DynamicResource BtTextColor}"
                FontAttributes="{DynamicResource
                BtFontStyle}" BackgroundColor="{DynamicResource
                BtCancelColor}" />
            </StackLayout>
        </Grid>
    </ContentPage>
```

Listing 4-15. Feedback Page Code Behind with Dynamic Resources

```
public partial class DynamicResourcesPage : ContentPage {
    void HandleSubject(object sender, Xamarin.Forms.FocusEventArgs e) {
        if (Subject.Text == string.Empty){
            Resources["PageBgColor"] = Resources["PageBgColorNoSubject"];
            Resources["BtSubmitColor"] = Resources["BtInactiveColor"];
        } else {
            Resources["PageBgColor"] = Resources["PageBgColorWithSubject"];
            Resources["BtSubmitColor"] = Resources["BtSubmitActiveColor"];
        }
    }
```

```
    void HandleFeedback(object sender, Xamarin.Forms.FocusEventArgs e) {
        var text = Feedback.Text;
        var placeHolderText = (string)Resources["FeedbackPlaceholder"];

        if (Feedback.Text == placeHolderText) {
            Feedback.Text = string.Empty;
            Feedback.TextColor = (Color)Resources["InputTextColor"];
            return;
        }

        if (Feedback.Text == string.Empty) {
            Feedback.Text = placeHolderText;
            Feedback.TextColor = (Color)Resources["InputPlaceholderColor"];
            return;
        }
    }

    public DynamicResourcesPage() {
        InitializeComponent();
        Feedback.Text = (string)Resources["FeedbackPlaceholder"];
        Feedback.TextColor = (Color)Resources["InputPlaceholderColor"];
        Subject.Text = "";
        Resources["PageBgColor"] = Resources["PageBgColorNoSubject"];
        Resources["BtSubmitColor"] = Resources["BtInactiveColor"];
    }
}
```

DynamicResource helps us create more interactive user interfaces.

Back to the resource dictionary, defining it as an external XAML file allows reuse across the entire application, a sophisticated coding technique.

Reusable Resource Dictionaries

Resource dictionaries can be defined as separate, reusable XAML documents that can be loaded into another XAML page or anywhere in the application.

In this example, we'll define the StyleExamples.MyResources resource dictionary as a standalone XAML file and reference it in ImportResourcesPage.xaml using the ResourceDictionary element.

Create a new XAML document called MyResources.xaml and replace the root element ContentPage that Visual Studio created with ResourceDictionary both in the XAML and the code behind.

Tip   Xamarin.Forms 3.0+ won't need a code behind, but this example is pre-3.0.

Copy the resources defined inside the DynamicResourcesPage.xaml to MyResources. xaml, as shown in Listing 4-16.

Listing 4-16.   External Resource Dictionary

```
<ResourceDictionary xmlns="http://xamarin.com/schemas/2014/forms"
xmlns:x="http://schemas.microsoft.com/winfx/2009/xaml"
x:Class="StyleExamples.MyResources">
    <x:String x:Key="SubjectPlaceholder">Enter Subject</x:String>
    <x:String x:Key="FeedbackPlaceholder">Type your message here
    </x:String>
    <x:String x:Key="InputPlaceholder">Enter Subject</x:String>
    <Color x:Key="PageBgColor">#4CAF50</Color>
    <Color x:Key="PageBgColorNoSubject">#85af87</Color>
    <Color x:Key="PageBgColorWithSubject">#4CAF50</Color>
    <Color x:Key="FormBgColor">#AAAAAA</Color>
    <Color x:Key="InputTextColor">Navy</Color>
    <Color x:Key="InputPlaceholderColor">Silver</Color>
    <Color x:Key="FeedbackBorderColor">Silver</Color>
    <FontAttributes x:Key="InputFontStyle">Italic</FontAttributes>
    <Color x:Key="BtTextColor">White</Color>
    <Color x:Key="BtSubmitColor">#4CAF50</Color>
    <Color x:Key="BtCancelColor">#f47442</Color>
    <Color x:Key="BtSubmitActiveColor">#4CAF50</Color>
    <Color x:Key="BtCancelActiveColor">#f47442</Color>
    <Color x:Key="BtInactiveColor">Gray</Color>
    <FontAttributes x:Key="BtFontStyle">Bold</FontAttributes>
</ResourceDictionary>
```

Now let's create a file that will reference MyResources.xaml. Copy DynamicResourcesPage.xaml to a new page called ImportResourcesPage.xaml. Use xmlns to add the namespace of MyResources, StyleExamples, to the ContentPage root element.

```
xmlns:local="clr-namespace:StyleExamples"
```

Replace the existing ResourceDictionary in ImportResourcesPage.xaml with a single ResourceDictionary element that imports MyResources using the MergedWith property, like this:

```
<ContentPage.Resources>
    <ResourceDictionary MergedWith="local:MyResources"/>
</ContentPage.Resources>
```

The resource dictionary MyResources can now be maintained centrally and used across the entire app.

Global Resource Dictionary

After defining a reusable resource dictionary, make it available application-wide by configuring App.xaml. Modify the App.xaml, as shown in Listing 4-17.

Listing 4-17. Global Resources

```
<Application xmlns="http://xamarin.com/schemas/2014/forms"
xmlns:x="http://schemas.microsoft.com/winfx/2009/xaml"
xmlns:local="clr-
namespace:StyleExamples" x:Class="StyleExamples.App">
    <Application.Resources>
        <ResourceDictionary MergedWith="local:MyResources"/>
    </Application.Resources>
</Application>
```

Now that you've defined static, dynamic, and/or reusable resources, how does Xamarin.Forms determine what resources to apply at runtime?

Lookup Behavior

The runtime resource lookup begins with views, then pages, and then proceeds toward application resources as needed, so the physical location of the resource dictionary in the app matters. First, the runtime searches for any resources defined in the *view* that is performing the lookup. Then, the runtime traverses the parents all the way to the *page*. If it cannot find anything, then the resources defined in the *application* are searched and finally the *platform* resources that contain default resources for controls.

Try to keep the size of resource dictionary small. Reuse in this context refers to write once use everywhere but not that a resource exists only once in the runtime. The runtime creates copies of a resource each time it is requested. Scenarios where resources are defined higher up in the hierarchy but only used further down in a page are an indication that the resource is not needed.

Overriding Resources

When you need to force the use of a resource when other view, page, or app versions of this resource are available, you can override resources. Define in `ImportResourcesPage.xaml` a local resource that reuses the key `PageBgColor` to assign a different color and override the one defined in `MyResources.xaml`, as shown in Listing 4-18.

Listing 4-18. Importing External Resource Dictionaries Using MergedWidth

```
<ContentPage.Resources>
    <ResourceDictionary MergedWith="local:MyResources">
        <Color x:Key="PageBgColor">Red</Color>
    </ResourceDictionary>
</ContentPage.Resources>
```

The locally defined `Color Red` is assigned to `PageBgColor` after `MyResources` is imported.

Merging Dictionaries

Resources can be organized in separate XAML documents. This approach reduces the lookup effort and improves the performance if only dictionaries relevant to a page are loaded.

Use the property element syntax `ResourceDictionary.MergedDictionaries` instead of the attribute `MergedWith` to load one or multiple external dictionaries, as shown in Listing 4-19.

Listing 4-19. Import Multiple Resource Dictionaries Using MergedDictionaries

```
<ContentPage.Resources>
    <ResourceDictionary.MergedDictionaries>
        <local:MyResources/>
        <!—other dictionaries here -->
    </ResourceDictionary>
</ContentPage.Resources>
```

Merged dictionaries are searched in the order they are listed in the XAML. Resources with the same key in subsequent dictionaries override previously declared resources.

Resources are great to avoid hardcoding properties in the application. However, using markup extensions clutters the XAML code, which makes it less readable. Also, each resource needs to be individually assigned to a property. Ensuring a consistent design becomes a challenge. All of this also has performance implications. At runtime, each resource is looked up individually and assigned to a property of a view.

Wouldn't it be nice if the design of a view could be defined once and for the rest of your app Xamarin.Forms would take care of the UI magic? Welcome to the World of Styles.

Styles

Styles leverage resource dictionaries to allow us to customize the look and feel of our UI in an elegant, reusable manner. A *style* is a combination of one or more property setters that are applied to a particular `View` targeted by the `Style`. Styles are defined as resources inside a resource dictionary. As resources, styles have the same functionality as other resources, such as static and dynamic lookup, reuse through external resource dictionaries, overriding locally styles defined higher up, and merging styles from different sources. All views that inherit from `VisualElement` have the `Style` property that can be used to lookup a style using `StaticResource` or `DynamicResource`.

However, styles can do even more: styles when provided a key are defined to target a specific view and are referred to as explicit styles. Without a key, a style is called an implicit style and is applied implicitly to all instances of the targeted view. Views can override the property value provided by the style locally, by assigning a new value to the property. Property setters defined in a style can lookup other resources in the dictionary to avoid duplicate XAML. Styles support inheritance, which allows styles to derive from other styles. Finally, Xamarin.Forms provides built-in device styles for the Label view that can be used in the application to dynamically respond to the user's accessibility settings.

Caution   Properties used in styles must be bindable properties and exist in the view itself and not just its base class.

Define a style that targets ContentPage and specify a Setter inside the Style that assigns a color to the page's background color property, as shown in Listing 4-20.

Listing 4-20. Setting the Background Color for a Content Page

```
<ContentPage.Resources>
    <ResourceDictionary>
        <Style x:Key="PageBgColor" TargetType="ContentPage">
            <Setter Property="BackgroundColor" Value="#4CAF50"/>
        </Style>
    </ResourceDictionary>
</ContentPage.Resources>
```

The TargetType attribute is mandatory for a Style.

Style Lookup

Being a resource, styles are looked up using either the StaticResource or DynamicResource markup extensions. All views that inherit from VisualElement have the Style property that can be used to lookup a style.

Assign a style to a ContentPage using either StaticResource, if the style will not change during the lifetime of the application.

```
<ContentPage Style="{StaticResource PageBgColor}"/>
```

Remember, as with StaticResource, a style must exist and subsequent changes of the style will not be reflected.

Use DynamicResource if the style will change as the app runs.

```
<ContentPage Style="{DynamicResource PageBgColor}"/>
```

With `DynamicResource` default values of the bindable properties are used if the style is missing. The style can be defined at runtime, and C# code can be used to change the style dynamically at runtime.

Explicit Styles

Explicit styles are `Style` resources in a resource dictionary that have a key, which is used by a view to reference the style. An explicit style is not applied to all instances of the targeted view. The view must explicitly reference it in its `Style` property.

To specify an explicit style, add a `Style` element inside the resource dictionary of a page, indicate the type of views it targets using the `TargetType` property, and assign a `Key` to the style so that it can be referenced as a resource.

Create a new page called `ExplicitStylePage.xaml` and define a `Style` that specifically sets the background color for the `ExplicitStylePage`.

1. Create a `Style` specifically for a `Button` that uses the style `ButtonStyle`, e.g.:

    ```
    <Style TargetType="Button" x:Key="ButtonStyle"/>
    ```

2. Inside the `Style` element, provide one or more `Setter` elements to assign values to individual properties. Define two `Setter` that assign a text and background color, e.g.:

    ```
    <Setter Property="TextColor" Value="White" />
    <Setter Property="BackgroundColor" Value="#4CAF50" />
    ```

3. Assign the `Style` to a view using the view's `Style` property.

    ```
    <Button Text="Styled Button" Style="{StaticResource
    ButtonStyle}"/>
    ```

Figure 4-5 shows the result for both platforms.

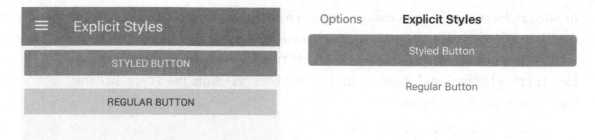

Figure 4-5. *Using explicit styles*

CODE COMPLETE: Using Explicit Styles

Listing 4-21 provides the complete code for the ExplicitStylePage.xaml.

Listing 4-21. Defining and Using Explicit Styles

```xml
<?xml version="1.0" encoding="UTF-8"?>
<ContentPage Title="Styles Page"
xmlns="http://xamarin.com/schemas/2014/forms"
xmlns:x="http://schemas.microsoft.com/winfx/2009/xaml"
x:Class="StyleExamples.ExplicitStylePage">
    <ContentPage.Resources>
        <ResourceDictionary>
            <Style TargetType="Button" x:Key="ButtonStyle">
                <Setter Property="TextColor" Value="White" />
                <Setter Property="BackgroundColor" Value="#4CAF50" />
            </Style>
        </ResourceDictionary>
    </ContentPage.Resources>
    <StackLayout Orientation="Vertical">
        <Button Text="Styled Button" Style="{StaticResource
        ButtonStyle}" />
        <Button Text="Regular Button" />
    </StackLayout>
</ContentPage>
```

Implicit Styles

Implicit styles are `style` resources in a resource dictionary that have no Key assigned and therefore are applied to all the views specified as the target type.

Create a new XAML page called `ImplicitStylePage.xaml` and copy the page `ExplicitStylePage.xaml`. Remove the Key `ButtonStyle` from the `Style`, like this, leaving only the TargetType:

```
<Style TargetType="Button"/>
```

This will apply the `style` to all `Buttons` defined in the `ContentPage`. Also, remove all `Buttons` and create a simple button with no `style`, like this:

```
<Button Text="Implicit Style Button"/>
```

Figure 4-6 shows the result for both platforms.

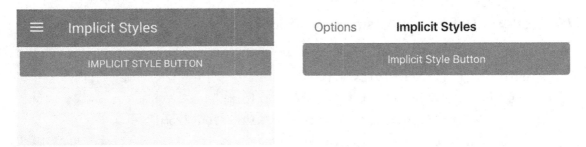

Figure 4-6. *Using implicit styles*

CODE COMPLETE: Using Implicit Styles

Listing 4-22 provides the complete code for the `ImplicitStylePage.xaml`.

Listing 4-22. Defining and Using Implicit Styles

```
<?xml version="1.0" encoding="UTF-8"?>
<ContentPage Title="Implicit Styles"
xmlns="http://xamarin.com/schemas/2014/forms"
xmlns:x="http://schemas.microsoft.com/winfx/2009/xaml"
x:Class="StyleExamples.ImplicitStylePage">
    <ContentPage.Resources>
        <ResourceDictionary>
            <Style TargetType="Button">
```

```
            <Setter Property="TextColor" Value="White" />
            <Setter Property="BackgroundColor" Value="#4CAF50" />
        </Style>
    </ResourceDictionary>
</ContentPage.Resources>
<StackLayout Orientation="Vertical">
    <Button Text="Implicit Style Button"/>
</StackLayout>
</ContentPage>
```

Note   The target type of a style must exactly match the type of the target view. Otherwise it is not applied. For example, a VisualElement style will not be applied to a Button implicitly.

To apply a style defined for a base class of a specific view, a style must be set explicitly. Define a style for the base class View, e.g.:

```
<Style TargetType="View" x:Key="ViewStyle"/>
```

View cannot be implicitly applied to Button. A Key must be provided to assign the style explicitly.

```
<Button Style="{StaticResource ViewStyle}"/>
```

Overriding Styles

When a view is instantiated, first the style is applied and then any local values assigned to its properties. This allows overriding styles locally, which is interesting when dealing with styling exceptions. You can override both explicit and implicit styles.

Create a XAML page called OverridingStylesPage.xaml. Copy ExplicitStylePage. xaml into it. Add another Button that uses the ButtonStyle but that has a local definition of the BackgroundColor, e.g.:

```
<Button Text="Overriding Styled Button" Style="{StaticResource
ButtonStyle}"
BackgroundColor="Black"/>
```

Figure 4-7 shows the result for both platforms.

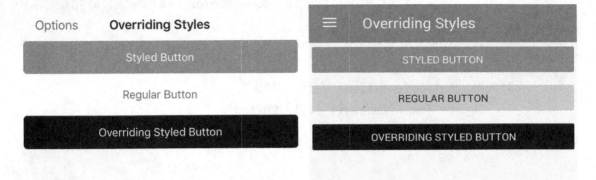

Figure 4-7. *Overriding styles*

CODE COMPLETE: Overriding Styles

Listing 4-23 provides the complete code for the OverridingStylesPage.xaml.

Listing 4-23. Defining and Using Implicit Styles

```xml
<?xml version="1.0" encoding="UTF-8"?>
<ContentPage xmlns="http://xamarin.com/schemas/2014/forms"
xmlns:x="http://schemas.microsoft.com/winfx/2009/xaml"
x:Class="StyleExamples.OverridingStylesPage">
    <ContentPage.Resources>
        <ResourceDictionary>
            <Style TargetType="Button" x:Key="ButtonStyle">
                <Setter Property="TextColor" Value="White" />
                <Setter Property="BackgroundColor" Value="#4CAF50" />
            </Style>
        </ResourceDictionary>
    </ContentPage.Resources>
    <StackLayout Orientation="Vertical">
        <Button Text="Styled Button" Style="{StaticResource
        ButtonStyle}" />
        <Button Text="Regular Button" />
        <Button Text="Overriding Styled Button" Style="{StaticResource
        ButtonStyle}"
```

```
            BackgroundColor="Black"/>
        </StackLayout>
    </ContentPage>
```

Using Resources in Styles

It is common for styles to share property settings for different views. The buttons in the feedback page share the same text color and font style. Defining these properties for each style individually results in duplicate XAML. The Value attribute of Setter allows lookup of resources using StaticResource or DynamicResource.

Create a XAML file called ButtonStylesWithResourcesPage.xaml with a resource dictionary. Define a Color and FontAttributes as separate resources in the dictionary. Define two Button styles SubmitButton and CancelButton that both reference the resources BtTextColor and BtFontStyle using the StaticResource markup extension as shown in Listing 4-24.

Listing 4-24. Using Resources

```
<ResourceDictionary>
    <Color x:Key="BtTextColor">Black</Color>
    <FontAttributes x:Key="BtFontStyle">Bold</FontAttributes>
    <Style x:Key="SubmitButton" TargetType="Button">
        <Setter Property="TextColor" Value="{StaticResource
        BtTextColor}" />
        <Setter Property="FontAttributes" Value="{StaticResource
        BtFontStyle}" />
    </Style>
    <Style x:Key="CancelButton" TargetType="Button">
        <Setter Property="TextColor" Value="{StaticResource
        BtTextColor}" />
        <Setter Property="FontAttributes" Value="{StaticResource
        BtFontStyle}" />
    </Style>
</ResourceDictionary>
```

The DynamicResource markup extension can be used as well, which makes BtTextColor and BtFontStyle optional at design time. The runtime uses default values for the TextColor and FontAttributes properties if these resources cannot be found. With StaticResource this would result in a runtime error.

Now, apply these styles to a submit and cancel button on the page, e.g.:

```
<Button Text="Submit" Style="{StaticResource SubmitButton}" />
<Button Text="Cancel" Style="{StaticResource CancelButton}" />
```

Figure 4-8 shows the buttons for each platform.

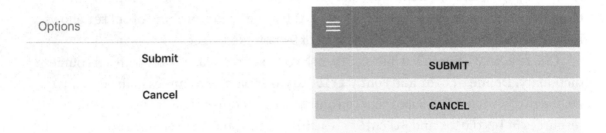

Figure 4-8. *Button styles using resources*

Both styles, SubmitButton and CancelButton now share resources but still maintain duplicate XAML code to do so. Style inheritance solves this problem.

CODE COMPLETE: Using Resources in Styles

Listing 4-25 shows the ButtonStylesWithResourcesPage.xaml.

Listing 4-25. ButtonStylesPage.xaml

```
<ContentPage xmlns="http://xamarin.com/schemas/2014/forms" xmlns:x="http://
schemas.microsoft.com/winfx/2009/xaml" x:Class="StyleExamples.
ButtonStylesWithResourcesPage">
    <ContentPage.Resources>
        <ResourceDictionary>
            <Color x:Key="BtTextColor">Black</Color>
            <FontAttributes x:Key="BtFontStyle">Bold</FontAttributes>
            <Style x:Key="SubmitButton" TargetType="Button">
                <Setter Property="TextColor" Value="{StaticResource
                BtTextColor}" />
```

```
            <Setter Property="FontAttributes" Value="{StaticResource
            BtFontStyle}" />
        </Style>
        <Style x:Key="CancelButton" TargetType="Button">
            <Setter Property="TextColor" Value="{StaticResource
            BtTextColor}" />
            <Setter Property="FontAttributes" Value="{StaticResource
            BtFontStyle}" />
        </Style>
    </ResourceDictionary>
  </ContentPage.Resources>
  <StackLayout Orientation="Vertical">
      <Button Text="Submit" Style="{StaticResource SubmitButton}" />
      <Button Text="Cancel" Style="{StaticResource CancelButton}" />
  </StackLayout>
</ContentPage>
```

In this example, you can see that we are setting for both the SubmitButton and
CancelButton the TextColor and FontAttributes properties. Let's examine how we can
avoid this through style inheritance.

Style Inheritance

Style inheritance allows a style to serve as the base style of other derived styles. The
derived style can override or add property settings.

Note   A derived style can only target the same or a subclass of the view targeted
by the base style. Also, an implicit style can derive from an explicit style, but an
explicit style cannot derive from an implicit style, because no Key is provided for an
implicit style.

Inheritance is handled differently depending on whether a style is derived statically
or dynamically.

Let's start with defining style inheritance statically.

Static Style Inheritance

Static style inheritance is used to define the inheritance at design time. Use the `BasedOn` property to provide a lookup for the base style.

When defining a static style inheritance, you create two styles that both target, for example, a specific type like a `Button`. However, the inheriting style derives from the first style using the `BasedOn` property in combination with `StaticResource` markup extension, e.g.:

```
<Style x:Key="Parent" TargetType="Button"/>
<Style x:Key="Child" TargetType="Button" BasedOn="{StaticResource
Parent}"/>
```

Note   Only the `StaticResource` markup extension can be used with the `BasedOn` property.

To demonstrate this, copy the `ButtonStylesWithResourcesPage.xaml` to a new XAML page called `ButtonStylesWithStaticInheritancePage.xaml`. Define a new style called `ButtonStyle` that both `SubmitButton` and `CancelButton` derive from, as shown in Listing 4-26.

Listing 4-26. Static Style Inheritance

```
<ResourceDictionary>
    <Color x:Key="BtTextColor">Black</Color>
    <FontAttributes x:Key="BtFontStyle">Bold</FontAttributes>
    <Style x:Key="ButtonStyle" TargetType="Button">
        <Setter Property="TextColor" Value="{StaticResource
        BtTextColor}" />
        <Setter Property="FontAttributes" Value="{StaticResource
        BtFontStyle}" />
    </Style>
    <Style x:Key="SubmitButton" TargetType="Button"
    BasedOn="{StaticResource
    ButtonStyle}" />
```

```
    <Style x:Key="CancelButton" TargetType="Button"
    BasedOn="{StaticResource
    ButtonStyle}" />
  </ResourceDictionary>
```

The changes are only in the resource dictionary. The buttons look the same as Figure 4-9 shows for each platform.

Figure 4-9. *Button styles with static style inheritance*

The XAML looks cleaner now but what if the inheritance can change at runtime? Use dynamic style inheritance in this case.

Dynamic Style Inheritance

Dynamic style inheritance defines style inheritance at runtime. Use the `BaseResourceKey` property to specify the name of the base style, which can be provided at runtime.

When defining a dynamic style inheritance, create two styles that both target a specific element type like a `Button`, a `Parent`, and a `Child` style. The inheriting child style uses the `BaseResourceKey` property to reference the name of the parent style without using the markup extensions `StaticResource` to lookup a resource, e.g.:

```
<Style x:Key="Parent" TargetType="Button"/>
<Style x:Key="Child" TargetType="Button" BaseResourceKey="Parent"/>
```

Note   `BaseResourceKey` does not use a dictionary lookup.

The `Style Parent` does not need to exist at design time. The runtime will use default settings of a view when instantiating the `Child` style, if not `Parent` can be found.

To demonstrate this, copy the `ButtonStylesWithStaticInheritancePage.xaml` to a new XAML page called `ButtonStylesWithDynamicInheritancePage.xaml`. Replace the `BasedOn` properties of `SubmitButton` and `CancelButton` with the `BaseResourceKey` property to indicate dynamic style inheritance, as shown in Listing 4-27.

Listing 4-27. Dynamic Style Inheritance

```
<ResourceDictionary>
    <Color x:Key="BtTextColor">Black</Color>
    <FontAttributes x:Key="BtFontStyle">Bold</FontAttributes>
    <Style x:Key="ButtonStyle" TargetType="Button">
        <Setter Property="TextColor" Value="{StaticResource
        BtTextColor}" />
        <Setter Property="FontAttributes" Value="{StaticResource
        BtFontStyle}" />
    </Style>
    <Style x:Key="SubmitButton" TargetType="Button"
    BaseResourceKey="ButtonStyle" />
    <Style x:Key="CancelButton" TargetType="Button"
    BaseResourceKey="ButtonStyle" />
</ResourceDictionary>
```

Once again, the changes are only in the resource dictionary. The buttons look the same as Figure 4-10 shows for each platform.

Figure 4-10. *Button styles with dynamic style inheritance*

A new style can be assigned in the code behind.

```
Resources["SubmitButton"] = Resources["InactiveButton"];
```

Styles Overview

Let's revisit the feedback page and apply the various styles discussed such as style inheritance, implicit and explicit styles, using resources, and defining styles as external dictionaries. We will first create a resource dictionary file that defines our styles using the techniques discussed in this chapter and then apply these styles to a feedback page and examine how the final result compares to the original feedback page.

Create a XAML page MyStyles.xaml and copy MyResources.xaml to it. Add the following styles to the dictionary:

1. Create an implicit Style for ContentPage views that sets the background color to the PageBgColor resource.

2. Entry and Editor have a base class InputView but do not share many properties at the base class level. Create a base Style called InputViewStyle for InputView that sets the VerticalOptions to FillAndExpand. Define two implicit styles for Entry and Editor that inherit from InputViewStyle and set for each TextColor to the InputTextColor and FontAttributes to InputFontStyle. For the Entry also add a setter for Placeholder to lookup the text from the SubjectPlaceholder resource.

3. Add another Setter to the ButtonStyle for HorizontalOptions and Setters for BackgroundColor and Text for the SubmitButton and CancelButton styles.

4. Create an implicit Style for Grid layouts with a default Padding, Margin, and BackgroundColor.

5. Create an explicit Style for StackLayout called FeedbackBorder to be used around the Editor to provide a border.

CODE COMPLETE: Defining Styles

Listing 4-28 shows the updated MyStyles.xaml. The resources are included from MyResources.xaml (Listing 4-16).

Listing 4-28. MyStyles.xaml

```xml
<ResourceDictionary xmlns="http://xamarin.com/schemas/2014/forms"
xmlns:x="http://schemas.microsoft.com/winfx/2009/xaml"
x:Class="StyleExamples.MyStyles">
    <Style TargetType="ContentPage">
        <Setter Property="BackgroundColor" Value="{DynamicResource
        PageBgColor}" />
    </Style>
    <Style x:Key="InputViewStyle" TargetType="InputView">
        <Setter Property="VerticalOptions" Value="FillAndExpand" />
    </Style>
    <Style TargetType="Entry" BaseResourceKey="InputViewStyle">
        <Setter Property="FontAttributes" Value="{DynamicResource
        InputFontStyle}" />
        <Setter Property="TextColor" Value="{DynamicResource
        InputTextColor}" />
        <Setter Property="Placeholder" Value="{DynamicResource
        SubjectPlaceholder}" />
    </Style>
    <Style TargetType="Editor" BaseResourceKey="InputViewStyle">
        <Setter Property="FontAttributes" Value="{DynamicResource
        InputFontStyle}" />
        <Setter Property="TextColor" Value="{DynamicResource
        InputTextColor}" />
    </Style>
    <Style x:Key="ButtonStyle" TargetType="Button">
        <Setter Property="HorizontalOptions" Value="FillAndExpand" />
        <Setter Property="TextColor" Value="{DynamicResource
        BtTextColor}" />
        <Setter Property="FontAttributes" Value="{DynamicResource
        BtFontStyle}" />
    </Style>
    <Style x:Key="SubmitButton" TargetType="Button"
    BaseResourceKey="ButtonStyle">
```

```
    <Setter Property="BackgroundColor" Value="{DynamicResource
    BtSubmitColor}" />
    <Setter Property="Text" Value="Submit" />
</Style>
<Style x:Key="CancelButton" TargetType="Button"
BaseResourceKey="ButtonStyle">
    <Setter Property="BackgroundColor" Value="{DynamicResource
    BtCancelColor}" />
    <Setter Property="Text" Value="Cancel" />
</Style>
<Style TargetType="Grid">
    <Setter Property="Padding" Value="30" />
    <Setter Property="Margin" Value="30" />
    <Setter Property="BackgroundColor" Value="{DynamicResource
    FormBgColor}" />
</Style>
<Style x:Key="FeedbackBorder" TargetType="StackLayout">
    <Setter Property="Orientation" Value="Vertical" />
    <Setter Property="BackgroundColor" Value="{DynamicResource
    FeedbackBorderColor}" />
    <Setter Property="Padding" Value="1" />
</Style>

<x:String x:Key="SubjectPlaceholder">Enter Subject</x:String>
<x:String x:Key="FeedbackPlaceholder">Type your message here
</x:String>
<x:String x:Key="InputPlaceholder">Enter Subject</x:String>
<Color x:Key="PageBgColor">#4CAF50</Color>
<Color x:Key="PageBgColorNoSubject">#85af87</Color>
<Color x:Key="PageBgColorWithSubject">#4CAF50</Color>
<Color x:Key="FormBgColor">#AAAAAA</Color>
<Color x:Key="InputTextColor">Navy</Color>
<Color x:Key="InputPlaceholderColor">Silver</Color>
<Color x:Key="FeedbackBorderColor">Silver</Color>
<FontAttributes x:Key="InputFontStyle">Italic</FontAttributes>
<Color x:Key="BtTextColor">White</Color>
```

159

```
    <Color x:Key="BtSubmitColor">#4CAF50</Color>
    <Color x:Key="BtCancelColor">#f47442</Color>
    <Color x:Key="BtSubmitActiveColor">#4CAF50</Color>
    <Color x:Key="BtCancelActiveColor">#f47442</Color>
    <Color x:Key="BtInactiveColor">Gray</Color>
    <FontAttributes x:Key="BtFontStyle">Bold</FontAttributes>
</ResourceDictionary>
```

Now let's use the styles we have defined. Duplicate the ImportResourcesPage.xaml and rename it to StylesPage.xaml. Replace local:MyResources with local:MyStyles to load MyStyles.xaml instead, that is:

```
<ResourceDictionary MergedWith="local:MyStyles"/>
```

For the styles to take effect, we remove all properties set directly and instead use the Style property to apply our styles from MyStyles.xaml. Apply the styles to your page:

1. Remove the BackgroundColor property assignment for the ContentPage. This is set now implicitly.

2. Remove Placeholder, TextColor, and FontAttributes property assignments from the Entry view. These are set now implicitly.

3. Remove VerticalOptions, TextColor, and FontAttributes property assignments from the Editor view. These are set now implicitly.

4. Remove HorizontalOptions, TextColor, FontAttributes, and BackgroundColor property settings from the two Buttons. Instead use the Style property of the Buttons to lookup the SubmitButton and CancelButton, respectively.

5. Remove the Padding, Margin, and BackgroundColor property settings from the Grid. These are now set implicitly.

6. Remove the Padding and BackgroundColor property settings from the StackLayout that includes the Editor. Instead set the Style property of the StackLayout to lookup the FeedbackBorder style.

CODE COMPLETE: Applying Styles

Listing 4-29 shows the resulting StylesPage.xaml. The Grid row and column definitions are included from Listing 4-9.

Listing 4-29. StylesPage.xaml

```
<ContentPage Title="Styles Page" xmlns:local="clr-namespace:StyleExamples"
xmlns="http://xamarin.com/schemas/2014/forms"
xmlns:x="http://schemas.microsoft.com/winfx/2009/xaml"
x:Class="StyleExamples.StylesPage">
    <ContentPage.Resources>
        <ResourceDictionary MergedWith="local:MyStyles"/>
    </ContentPage.Resources>
    <ContentPage.Content>
        <Grid>
            <Grid.RowDefinitions>
                <RowDefinition Height="Auto"/>
                <RowDefinition Height="*"   />
                <RowDefinition Height="Auto"/>
            </Grid.RowDefinitions>
            <Grid.ColumnDefinitions>
                <ColumnDefinition Width="*" />
            </Grid.ColumnDefinitions>
            <Entry x:Name="Subject" Grid.Row="0" Focused="HandleSubject"
            Unfocused="HandleSubject" />
            <StackLayout Style="{StaticResource FeedbackBorder}" Grid.
            Row="1">
                <Editor x:Name="Feedback" Focused="HandleFeedback"
                Unfocused="HandleFeedback" />
            </StackLayout>
            <StackLayout Orientation="Horizontal" Grid.Row="2">
                <Button Style="{StaticResource SubmitButton}" />
                <Button Style="{StaticResource CancelButton}" />
```

```
            </StackLayout>
        </Grid>
    </ContentPage.Content>
 </ContentPage>
```

Figure 4-11 shows the result for both platforms.

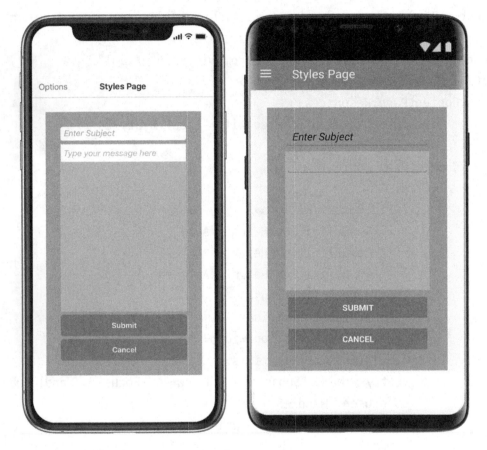

Figure 4-11.   *Feedback page using styles*

Compare StylesPage.xaml with the original FeedbackPage.xaml in Listing 4-1.
They are almost identical. StylesPage has only a few additional property settings for the
Buttons and the StackLayout to compensate for the lack of a Border property for the
Editor.

Using styles removes the clutter from the XAML and makes it more maintainable and
consistent across the entire application.

Xamarin.Forms provides device styles for Label to allow an application to respond to accessibility settings of a user. Let's explore this next.

Device Styles

Xamarin.Forms provides for the Label control six built-in styles that adjust dynamically to accessibility settings of the device, referred to as *device styles*:

1. TitleStyle

2. SubTitleStyle

3. BodyStyle

4. CaptionStyle

5. ListItemTextStyle

6. ListItemDetailTextStyle

The device styles can be used like any other style directly on the Label view using the Style property, e.g.:

```
<Label Style="{DynamicResource TitleStyle}">
```

The device styles can also serve as the base style for other Label views using the BaseResourceKey of a Style element, e.g.:

```
<Style x:Key="MyTitleStyle" TargetType="Label"
BaseResourceKey="TitleStyle">
    <Setter Property="TextColor" Value="#4CAF50" />
</Style>
```

The second option is interesting as it allows an application to respond to accessibility settings of a user.

Note   Use DynamicResource for looking up styles to ensure the view is updated if the user changes the accessibility settings.

Figure 4-12 shows how built-in device styles are rendered on iOS and Android.

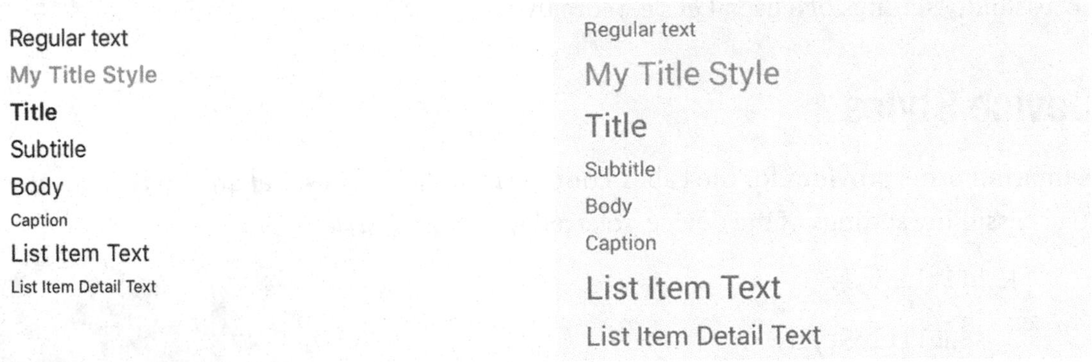

Regular text

My Title Style

Title

Subtitle

Body

Caption

List Item Text

List Item Detail Text

Regular text

My Title Style

Title

Subtitle

Body

Caption

List Item Text

List Item Detail Text

Figure 4-12. *Using device styles*

CODE COMPLETE: Using Device Styles

Listing 4-30 provides the complete code for the DeviceStylePage.xaml.

Listing 4-30. StylesPage.xaml

```
<ContentPage xmlns="http://xamarin.com/schemas/2014/forms"
xmlns:x="http://schemas.microsoft.com/winfx/2009/xaml"
x:Class="StyleExamples.DeviceStylesPage">
    <ContentPage.Resources>
        <ResourceDictionary>
            <Style x:Key="MyTitleStyle" TargetType="Label"
            BaseResourceKey="TitleStyle">
                <Setter Property="TextColor" Value="#4CAF50" />
            </Style>
        </ResourceDictionary>
    </ContentPage.Resources>
    <StackLayout Padding="20,20">
        <Label Text="Regular text" />
        <Label Text="My Title Style" Style="{DynamicResource
        MyTitleStyle}" />
        <Label Text="Title" Style="{DynamicResource TitleStyle}" />
        <Label Text="Subtitle" Style="{DynamicResource
        SubtitleTextStyle}" />
```

```
        <Label Text="Body" Style="{DynamicResource BodyStyle}" />
        <Label Text="Caption" Style="{DynamicResource CaptionStyle}" />
        <Label Text="List Item Text" Style="{DynamicResource
        ListItemTextStyle}" />
        <Label Text="List Item Detail Text" Style="{DynamicResource
        ListItemDetailTextStyle}" />
      </StackLayout>
  </ContentPage>
```

The feedback page defined styles for selected controls as a reusable resource dictionary. Creating a collection of well-designed and cohesive styles is an art in and of itself. A baseline to start from is themes that are available for Xamarin.Forms.

Themes

Xamarin.Forms *themes* are collections of styles for common visual elements and include style options for standard controls. Themes are a great way to learn about styles, and they provide two ready-made templates. Many platforms support a light and a dark mode. The light mode provides high contrast and is useful during day time. For low-light conditions or working at night, a dark mode can be more pleasant. Xamarin.Forms *Light* and a *Dark* theme NuGet packages can be added to a project to implement a light or a dark theme.

Using the dark or light theme helps bootstrap the creation of your own custom themes, while you only override the styles as needed.

Note   Themes have been in Preview for years now and are best used as a learning tool for styles unless they are released to Stable.

Using Themes

Using themes is a four-step process:

1. Import the Light or Dark theme NuGet packages.

2. Initialize themes in the platform-specific projects.

3. Add the theme namespace in the page or application.

4. Load the theme as a resource dictionary.

The coding for using the Light and Dark theme is almost identical. Let's begin with the Dark theme for our main example and then tackle the Light theme at the end. Here are the four steps in detail:

1. Import the Dark theme into your project by adding the Xamarin. Forms.Theme.Base NuGet package as well as the corresponding Dark package to both platform-specific projects (iOS and Android).

2. Themes are still in preview and occasionally don't load properly due to an error. Use the following steps in each platform-specific project to initialize them:

    In the iOS platform-specific project, add the following lines of code after the LoadApplication method in the AppDelegate.cs file:

    ```
    var x = typeof(Xamarin.Forms.Themes.DarkThemeResources);
    x = typeof(Xamarin.Forms.Themes.iOS.UnderlineEffect);
    ```

    Similarly, in the Android platform-specific project, add the following lines of code after the LoadApplication method in the MainActivity.cs file:

    ```
    var x = typeof(Xamarin.Forms.Themes.DarkThemeResources);
    x = typeof(Xamarin.Forms.Themes.Android.UnderlineEffect);
    ```

3. Add the namespace to App.xaml by providing the namespace Xamarin.Forms.Themes and the assembly Xamarin.Forms.Theme. Dark, e.g.,

    ```
    xmlns:theme="clr-namespace:Xamarin.Forms.Themes;
        assembly=Xamarin.Forms.Theme.Dark"
    ```

4. Load a dark theme as an external resource dictionary in the App. xaml to use the theme globally, as shown in Listing 4-31.

Listing 4-31. Using the Dark Theme

```
<Application xmlns="http://xamarin.com/schemas/2014/forms"
xmlns:x="http://schemas.microsoft.com/winfx/2009/xaml"
x:Class="mynamespace.App" xmlns:theme="clr-
namespace:Xamarin.Forms.Themes;assembly=Xamarin.Forms.Theme.Dark">
    <Application.Resources>
        <ResourceDictionary MergedWith="theme:DarkThemeResources" />
    </Application.Resources>
</Application>
```

Tip   Using the light theme follows the same process. Just replace the word "Dark" with "Light" and you are good to go. More on this soon.

Let's add some styling options for supported controls to show what the themes are all about.

Theme Styling Options

Both light and dark themes provide style options for selected controls. Style options are available for the following controls:

- **BoxView styles:** HorizontalRule, Circle, and Rounded.

- **Image styles:** Circle, Rounded, and Thumbnail. Rounded and Thumbnail currently behave the same.

- **Button styles:** Default, Primary, Success, Info, Warning, Danger, Link, Small, and Large.

- **Label styles:** Header, Subheader, Body, Link, and Inverse.

To apply a style option to a view, use the view's StyleClass property. For example, if you want to add a header to your application, set StyleClass to the style option Header on your Label.

```
<Label Text="Header" StyleClass="Header"/>
```

Let's look how these style options look like in the dark and the light theme.

Dark Theme

Let's create a page that uses all the style options in the dark theme available for Button and Label. Create a page called DarkThemePage.xaml and import the dark theme, as shown in Listing 4-32. Add in the page nine buttons and five labels, each using one of the preceding styling options.

Listing 4-32. Dark Theme Page

```
<ContentPage xmlns="http://xamarin.com/schemas/2014/forms"
xmlns:x="http://schemas.microsoft.com/winfx/2009/xaml"
x:Class="StyleExamples.DarkThemePage" xmlns:theme="clr-
namespace:Xamarin.Forms.Themes;assembly=Xamarin.Forms.Theme.Dark">
    <ContentPage.Resources>
        <ResourceDictionary MergedWith="theme:DarkThemeResources" />
    </ContentPage.Resources>
    <StackLayout Padding="20">
        <Button Text="Button Default" StyleClass="Default" />
        <Button Text="Button Primary" StyleClass="Primary" />
        <Button Text="Button Success" StyleClass="Success" />
        <Button Text="Button Info" StyleClass="Info" />
        <Button Text="Button Warning" StyleClass="Warning" />
        <Button Text="Button Danger" StyleClass="Danger" />
        <Button Text="Button Link" StyleClass="Link" />
        <Button Text="Button Default Small" StyleClass="Small" />
        <Button Text="Button Default Large" StyleClass="Large" />
        <Label Text="Label Header" StyleClass="Header" />
        <Label Text="Label Subheader" StyleClass="Subheader" />
        <Label Text="Label Body" StyleClass="Body" />
        <Label Text="Label Link" StyleClass="Link" />
        <Label Text="Label Inverse" BackgroundColor="White"
        StyleClass="Inverse"/>
    </StackLayout>
</ContentPage>
```

Figure 4-13 shows the available style options for the dark theme on iOS and Android.

Figure 4-13. *Dark theme with available style options*

Light Theme

Now for the Light theme, first you need to carry out the four steps we used earlier for the "Dark Theme" under "Using Themes" to initialize the Light theme, replacing "Dark" with "Light".

Next create a page called LightThemePage.xaml and import the Light theme, as shown in Listing 4-33. Add in the page the same nine buttons and five labels, each using one of the options.

Listing 4-33. Light Theme Page

```
<ContentPage xmlns="http://xamarin.com/schemas/2014/forms"
xmlns:x="http://schemas.microsoft.com/winfx/2009/xaml"
x:Class="StyleExamples.LightThemePage" xmlns:theme="clr-
namespace:Xamarin.Forms.Themes;assembly=Xamarin.Forms.Theme.Light">
    <ContentPage.Resources>
        <ResourceDictionary MergedWith="theme:LightThemeResources" />
    </ContentPage.Resources>
    <StackLayout Padding="20">
        <Button Text="Button Default" StyleClass="Default"
        BackgroundColor="Black"/>
        <Button Text="Button Primary" StyleClass="Primary" />
        <Button Text="Button Success" StyleClass="Success" />
        <Button Text="Button Info" StyleClass="Info" />
        <Button Text="Button Warning" StyleClass="Warning" />
        <Button Text="Button Danger" StyleClass="Danger" />
        <Button Text="Button Link" StyleClass="Link" />
        <Button Text="Button Default Small" StyleClass="Small" />
        <Button Text="Button Default Large" StyleClass="Large" />
        <Label Text="Label Header" StyleClass="Header" />
        <Label Text="Label Subheader" StyleClass="Subheader" />
        <Label Text="Label Body" StyleClass="Body" />
        <Label Text="Label Link" StyleClass="Link" />
        <Label Text="Label Inverse" BackgroundColor="White"
        StyleClass="Inverse"/>
    </StackLayout>
</ContentPage>
```

The Light theme with style options applied looks like Figure 4-14.

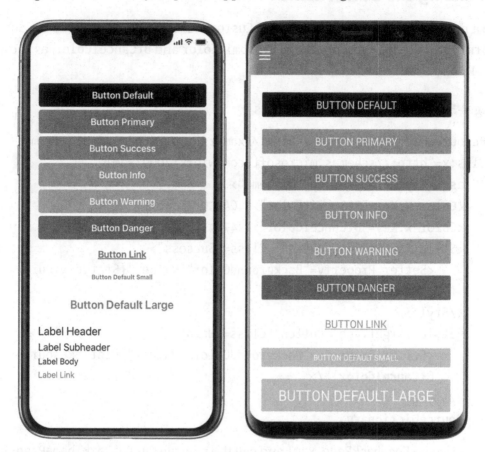

Figure 4-14. *Light theme with available style options*

Custom Themes

Custom themes are themes you define based on the dark and the light theme. After using one of the two themes, customize it. Define a style that derives from the style option using the Class property of the Style element and override properties of the style option with one or more property settings, e.g.:

```
<Style TargetType="Label" Class="Header">
    <Setter Property="TextColor" Value="Red"/>
</Style>
```

Now, let's go back to the original feedback page and define a custom theme to style it.

Customizing the Dark Theme

Create a new resource dictionary file called `CustomTheme.xaml` and override the Success and Warning Style for Button with the BtSubmitColor and BtCancelColor, as shown in Listing 4-34.

Listing 4-34. Defining Custom Themes

```
<ResourceDictionary xmlns="http://xamarin.com/schemas/2014/forms"
xmlns:x="http://schemas.microsoft.com/winfx/2009/xaml"
x:Class="StyleExamples.CustomTheme">
    <Color x:Key="BtSubmitColor">#4CAF50</Color>
    <Color x:Key="BtCancelColor">#f47442</Color>
    <Style TargetType="Button" Class="Success">
        <Setter Property="BackgroundColor" Value="{StaticResource
        BtSubmitColor}"/>
    </Style>
    <Style TargetType="Button" Class="Warning">
        <Setter Property="BackgroundColor" Value="{StaticResource
        BtCancelColor}"/>
    </Style>
</ResourceDictionary>
```

Duplicate the `FeedbackPage.xaml` and call the new file `CustomDarkThemePage.xaml`. Load the custom theme into the `CustomDarkThemePage.` Assign the Success and Warning styles to the submit and cancel buttons, e.g.:

```
<Button Text="Cancel" StyleClass="Warning" />
<Button Text="Submit" StyleClass="Success" />
```

Figure 4-15 shows the customized dark theme applied to the feedback page.

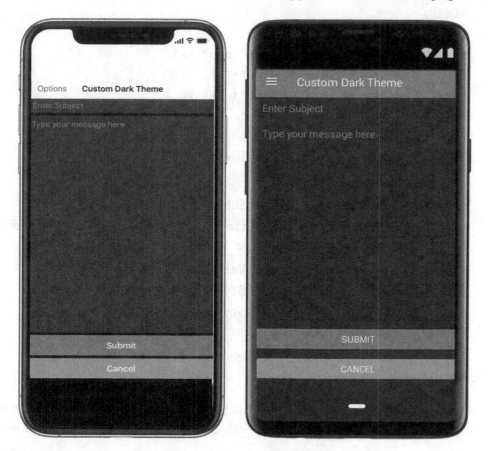

Figure 4-15. *Custom dark theme applied to the feedback page*

CODE COMPLETE: Customizing the Dark Theme

Listing 4-35 provides the complete code for the `CustomDarkThemePage.xaml`.

Listing 4-35. CustomDarkThemePage.xaml

```
<ContentPage Title="Custom Dark Theme"
xmlns="http://xamarin.com/schemas/2014/forms"
xmlns:x="http://schemas.microsoft.com/winfx/2009/xaml"
x:Class="StyleExamples.CustomDarkThemePage" xmlns:theme="clr-
namespace:Xamarin.Forms.Themes;assembly=Xamarin.Forms.Theme.Dark">
    <ContentPage.Resources>
        <ResourceDictionary MergedWith="theme:DarkThemeResources" />
```

```
        </ContentPage.Resources>
        <Grid>
            <Grid.RowDefinitions>
                <RowDefinition Height="Auto" />
                <RowDefinition Height="*" />
                <RowDefinition Height="Auto" />
            </Grid.RowDefinitions>
            <Grid.ColumnDefinitions>
                <ColumnDefinition Width="*" />
            </Grid.ColumnDefinitions>
            <Entry Placeholder="Enter Subject" Grid.Row="0" />
            <Editor x:Name="Feedback" Grid.Row="1" Unfocused="HandleFeedback"
            Focused="HandleFeedback" />
            <StackLayout Orientation="Vertical" Grid.Row="2">
                <Button Text="Cancel" StyleClass="Warning" />
                <Button Text="Submit" StyleClass="Success" />
            </StackLayout>
        </Grid>
    </ContentPage>
```

Up until now, the XAML syntax was used to style an application. An alternative and common syntax for web pages is Cascading Style Sheets, which is supported by Xamarin. Forms as well.

Cascading Style Sheets (CSS)

Cascading Style Sheets (CSS) is a language to describe the presentation of Hypertext Markup Language (HTML) web pages. Xamarin.Forms has adopted this notation as an alternative to the XAML syntax. Internally, the CSS is parsed and the same style engine is used to apply the design.

CSS is comprised of a set of rules, each starting with one or more *Selectors* separated by a comma and followed by one or more property-value pairs inside curly braces.

Tip   Anything you can do with XAML styles, you can do with CSS and vice versa.

Caution   Use either styles or CSS but not a combination of both when developing an application to simplify troubleshooting.

Selectors

A *selector* points to the XAML element for which the property settings apply. The basic anatomy of a CSS rule is shown in Listing 4-36.

Listing 4-36. Anatomy of a CSS Rule

```
Selector {
    Property1: Value1;
    Property2: Value2;
}
```

If a matching XAML element is found, then the values are assigned to its respective properties, such as `Value1` to `Property1` and `Value2` to `Property2`. This is very similar to a XAML `Style` element and `Setters`. A selector specifies the type of page, layout, or control and possibly the relationship between them that needs to be satisfied before a style can be applied.

The lists of supported selectors, properties, and property values are provided at the end of the section as a reference. Selectors can be combined without any limitation. All matching styles are applied in the order of the definition. Styles applied on the control itself are applied last. This is referred to as cascading, which means in this context that the rule that is the most specific is applied last.

Note   Selector names are case sensitive. Property names must be lower case. Property values are not case sensitive.

Let's revisit the original feedback page and use CSS to style it.

Using CSS

Use CSS notation to style Xamarin.Forms elements. Style specific classes with `.StyleClassName` notation, views with `#ViewName`, and class types with `^ClassName`.

Let's style our Feedback app using CSS. First you will need a CSS file. Create a style sheet called `Styles.css` in the project and use the Build Action to define the file as an `EmbeddedResource`.

We want to define our submit button style with a white and bold font and a green background color. For this, use the selector notation. `StyleClassName` to define a CSS rule for the `SubmitButton` style class. Use the property `color` for `TextColor`, `font-style` for `FontAttributes`, and `background-color` for `BackgroundColor` to specify the values, as shown in Listing 4-37.

Listing 4-37. CSS Rule for the SubmitButton Style Class

```
.SubmitButton {
    color: white;
    font-style: bold;
    background-color: #4CAF50;
}
```

Repeat the same for the style class `CancelButton`, defining a selector but instead using our orange background color, as shown in Listing 4-38.

Listing 4-38. CSS Rule for the CancelButton Style Class

```
.CancelButton {
    color: white;
    font-style: bold;
    background-color: #f47442;
}
```

A selector can target named views in the XAML. Use the notation `#ViewName` to define the CSS rule for the `Entry` and `Editor` controls named `Subject` and `Feedback` using the `color`, `font-style`, and `background-color` properties to turn the font of the subject and feedback views italic with a navy color on a white background, as shown in Listing 4-39.

Listing 4-39. CSS Rule for Views Named Subject and Feedback

```
#Subject,#Feedback{
    color: navy;
    font-style: italic;
    background-color: white;
}
```

You can provide a border to the feedback view by defining a style `FeedbackBorder` with a padding of 1 and a silver background color, as shown in Listing 4-40.

Listing 4-40. CSS Rule to Define a Border for StackLayout That Contains the Editor View

```
.FeedbackBorder {
    padding: 1;
    background-color: silver;
}
```

Define styles targeting all views of the same type using the `^ClassName` notation. To apply a green background color to all `ContentPage` views and a grey color to all `Grid` views and a 30-pixel padding to both view types, use the `background-color` and `padding` properties, as demonstrated in Listing 4-41.

Listing 4-41. CSS Rule for ContentPages and Grids

```
^ContentPage {
    background-color: #4CAF50;
    padding: 30 30;
}
^Grid {
    background-color: #AAAAAA;
    padding: 30 30;
}
```

Create a new XAML file called `CSSPage.xaml` and copy `StylesPage.xaml` into it. Replace `MyStyles` by loading the CSS as a resource dictionary using the `StyleSheet` syntax, as shown in Listing 4-42.

Listing 4-42. Loading a CSS into XAML

```
<ContentPage Title="Cascading Style Sheet"
xmlns="http://xamarin.com/schemas/2014/forms"
xmlns:x="http://schemas.microsoft.com/winfx/2009/xaml" xmlns:local="clr-
namespace:CSSExample" x:Class="CSSExample.CSSPage">
    <ContentPage.Resources>
        <StyleSheet Source="Styles/Styles.css" />
    </ContentPage.Resources>
    ...
</ContentPage>
```

Remove the `Style` property settings for `StackLayout` and the two buttons and replace them with `StyleClass` properties pointing to the `FeedbackBorder`, `SubmitButton`, and `CancelButton` as specified in `Styles.css`.

Figure 4-16 shows the feedback page using CSS.

Figure 4-16. *Feedback page using CSS*

CODE COMPLETE: Using CSS

Listings 4-43 and Listing 4-44 provide the complete code for the Styles.css and CSSPage.xaml.

Listing 4-43. Styles.css

```
^ContentPage {
    background-color: #4CAF50;
    padding: 30 30;
}
```

```css
#Subject,#Feedback{
    color: navy;
    font-style: italic;
    background-color: white;
}

    .FeedbackBorder {
    padding: 1;
    background-color: silver;
}

.SubmitButton {
    color: white;
    font-style: bold;
    background-color: #4CAF50;
}

.CancelButton {
    color: white;
    font-style: bold;
    background-color: #f47442;
}

.InactiveButton {
    color: white;
    font-style: bold;
    background-color: gray;
}

^Grid {
    background-color: #AAAAAA;
    padding: 30 30;
}
```

Listing 4-44. CSSPage.xaml

```xml
<ContentPage Title="Cascading Style Sheet"
xmlns="http://xamarin.com/schemas/2014/forms"
```

```
    xmlns:x="http://schemas.microsoft.com/winfx/2009/xaml" xmlns:local="clr-
    namespace:CSSExample" x:Class="CSSExample.CSSPage">
        <ContentPage.Resources>
            <StyleSheet Source="Styles/Styles.css" />
        </ContentPage.Resources>
        <Grid>
            <Grid.RowDefinitions>
                <RowDefinition Height="Auto" />
                <RowDefinition Height="*" />
                <RowDefinition Height="Auto" />
            </Grid.RowDefinitions>
            <Grid.ColumnDefinitions>
                <ColumnDefinition Width="*" />
            </Grid.ColumnDefinitions>
            <Entry Placeholder="Enter Subject" x:Name="Subject" Grid.Row="0"
            Focused="HandleSubject" Unfocused="HandleSubject" />
            <StackLayout StyleClass="FeedbackBorder" Grid.Row="1"
            Orientation="Vertical">
                <Editor x:Name="Feedback" Focused="HandleFeedback"
                Unfocused="HandleFeedback" VerticalOptions="FillAndExpand" />
            </StackLayout>
            <StackLayout Orientation="Vertical" Grid.Row="2">
                <Button Text="Submit" StyleClass="SubmitButton" />
                <Button Text="Cancel" StyleClass="CancelButton" />
            </StackLayout>
        </Grid>
    </ContentPage>
```

Xamarin.Forms CSS Definition

The following is a Rosetta Stone of CSS, translating between XAML and CSS for the supported selectors. Again, anything you can do in CSS, you can do in XAML, and the other way around. Tables 4-1 and 4-2 list supported CSS selectors, properties, and property values in Xamarin.Forms.

Table 4-1. Supported CSS Selectors

Control	CSS Example	Corresponding XAML	Description
`.class`	`.Note`	`<Label StyleClass="Note">`	Class Selector. Selects any element classified as Note
`#id`	`Message`	`<Label x:Name="Message">`	Id Selector. Selects the element with the unique name Message
`*`	`*`	`--`	Universal Selector. Selects any visual element
`Element`	`Label`	`<Label>`	Element Selector. Selects all visual elements of a particular type
`Element Element`	`StackLayout Label`	`<StackLayout><Label/></StackLayout>`	Descendent Selector. Selects all `Label`s inside a `StackLayout`
`Element>Element`	`StackLayout>Label`	`<StackLayout><Label/></StackLayout>`	Child Selector. Selects all `Label`s where the parent is a `StackLayout`
`Element+Element`	`Label+Button`	`<Label/><Button/>`	Adjacent Sibling Selector. Selects all `Button`s immediately placed after a `Label`
`Element~Element`	`Label+Label`	`<Label/><Button/>`	Sibling Selector. Selects all `Button`s that follow a `Label` which have the same parent
`Element,Element`	`Label,Button`	`<Label>` `<Button>`	List of Selectors. Selects all `Label` and `Button` elements
`^Element`	`^VisualElement`	`--`	Base Type Selector. Selects any element that is based on `VisualElement`. This selector is only available in Xamarin.Forms

Table 4-2. Properties and Values Supported by Xamarin.Forms

Property	Visual Element	Value	Example
background-color	VisualElement	Color type: Name, HEX, RGB, RGBA, HSL and HSLA values	background-color: red;
background-image	Page	string	background-image:logo.png;
border-color	Button, Frame	Color type	border-color:#222222;
border-width	Button	double	border-width:.25;
color	Button, DatePicker, Editor, Entry, Label, Picker, SearchBar, TimePicker	Color type	color:rgba(0,125,3,0.2);
direction	VisualElement	ltr, rtl,initial	direction:rtl;
font-family	Button, DatePicker, Editor, Entry, Label, Picker, SearchBar, TimePicker, Span	string	font-family:Arial;
font-size	Button, DatePicker, Editor, Entry, Label, Picker, SearchBar, TimePicker, Span	double NamedSize type: default, micro, small, medium, large	font-size:Large;
font-style	Button, DatePicker, Editor, Entry, Label, Picker, SearchBar, TimePicker, Span	bold, italic	font-style:italic;

(continued)

183

Table 4-2. (*continued*)

Property	Visual Element	Value	Example
height min-height width min-width	VisualElement	double	height:50;
margin margin-left margin-top margin-right margin-button	View	Thickness type double	margin:10 20; margin-right:3;
padding padding-left padding-top padding-right padding-bottom	Layout, Page	Thickness type double	padding: 10 20; padding-bottom:5;
opacity	VisualElement	double	opacity:.5;
text-align	Entry, EntryCell, Label, SearchBar	left, right, center, start, end	text-align:right;
visibility	VisualElement	true, visible, false, hidden, collapse	visibility: false;

All properties accept `initial` as the value to reset the value set by another style, e.g.:

```
background-color: initial;
```

`Thickness` data type allows one (uniform), two (vertical horizontal), three (top, horizontal, bottom), and four (top, right, bottom, left) values separated by white space.

Summary

Using resources inside resource dictionaries is a powerful way to reduce duplicate XAML and improve the maintainability of an application. Any object can be defined as a resource inside a dictionary. Resources are looked up by their key either once when the XAML element using the resource is initialized the first time using the `StaticResource` markup extension or continuously using `DynamicResource`. The lookup behavior for resources allows resources defined at a lower level to override those defined higher up in the application. Resources can be stored in external dictionaries for reuse across multiple pages or the entire application. Style resources address the limitations of using resources directly for defining UI designs. This allows creating more performant, readable, and coherent applications. Styles can be defined implicitly or explicitly, can be overridden locally, and support both dynamic and static inheritance. Xamarin. Forms provides built-in device styles for `Label` to respond to the accessibility settings of users and comes with two pre-defined themes to support a dark and the light mode. Alternatively to the XAML syntax, the CSS notation can be used, which at runtime is translated to styles in a resource dictionary.

That's Xamarin.Forms design using resources, styles, and CSS. Let's move on to user interaction!

CHAPTER 5

User Interaction Using Controls

Users choose dates, times, text, integers, doubles, and other values on mobile devices by using tactile controls. Touch-sensitive screens have user interaction that differs slightly from mouse-driven UIs: most is done with the thumbs and forefingers on the touchscreen. From the user's standpoint, this results in a hands-on control-panel interface with switches, icons, sliders, keyboards, and pickers that sometimes look—but, more important, feel—like physical mechanisms.

Chapter 1 covered some of the basic Xamarin.Forms views such as the Label, Button, and Image. In this chapter, you'll explore additional controls available on each platform, the gestures and events that make them work, and their outputs.

Many of the controls in this chapter are picker-style (pick a date, pick an option, pick a time, etc.). These controls tend to look and work better when displayed in a *modal dialog box*, a pop-up box that overlays the app and maintains focus until dismissed by the user. Xamarin.Forms handles this for you by automatically placing pickers in dialogs. You can enhance your controls using Xamarin.Forms' commands, triggers, and behaviors.

This chapter is a gallery and a reference for the most commonly used selection controls.

Xamarin.Forms Views

These are more of the basic Xamarin.Forms views:

- *Picker:* A pop-up to select a value from a simple list
- *DatePicker:* A pop-up for selecting month, date, and year
- *TimePicker:* A pop-up for selecting hour, minute, and AM/PM

© Dan Hermes 2019
D. Hermes and N. Mazloumi, *Building Xamarin.Forms Mobile Apps Using XAML*,
https://doi.org/10.1007/978-1-4842-4030-4_5

- *Stepper:* Increment/decrement buttons for discrete values

- *Slider:* Sliding input lever for continuous values

- *Switch:* Boolean on/off control

Xamarin.Forms views provide a range of controls that mimic and extend their iOS and Android counterparts. All of the views covered here allow selection and populate at least one property with a data value specified by the user, sometimes more. Let's look at each view in turn.

Xamarin.Forms views often provide the selected value in two places: a handler event property (e.g., e.NewValue) provides the most recent value, and a general-use property on the view provides the selected value for use throughout the page. You will create two labels to display both of those values: EventValue and PageValue.

Create a new page called Controls.xaml and declare StackLayout with two Label views to hold the results of control selection.

```
<StackLayout HorizontalOptions="Center">
    <Label x:Name="EventValue" Text="Value in Event" />
    <Label x:Name="PageValue" Text="Value in Page" />
</StackLayout>
```

Center all of the controls in the StackLayout by using HorizontalOptions = "Center".

All of the Xamarin.Forms examples in this chapter can be found in the source listing Controls in the ControlExamples solution, shown in Listing 5-1 at the end of this section.

As you move on to other controls, remember to add each view to your StackLayout as you go!

Picker

The Picker view provides a pop-up to select a value from a simple list.

Note   The Picker view is used for quick selection of short words, phrases, or numbers. Complex lists with composite cells containing multiple strings and images are covered in the next chapter.

First, create the picker and give it a title, "Options," to identify what the user needs to pick:

```
<Picker x:Name="ThePicker" Title="Options" SelectedIndexChanged="Picker
SelectedIndexChanged">
</Picker>
```

Next, populate the picker's ItemsSource with options:

```
<Picker x:Name="ThePicker" Title="Options" SelectedIndexChanged="Picker
SelectedIndexChanged">
    <Picker.ItemsSource>
        <x:Array Type="{x:Type x:String}">
            <x:String>First</x:String>
            <x:String>Second</x:String>
            <x:String>Third</x:String>
            <x:String>Fourth</x:String>
        </x:Array>
    </Picker.ItemsSource>
</Picker>
```

Option names are placed into the list and then added to the ItemsSource collection in the picker.

A Picker first presents as an Entry control, which in Figure 5-1 starts as a data entry field, similar to Xamarin.Forms.Entry, displaying the value of the Title property.

Figure 5-1. *Entry views often have inline labels instead of side labels*

When this Entry field is tapped, a modal dialog appears, containing the list of items (Figure 5-2).

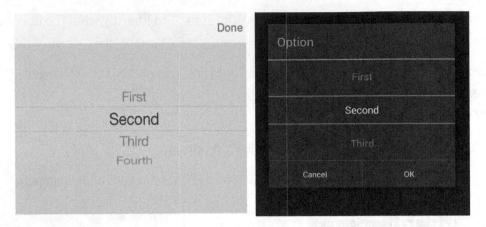

Figure 5-2. *Each picker looks a bit different, depending on the platform*

The list spins when swiped, and the highlighted value becomes the selected value. The selection is automatically populated into the original entry field, so the user can see the effect of the change. The SelectedIndexChanged event was assigned the PickerSelectedIndexChanged handler method:

```
<Picker x:Name="ThePicker" Title="Options"
SelectedIndexChanged="PickerSelectedIndexChanged">
```

Choosing a value using the picker calls the PickerSelectedIndexChanged method:

```
void PickerSelectedIndexChanged(object sender, EventArgs e)
{
    PageValue.Text = (string)ThePicker.ItemsSource[ThePicker.
    SelectedIndex];
}
```

This implementation assigns the selected string to the Text property of the PageValue label.

Tip The selected index in the ThePicker.SelectedIndex property is a zero-based integer index. If Cancel is selected, the SelectedIndex remains unchanged.

DatePicker

The DatePicker view creates a pop-up for selection of month, date, and year. Create a DatePicker view like this:

```
<DatePicker x:Name="TheDatePicker" Format="D" VerticalOptions="Center
AndExpand" DateSelected="DatePickerDateSelected">
</DatePicker>
```

The Format property is set to D for the full month/day/year display. More date formats are provided later in this section.

The DatePicker view starts as a data entry field (Figure 5-3), similar to Xamarin. Forms.Entry displaying the value of the Date property.

Figure 5-3. *DatePicker begins as an Entry view waiting for a tap*

When the date field is tapped, a dialog appears (Figure 5-4).

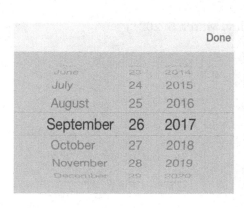

Figure 5-4. *DatePicker is a dialog*

Each column spins individually when swiped, and the highlighted values become the selected values. When Done is tapped, the selected date is automatically populated into the original entry field, so the user can see the effect of the change. The DateSelected event was assigned the PickerSelectedIndexChanged handler method:

```
<DatePicker x:Name="TheDatePicker" Format="D" VerticalOptions="CenterAnd
Expand" DateSelected="DatePickerDateSelected">
```

Choosing a value using the picker calls the DatePickerDateSelected method:

```
void DatePickerDateSelected (object sender, DateChangedEventArgs e)
{
    EventValue.Text = e.NewDate.ToString();
    PageValue.Text = TheDatePicker.Date.ToString();
}
```

The properties e.OldDate and e.NewDate are available within this event to provide the old and new selected date values. In general cases, however, the value entered by the user is stored in the Date property. All of these properties use type DateTime.

The format of the Date field is customizable with the Format property—for example:

```
<DatePicker.Format>MM-dd-yyyy</DatePicker.Format>
```

Other values are as follows:

- D: Full month, day, and year (Monday, March 5, 2021)

- d: Month, day, and year (3/5/2021)

- M: Month and day (March 5)

- Y: Month and year (March 2021)

- yy: Last two digits of the year (21)

- yyyy: Full year (2021)

- MM: Two-digit month (03)

- MMMM: Month (March)

- dd: Two-digit day (05)

- ddd: Abbreviated day of the week (Mon)

- dddd: Full day of the week (Monday)

You set a date range for selection by using MaximumDate and MinimumDate:

```
<DatePicker.MinimumDate>
    <sys:DateTime x:FactoryMethod="Parse">
        <x:Arguments>
            <x:String>Jan 1 2018</x:String>
        </x:Arguments>
    </sys:DateTime>
</DatePicker.MinimumDate>

<DatePicker.MaximumDate>
    <sys:DateTime x:FactoryMethod="Parse">
        <x:Arguments>
            <x:String>Dec 31 2025</x:String>
        </x:Arguments>
    </sys:DateTime>
</DatePicker.MaximumDate>
```

Tip   On Android, the `Format` and `MaximumDate/MinimumDate` properties affect the `DatePicker` entry field but not the modal selection dialog at the time of this writing.

TimePicker

The `TimePicker` view creates a pop-up for selecting hour, minute, and AM/PM. Create a `TimePicker` view like this:

```
<TimePicker x:Name="TheTimePicker" Format="T" VerticalOptions="Center
AndExpand" PropertyChanged="TimePickerPropertyChanged"></TimePicker>
```

The `Format` property set to `T` displays the full time. More time formats follow.

The `TimePicker` view starts as a data entry field similar to `Xamarin.Forms.Entry`, displaying the value of the `Time` property (Figure 5-5).

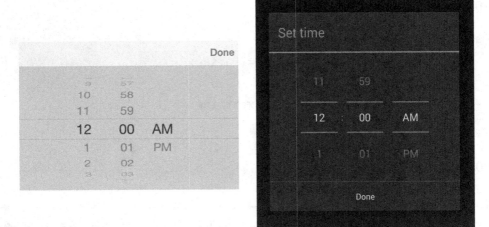

12:00:00 AM   12:00:00 AM

Figure 5-5. *TimePicker waits for a tap*

When the time field is tapped, a modal dialog appears (Figure 5-6).

Done

9   57
10   58
11   59
12   00   AM
1   01   PM
2   02
3   03

Set time

11   59

12   :   00   AM

1   01   PM

Done

Figure 5-6. *TimePicker is a dialog box*

Each column spins individually when swiped, and the highlighted values become the selected values. When Done is tapped, the selected time is automatically populated into the original entry field, so the user can see the effect of the change.

There is no *TimeSelected* event that triggers when a value is selected. Instead, use the PropertyChanged event in Xamarin.Forms data binding to track changes to this view.

```
<TimePicker x:Name="TheTimePicker" Format="T" VerticalOptions="Center
AndExpand" PropertyChanged="TimePickerPropertyChanged">
```

The `TimePickerPropertyChanged` method is called when the time is selected in the picker:

```
void TimePickerPropertyChanged (object sender, PropertyChangedEventArgs e)
{
    if (e.PropertyName == TimePicker.TimeProperty.PropertyName)
    {
        PageValue.Text = TheTimePicker.Time.ToString();
    }
}
```

The `TimePicker.Time` property is set with the selected value as type `TimeSpan`.

The format of the `Time` field is customizable with the `Format` property (e.g., `Format = "T"`). Other values are as follows:

- T: Full time with hours, minutes, seconds, and AM/PM (9:30:25 AM)

- t: Full time with hours, minutes, and AM/PM (9:30 AM)

- hh: Two-digit hours (09)

- mm: Two-digit minutes (30)

- ss: Two-digit seconds (25); seconds are not selectable in the dialog box

- tt: AM/PM designator (AM)

Stepper

The `Stepper` view creates increment and decrement buttons for discrete adjustments to the values:

```
<Stepper x:Name="TheStepper" Minimum="0" Maximum="10" Increment="1"
HorizontalOptions="Center" VerticalOptions="CenterAndExpand"
ValueChanged="StepperValueChanged"></Stepper>
```

`Minimum`, `Maximum`, and `Increment` properties are set for the steppable value. The start value can optionally be set in the `Value` property.

Figure 5-7 shows what the Stepper view looks like.

Figure 5-7. *Plus and minus for increment and decrement*

Tapping a plus or minus button changes the adjustable value and fires the ValueChanged event, called StepperValueChanged in this case.

```
void StepperValueChanged (object sender, ValueChangedEventArgs e)
{
    EventValue.Text = String.Format("Stepper value is {0:F1}",
    e.NewValue);
    PageValue.Text = TheStepper.Value.ToString();
}
```

The properties e.OldValue and e. NewValue are available within this event to provide the old and new selected values. In general cases, however, the value entered by the user is stored in the Stepper's Value property. All these properties are type Double.

Slider

The Slider view is a sliding input control providing a continuum of selection:

```
<Slider x:Name="TheSlider" Minimum="0" Maximum="100" Value="50"
VerticalOptions="CenterAndExpand" ValueChanged="SliderValueChanged"
WidthRequest="300"></Slider>
```

Minimum and Maximum properties are set for the slidable value. The start value can be set in the Value property. The value changes by increments by one-tenth of a unit (0.1) as the slider is moved. The WidthRequest property sets the width of the view without changing minimum or maximum values.

Figure 5-8 shows what the Slider view looks like (with Value = 100).

Figure 5-8. *Slider view at its max value*

Sliding the slider changes the adjustable value and fires the `ValueChanged` event, named `SliderValueChanged` in this case:

```
void SliderValueChanged (object sender, ValueChangedEventArgs e)
{
    EventValue.Text = String.Format("Slider value is {0:F1}",
    e.NewValue);
    PageValue.Text = TheSlider.Value.ToString();
}
```

The properties `e.OldValue` and `e.NewValue` are available within this event to provide the old and new selected values. In general cases, the slidable value is also stored in the `Value` property. All these properties are of type `Double`.

Switch

The `Switch` view is a Boolean on/off control:

```
<Switch x:Name="TheSwitch" HorizontalOptions="Center" VerticalOptions="
CenterAndExpand" Toggled="SwitchToggled"></Switch>
```

Figure 5-9 shows what the `Switch` view looks like off.

Figure 5-9. *Switch off*

And Figure 5-10 shows what the same view looks like on.

Figure 5-10. *Switch on*

Tapping the switch changes the Boolean value and fires the Toggled event, SwitchToggled in this case:

```
void SwitchToggled (object sender, ToggledEventArgs e)
{
    EventValue.Text = String.Format("Switch is now {0}", e.Value ?
    "On" : "Off");
    PageValue.Text = TheSwitch.IsToggled.ToString();
}
```

The property e.Value is available within this event to provide the new switch value. In general cases, the value is also stored in the IsToggled property. These properties are of type Boolean.

Scale, Rotation, Opacity, Visibility, and Focus

You can alter the appearance and behavior of Xamarin.Forms views by using members of the View superclass, VisualElement. Here are some key properties that can be set on a view:

- Scale: Change the size of a view without affecting the views around it. The default value is 1.0.

  Scale = "0.7"

- IsVisible: Make a view invisible or visible again.

  IsVisible = "False"

- IsEnabled: Disable and reenable a view.

  IsEnabled = "False"

- Opacity: Fade a view in and out. The default value is 1.0.

  Opacity = "0.5"

- Rotation: View rotation can be achieved on all axes by using the Rotation, RotationX, and RotationY properties. These rotate the view around the point set by AnchorX and AnchorY.

Using C#, give focus to a view by using the Focus() method, which returns true if successful.

```
var gotFocus = entry.Focus();
```

This example sets focus on an Entry view (which pops up the keyboard).

Tip Use the animation extensions on Xamarin.Forms controls and UI elements to handle fades, rotation, scaling, and translation. The ViewExtensions' methods include TranslateTo, ScaleTo, RelScaleTo, RotateTo, RelRotateTo, RotateXTo, RotateYTo, and FadeTo. Fade in an image over four seconds like this: await image.FadeTo (1, 4000);

CODE COMPLETE: Xamarin.Forms Views

Listing 5-1 contains the complete code for all Xamarin.Forms selection control examples in this chapter. Figure 5-11 shows the full example screen.

Figure 5-11. *Xamarin.Forms selection views*

Listing 5-1. Controls.xaml in the ControlExamples Project of the
ControlExamples Solution

```xml
<?xml version="1.0" encoding="UTF-8"?>
<ContentPage xmlns="http://xamarin.com/schemas/2014/forms"
xmlns:x="http://schemas.microsoft.com/winfx/2009/xaml"
x:Class="ControlExamples.Xaml.Controls"
Title="Xamarin.Forms XAML Controls - Ch. 5"
>
<ContentPage.Padding>
    <OnPlatform x:TypeArguments="Thickness">
        <OnPlatform.iOS>10,20,10,5</OnPlatform.iOS>
        <OnPlatform.Android>10,0,10,5</OnPlatform.Android>
    </OnPlatform>
</ContentPage.Padding>
    <StackLayout HorizontalOptions="Center">
        <Label x:Name="EventValue" Text="Value in Event" />
        <Label x:Name="PageValue" Text="Value in Page" />
        <Picker x:Name="ThePicker" Title="Options" SelectedIndexChanged=
        "PickerSelectedIndexChanged">
            <Picker.Items>
                <x:String>First</x:String>
                <x:String>Second</x:String>
                <x:String>Third</x:String>
                <x:String>Fourth</x:String>
            </Picker.Items>
        </Picker>
        <DatePicker x:Name="TheDatePicker" Format="D" VerticalOptions=
        "CenterAndExpand" DateSelected="DatePickerDateSelected"></DatePicker>
        <TimePicker x:Name="TheTimePicker" Format="T" VerticalOptions=
        "CenterAndExpand" PropertyChanged="TimePickerPropertyChanged">
        </TimePicker>
        <Stepper x:Name="TheStepper" Minimum="0" Maximum="10" Increment="1"
        HorizontalOptions="Center" VerticalOptions="CenterAndExpand"
        ValueChanged="StepperValueChanged"></Stepper>
```

```
    <Slider x:Name="TheSlider" Minimum="0" Maximum="100" Value="50"
    VerticalOptions="CenterAndExpand" ValueChanged="SliderValueChanged"
    WidthRequest="300"></Slider>
        <Switch x:Name="TheSwitch" HorizontalOptions="Center" VerticalOptions=
        "CenterAndExpand" Toggled="SwitchToggled"></Switch>
    </StackLayout>
</ContentPage>
```

Note   Again, the two labels used in this example, EventValue and PageValue, reflect the two ways in which selection values can be retrieved: in a handler *event* property (e.g., e.NewValue), which provides the most recent value, or in a general-use property on the view (e.g., TheControl.Value), which provides the selected value for use throughout the *page*.

Now that you can use Xamarin.Forms controls, how can you group them into UI components for reuse throughout your app? By using old and familiar custom controls, of course.

Custom Controls

Every XAML page you create is really a custom class. Using C# you create a page by inheriting the ContentPage class in the code behind. Using XAML you specify a ContentPage as the root of your XAML and declare your namespace and class name using the x:Class attribute. Creating custom controls is no different. Xamarin.Forms provides two base classes for this purpose: ContentView and ViewCell. ContentView is useful if you want to create your own reusable controls. If you want to define a template for items in a list, then use ViewCell. Listing 5-2 shows a simple custom control based on ContentView.

Listing 5-2. Custom ContentView Control Called MyControl

```
<ContentView xmlns="http://xamarin.com/schemas/2014/forms"
xmlns:x="http://schemas.microsoft.com/winfx/2009/xaml"
x:Class="mycontrols.MyControl">
        <Label x:Name="MyLabel" />
</ContentView>
```

The custom control MyControl in the namespace mycontrols is a Label View. You can use as a View any of the Xamarin.Forms Views available to you and create beautiful and reusable controls. You derive from ContentView and inside of it build your control using layouts, buttons, labels, images, etc. Listing 2-33 demonstrates how you use this control inside your XAML pages. Here you use MyControl declared in Listing 5-3.

Listing 5-3. Using a Custom Control in XAML

```
<ContentPage xmlns="http://xamarin.com/schemas/2014/forms"
xmlns:x="http://schemas.microsoft.com/winfx/2009/xaml"
xmlns:my="clr-namespace:mycontrols"
x:Class="mynamespace.MyClass">
    <my:MyControl/>
</ContentPage>
```

After specifying your namespace mycontrols with the prefix my, you are able to use your custom control inside the page, that is, <my:MyControl/>.

Custom controls enable XAML code reuse. Use control templates for a separation between the appearance of a page and its content.

Control Templates

Control templates are generalized reusable user interfaces meant to be used along with page-specific content. Define a control template as a resource in a resource dictionary and use them in your XAML pages. Control templates can increase consistency of your visual design across several pages or across your entire application. Custom templates can be used application-wide or on a single page. Some examples include app-wide header and footer definitions or repeated blocks of UI on a single page. We'll use an application-wide header and footer example here.

A ControlTemplate is created using a ContentPage or ContentView and their respective base classes, TemplatedPage and TemplatedView. Listing 5-4 shows how a control template with the Key MyTemplate is defined as a resource of the Application. Create a ControlTemplate and add a StackLayout with a header label and a footer label.

Listing 5-4. Defining a Control Template

```
<Application xmlns=http://xamarin.com/schemas/2014/forms
xmlns:x="http://schemas.microsoft.com/winfx/2009/xaml"
x:Class="SimpleTheme.App">
    <Application.Resources>
            <ResourceDictionary>
                <ControlTemplate x:Key="MyTemplate">
                    <StackLayout>
                        <Label Text="Header"/>
                    <ContentPresenter/>
                     <Label Text="Footer"/>
                     </StackLayout>
                </ControlTemplate>
            </ResourceDictionary>
    </Application.Resources>
</Application>
```

In between the header and footer is the ContentPresenter, a placeholder for page-specific content added later, shown in Listing 5-5. Create a new page with a `ControlView` and set the `ControlView.ControlTemplate` property to the `ControlTemplate` `Key`, `MyTemplate` in this case. Add page-specific controls you want in the body of the page inside the `ContentView`, such as a `Label` with text "Page Body."

Listing 5-5. Using a Control Template in a Page

```
<ContentPage xmlns="http://xamarin.com/schemas/2014/forms"
xmlns:x="http://schemas.microsoft.com/winfx/2009/xaml"
x:Class="SimpleTheme.HomePage">
    <ContentView x:Name="contentView" Padding="0,20,0,0"
                ControlTemplate "MyTemplate">
        <Label Text="Page Body"/>
    </ContentView>
</ContentPage>
```

The ContentPresenter element inside the ControlLayout is replaced with whatever you have defined in your ContentView. The resulting page would be comprised of a StackLayout with three Labels: Header, Page Body, and Footer.

Tip   Another type of template is the data template useful for creating list items, which we'll cover in Chapter 6.

Commands

Xamarin.Forms offers *commands* as an alternative to events and event handlers. Event handlers reside in the C# code behind tightly coupled to your XAML file, making them non-reusable. Xamarin.Forms provides your controls with a bindable property Command and a corresponding CommandProperty.

Command is of type ICommand which requires an implementation of the methods Execute and CanExecute and also defines the event CanExecuteChanged. The CommandParameter object allows your Execute to receive an additional argument that is used during its execution.

You can define classes with properties that implement the ICommand interface and bind them to the bindable property Command provided by Xamarin.Forms to react to user interactions. Anytime interaction takes place, your command property is notified. First the CanExecute method will be called, and if the result is true, the Execute method runs. You can also provide a delegate to handle scenarios where CanExecute changes. To simplify the creation of custom commands, Xamarin.Forms defines two classes that implement ICommand: Command and Command<T>. These helpers also define a ChangeCanExecute method that you call to fire a CanExecuteChanged event.

Create a class called MyClass with a command called MyCommand that executes when the user presses a Button as shown in Listing 5-6.

Listing 5-6. Creating a Command

```
namespace mycommands {
        class MyClass {
                public ICommand MyCommand { protected set; get; }
```

```
public MyClass() {
        MyCommand = new Command({
                Console.WriteLine("Hello");
        });
}
}
}
```

This defines a class MyClass with a command MyCommand and writes "Hello" to the
Console. Command also allows async calls. Listing 5-7 shows how to bind a Button to our
MyCommand using the view's Command parameter and BindingContext.

Listing 5-7. Binding a Command to a Button

```
<Button Text="Click Me"
        Command="{Binding MyCommand}">
        <Button.BindingContext>
                <my:MyClass/>
        </Button.BindingContext>
</Button>
```

Assuming that you have specified the namespace mycommands with the prefix my in
the ContentPage of your XAML file, you can define a Button and set its BindingContext
to our custom class MyClass.

Tip   Execute a Command as a method by calling that method in the Command
definition.

Commands offer an alternative to the traditional event handling. However, not
all classes and types of user interactions are supported. The vast majority of controls
inherit from View class, and a view specifies the property GestureRecognizers of
type IList<GestureRecognizer> that allows you to register classes that implement
the IGestureRecognizer interface. The GestureRecognizer class that implements
the IGestureRecognizer interfaces has three children: TagGestureRecognizer,
PanGestureRecognizer, and ClickGestureRecognizer. TagGestureRecognizer and
ClickGestureRecognizer have a bindable property Command of type ICommand and
CommandParameter of type object.

Classes that inherit from Element, which is higher in the hierarchy, don't have gesture recognizers. For MenuItem (and hence also ToolbarItem) and for TextCell (and hence also ImageCell), Xamarin.Forms directly defines the Command and CommandParameter bindable properties. A MenuItem notifies your command when it is activated, and TextCell notifies your command when any property of it is changing or changed or was tapped. The Views SearchBar, ListView, and Button in addition to the GestureRecognizers also implement their own Command property, that is, SearchCommand, RefreshCommand, and Command. The Views SearchBar and Button also provide for a command parameter, SearchParameter, and CommandParameter of type object. This means that you cannot use classes that represent pages like ContentPage for commanding.

So, before you opt for an event, consider using a Command. First explore Binding, or whether you can use commands provided on Views, through GestureRecognizers, or controls that have a Command property.

Executing code is as a Command is useful, but what if it needs parameters?

CommandParameters

Now that you can bind the Command property of Button to your MyCommand, it's time to pass in a parameter. Begin with passing the "Hello" string into your command via CommandParameter. Replace the line containing the Command definition in Listing 5-6 to pass value s into the Command and display it in the Writeline.

```
MyCommand = new Command<string>(s => {Console.WriteLine(s); });
```

MyCommand now expects a string command parameter in s and writes the string to the Console. Working from Listing 5-7, pass your old "Hello" into the Button's CommandParameter attribute.

```
<Button Text="Click Me" Command="{Binding MyCommand}"
CommandParameter="Hello">
```

When the button is clicked and MyCommand is called, the "Hello" string is passed into the Command through the CommandParameter.

Tip   Need multiple parameters? Create a class and populate it with properties to pass into your Command.

Another approach to respond to user interactions and states of your UI is with triggers.

Triggers

Triggers respond to changes on a control or other element in your page. A trigger is composed of one or more conditions and an action. All controls, with the exception of cells, which do not inherit from the *VisualElement* class, have a `Triggers` property, where you can register your trigger. There are four types of triggers based on the type of condition: `Property`, `Data`, `Multi`, and `Event`.

All of these trigger types require the use of the `TargetType` property.

TargetType

Use `TargetType` when you define your trigger to specify the control type the trigger applies to, which is an `Entry` control in this example:

```
<Trigger TargetType="Entry" Property="IsEnabled" Value="true">
```

You can also use `TargetType` to define a trigger as a resource in your resource dictionary instead of registering it with the `Triggers` property of a specific control (Listing 5-8). For this you have to use a `Style` element as the container and register your trigger to its `Triggers` property. The `Style` element also has a `TargetType` that you need to specify for this to take effect. This allows you to change its properties for all controls of that type.

Listing 5-8. Using TargetType to Create a Page-Wide Property Trigger

```
<ContentPage xmlns="http://xamarin.com/schemas/2014/forms"
    xmlns:x="http://schemas.microsoft.com/winfx/2009/xaml"
    xmlns:my="clr-namespace:MyTriggers"
    x:Class="mynamespace.MyClass">
    <ContentPage.Resources>
        <ResourceDictionary>
            <Style TargetType="Entry">
                    <Style.Triggers>
```

```
                    <Trigger TargetType="Entry"
                            Property="IsFocused" Value="true">
                        <Setter Property="BackgroundColor" Value="Red" />
                    </Trigger>
                </Style.Triggers>
            </Style>
        </ResourceDictionary>
    </ContentPage.Resources>
    ...
</ContentPage>
```

Insert your UI at the ellipses and include one or more Entry controls. This is a page-wide implementation of a Property Trigger.

Property Trigger

This trigger is useful when you want your control to respond to changes of its own properties. Inside your control, create an Entry.Triggers tag that contains your Triggers. Create a `Trigger` with the property name/value pair you want to trigger on. The `Trigger` element has the properties `Property` and `Value`:

```
<Trigger Property="IsFocused" Value="true">
```

Set `Trigger.TargetType` to your view, Entry in this case, and a change to the `Property` that matches your `Value` executes the `Setter` within the trigger. In this case, when `Entry` gets focus, the `Entry` background is set to `Red,` as shown in Listing 5-9.

Listing 5-9. Creating a Property Trigger

```
<Entry>
    <Entry.Triggers>
        <Trigger TargetType="Entry"
            Property="IsFocused" Value="True">
            <Setter Property="BackgroundColor" Value="Red" />
        </Trigger>
    </Entry.Triggers>
</Entry>
```

Data Trigger

Use this trigger when you want your control to respond to changes that take place on *other* elements in the user interface. The DataTrigger element expects the properties Binding and Value.

```
<DataTrigger Binding="{Binding Source={x:Reference
entry},Path=IsFocused}" Value="true">
```

This trigger fires when another entry control gets the focus (Listing 5-10). With the binding markup extension, you also have access to the Converter property for more advanced computations. DataTrigger requires that you specify the TargetType property to the control you are registering the trigger with.

Listing 5-10. Creating a Data Trigger

```
<StackLayout>
    <Label x:Name="label" Text="{Binding Text,Source={x:Reference
    entry}}"/>
    <Entry x:Name="entry">
        <Entry.Triggers>
            <DataTrigger TargetType="Entry" Binding="{Binding Text.
            Length,Source={x:Reference label},Converter={my:IsEmptyString
            Converter}}" Value="true">
                <Setter Property="TextColor" Value="Green"/>
            </DataTrigger>
        </Entry.Triggers>
    </Entry>
</StackLayout>
```

Multi Trigger

Use multi triggers if you need several conditions to be met before an action takes place. The MultiTrigger element has a Conditions property that can have multiple BindingCondition and PropertyCondition elements. A BindingCondition expects the properties Binding and Value and a PropertyCondition the properties Property and Value. With the binding markup extension, you also have access to the Converter property for more advanced computations. Listing 5-11 shows that MultiTrigger requires that you specify the TargetType property to the control you are registering the trigger with.

Listing 5-11. Creating a Multi Trigger

```
<StackLayout>
        <Label x:Name="label" Text="{Binding Text,
        Source={x:Reference entry}}"/>
        <Entry x:Name="entry">
            <Entry.Triggers>
                <MultiTrigger TargetType="Entry">
                    <MultiTrigger.Conditions>
                        <BindingCondition Binding="{Binding Text.
                        Length,Source={x:Reference label},Converter={my
                        :IsEmptyStringConverter}}" Value="true"/>
                        <PropertyCondition Property="IsFocused"
                        Value="true"/>
                    </MultiTrigger.Conditions>
                    <Setter Property="FontSize" Value="Large"/>
                </MultiTrigger>
            </Entry.Triggers>
        </Entry>
</StackLayout>
```

Event Trigger

You can subscribe to events that are fired in your control. The handler needs to be written in C# by implementing inheriting from the `TriggerAction<T>` class. T represents the type of control this action is related to. In the C# code, you override the `Invoke (T t)` method and can change the properties of your control t.

There are two types of actions that you can define: `Setters` and `TriggerAction<T>` classes. For property, data, and multi triggers, you can use a `Setter` element to define the action that needs to happen when a condition is met. A `Setter` allows you to change the `Value` of a `Property` of your control, e.g., `<Setter Property="IsEnabled" Value="false"/>` disables your control. All trigger types allow instead of `Setters` registering one or more `TriggerAction(T)` implementations that you register with the trigger's `EnterActions` or `ExitActions` properties. You define your `TriggerAction<T>` classes in C# by inheriting from `TriggerAction(T)` and overriding the `Invoke(T t)` method. T represents the type of control the action applies to (Listing 5-12).

Listing 5-12. Creating an Event Trigger

```
<StackLayout>
        <Label x:Name="label" Text="{Binding Text,Source={x:Reference
        entry}}"/>
        <Entry x:Name="entry">
            <Entry.Triggers>
                <EventTrigger Event="PropertyChanged">
                    <my:EntryTextLogger/>
                </EventTrigger>
            </Entry.Triggers>
        </Entry>
</StackLayout>
```

Finally, a very powerful concept is the `Trigger` property `TargetType`.

CODE COMPLETE: Triggers

Listing 5-13 contains the complete code listing for Xamarin.Forms trigger examples in this chapter.

Listing 5-13. Property Trigger, DataTrigger, MultiTrigger, and EventTrigger

```
<ContentPage xmlns="http://xamarin.com/schemas/2014/forms"
xmlns:x="http://schemas.microsoft.com/winfx/2009/xaml"
xmlns:my="clr-namespace:MyTriggers"
x:Class="mynamespace.MyClass">
<ContentPage.Resources>
    <ResourceDictionary>
        <Style TargetType="Entry">
                        <Style.Triggers>
                <Trigger TargetType="Entry"
                        Property="IsFocused" Value="true">
                    <Setter Property="BackgroundColor" Value="Yellow" />
                </Trigger>
            </Style.Triggers>
        </Style>
    </ResourceDictionary>
</ContentPage.Resources>
```

```
<StackLayout>
        <Label x:Name="label" Text="{Binding Text,Source={x:Reference
        entry}}"/>
        <Entry x:Name="entry">
            <Entry.Triggers>
                <DataTrigger TargetType="Entry" Binding="{Binding Text.
                Length,Source={x:Reference label},Converter={my:IsEmpty
                StringConverter}}" Value="true">
                    <Setter Property="TextColor" Value="Green"/>
                </DataTrigger>
                <EventTrigger Event="PropertyChanged">
                    <my:EntryTextLogger/>
                </EventTrigger>
                <MultiTrigger TargetType="Entry">
                    <MultiTrigger.Conditions>
                        <BindingCondition Binding="{Binding Text.
                        Length,Source={x:Reference label},Converter=
                        {my:IsEmptyStringConverter}}" Value="true"/>
                        <PropertyCondition Property="IsFocused"
                        Value="true"/>
                    </MultiTrigger.Conditions>
                    <Setter Property="FontSize" Value="Large"/>
                </MultiTrigger>
            </Entry.Triggers>
        </Entry>
    </StackLayout>
</ContentPage>
```

Listing 5-13 shows a page with a ResourceDictionary that has a Style object which includes a Trigger, which is only applicable to Entry controls, changing their BackgroundColor to Yellow if they get the focus. The page contains a StackLayout with a Label and an Entry. The Text of the Label property is bound to the Text property of the Entry. Anything you write in the Entry is shown in the Label. The Entry has three triggers: DataTrigger, EventTrigger, and MultiTrigger. The DataTrigger is bound to the Text of the Label and changes the TextColor of the Entry to Green as soon as the Text property of the Label contains text. We use a IsEmptyStringConverter that we will implement in a moment that returns true if the Label has some text. The EventTrigger uses a custom EntryTextLogger TriggerAction class that logs the user entry to Console. Finally, we have a MultiTrigger defined with one BindingCondition and one PropertyCondition monitoring the Label Text and whether the Entry has focus and changing the Entry FontSize to Large. Listing 5-14 shows the ValueConverter and TriggerAction we use in this example.

Listing 5-14. Value Converter Example

```
namespace MyTriggers {
    class IsEmptyStringConverter : IValueConverter {
        public object Convert(object value, Type targetType,
        object parameter, CultureInfo culture) {
            return ((int)value>0) ? true : false;
        }
        public object ConvertBack(object value, Type targetType,
        object parameter, CultureInfo culture) {
            throw new NotSupportedException();
        }
    }

    public class EntryTextLogger : TriggerAction<Entry> {
        public EntryTextLogger() { }
        protected override void Invoke(Entry entry) {
            Console.WriteLine(entry.Text);
        }
    }
}
```

The IsEmptyStringConverter we have defined in Listing 5-14 is very simple. It checks whether the integer value that was provided is greater null or not and returns true or false. The TriggerAction<Entry> is also very simple. The Invoke(Entry entry) method simply writes the value of Text to the Console. As you have learned, you can define auto-implemented properties to pass additional data to your TriggerAction class. Our EntryTextLogger could, for instance, have a DebugMode property that only writes to Console if set to true, e.g., <my:EntryTextLogger DebugMode="true"/>.

Behaviors

Behaviors let you extend the functionality of controls without subclassing them using Attached Properties or Behavior<T> classes.

Attached Properties

Extend behavior of a visual element using attached properties. Bindable properties are properties of UI elements that can be bound to data sources in code, such as arrays, collections, or view models.

Note   Learn about BindableProperty in Chapter 9.

Attached properties are a particular type of bindable property defined as a static property in a static class with corresponding static GetPropertyName and SetPropertyName methods. The difference between an attached property and a regular bindable property is that these properties are defined in one class but used in others.

Recognize an attached property by the class.propertyname notation in your XAML. As discussed in Chapter 9, the propertyChanged delegate can respond to changes on that property receiving a reference to the BindableObject that makes use of the attached property as well as the new and old value assigned. Since you have a reference to the control in your propertyChanged delegate, you can take full control over the object, change its properties, or enhance its behavior. The key restriction with attached properties is that they must be defined in a static class with static properties and methods, which means that they cannot have state, which is why it is recommended to use Behavior classes in many cases.

Assign an attached property to your control by using the attribute myprefix:MyStaticClass.PropertyName="true" on the element, and set it to false if you want to detach it again.

```
<Entry my:MyClass.PropertyName="true"/>
```

This requires that you have defined in your namespace with the prefix my a public static class MyClass with the public static BindableProperty MyAttachedProperty.

Implement your attached property within the Attached Behavior called MyBehavior as shown in Listing 5-15.

Listing 5-15. Attached Property Implementation

```
public static class MyBehavior
{
    public static readonly BindableProperty PropertyNameProperty =
        BindableProperty.CreateAttached (
            "PropertyName",
            typeof(bool),
            typeof(MyBehavior),
            false,
            propertyChanged:OnPropertyNameChanged);

    public static bool GetPropertyName (BindableObject view)
    {
        return (bool)view.GetValue (PropertyNameProperty);
    }

    public static void SetPropertyName (BindableObject view, bool value)
    {
        view.SetValue (PropertyNameProperty, value);
    }

    static void OnPropertyNameChanged (BindableObject view, object
    oldValue, object newValue)
    {
        var entry = view as Entry;
        if (entry == null) {
            return;
        }
            /* Validate Entry */
    }
}
```

This implementation also uses an Attached Behavior OnPropertyNameChanged that is triggered on the change of PropertyName.

Behavior

Behaviors are associated with a control, and every subclass of VisualElement has a Behaviors property where you can register your Behavior subclass.

Create a class that inherits from Behavior or Behavior<T>., where T is the type of the control tied to your behavior. Override the OnAttachedTo and OnDetachingFrom methods to provide your behavior implementation (Listing 5-16). Lastly, implement your behavior functionality.

Listing 5-16. Behavior Implementation

```
public class MyBehavior : Behavior<View>
{
    protected override void OnAttachedTo (View bindable)
    {
        base.OnAttachedTo (bindable);
        // Initialize
    }
    protected override void OnDetachingFrom (View bindable)
    {
        base.OnDetachingFrom (bindable);
        // Clean up
    }
    // Behavior Implementation
}
```

Using an Entry control in this example, register your behavior, MyBehavior, as shown in Listing 5-17.

Listing 5-17. Consuming a Behavior

```
<Entry Placeholder="Enter Name">
    <Entry.Behaviors>
        <my:MyBehavior />
    </Entry.Behaviors>
</Entry>
```

Tip   When you're finished with your behavior, you can only detach it using code. Detach by calling `myControl.Behaviors.Clear()` prior to your page going out of scope.

Behaviors can have a state, as opposed to attached properties, and you should not use resource dictionaries to share them if you want to manage state.

Note   If you prefer a `Style` in the resource dictionary to set your `Behavior` as a property of your visual element, then you need to combine the `Behavior` with the attached property technique.

```
<Setter Property="my:MyClass.PropertyName" Value="true"/>
```

Tip   EffectBehavior is another type of behavior used to define reusable visual effects for your user interface controls. We will explain this type more in depth in Chapter 8 when we talk about effects.

In this section, we covered how to extend the behavior of visual elements without the need to use the underlying C# file of your XAML file. These are valid but not reusable approaches because the behavior is bound to a specific control. However, what makes Behaviors really interesting is that all `VisualElements` have a `Behaviors` property that you can use to overcome the shortcomings of classes in Xamarin.Forms that don't support commands. Typically a `Behavior` class uses reflection to register a generic event handler with the control and provides properties in XAML to specify the event name as well as the `Command` the behavior should execute when the event is fired, as shown in Listing 5-18.

Listing 5-18. Event-to-Command Example

```
<Entry.Behaviors>
        <my:EventToCommand Event="TextChanged"
            Command="{Binding MyCommand}"/>
</Entry.Behaviors>
```

There are several libraries that eliminate the need to write event handlers entirely and replace them with commands. Check out Event-To-Command `Behavior` implementations for more details.

That completes our tour of Xamarin.Forms views!

Summary

Many controls share a common goal: allowing the user to pick a value. Simple selection controls require us to specify minimum and maximum values and set a default value. Pickers/spinners work best inside a modal dialog, and we use them to select from a list or choose dates and times. Xamarin.Forms handles the dialog pop-ups for you. The selection controls in this chapter typically provide a *value changed* or click event of some kind to allow your code to respond to changes in values.

Xamarin.Forms `Views` become more powerful every year, with features to help us make them interactive with minimal, `elegant code`. *Commands* provide an alternative to events useful for building a testable architecture. Commands help consolidate behaviors in a view model providing bindable properties and commands that can be unit tested independent of the user interface. *Triggers* can fire under a broad array of circumstances driving logic within the app. For example, data triggers can be used within views to update presentation based upon information in the data model. *Behaviors* supply a way to let you extend the functionality of controls without subclassing them.

While indispensable, the controls in this chapter are simple ones. In the next chapter, you'll dive deeper into the heart of mobile UI selection, where both the data and the selection can be richer and more complex when using lists and tables.

CHAPTER 6

Making a Scrollable List

Choosing quickly from a long list of items is one of the key offerings of the mobile UI. The limited real estate on mobile phone screens makes data grids a challenge and leads to extensive and creative use of lists. Grouping of items, scrolling, gesture sensitivity, and images make lists one of the most versatile and reusable data-bound tools available. Lists are to mobile development what the data grid is to web development.

This chapter covers the `ListView` class which allows us to make a scrollable, selectable list. The primary considerations include binding to an array or data model, handling item selection, customizing the look of rows, grouping headers, and perhaps most importantly: performance.

Xamarin.Forms ListView

Lists in Xamarin.Forms are created using the `ListView` control bound to an array or data model. The Xamarin.Forms `ListView` class provides a scrollable, selectable list. List rows are customizable using layouts, images, and views such as buttons. `ListView` supports grouping, headers, footers, jump lists, and pull-to-refresh. Deleting and applying operations to list rows are supported using Context Actions.

The lists in this chapter are read-only, which means that they are bound to a data source for viewing and selecting, but the rows are not edited, deleted, or added. We touch on some editable list UI techniques in the "Customizing List Rows" and "Using Context Actions" sections, but do not cover changes to the data model or two-way data binding so that these changes can be reflected in the list. For editable `ListView` data binding, see Chapter 9.

We can bind directly to a collection or list using the ItemsSource property with the default list template. We can also bind to data models and create custom rows with the `ListView`'s built-in adapter class called ItemTemplate. Let's try both approaches: `ItemsSource` and `ItemTemplate`. Beginning with `ItemsSource`, let us proceed by binding `ListView` to a simple data source.

© Dan Hermes 2019
D. Hermes and N. Mazloumi, *Building Xamarin.Forms Mobile Apps Using XAML*,
https://doi.org/10.1007/978-1-4842-4030-4_6

> **Tip** We don't cover them in this book as they're just being released as it's going to print, but the next generation of ListView may be the CollectionView.

Binding to a List of Strings

The simplest ListView implementation is binding to a List of Strings.

Instantiate a ListView class on your page and point it to the default data source using the ItemsSource property:

```
<ListView ItemsSource="{Binding .}" />
```

ItemsSource is defined as the local BindingContext, indicated by a period ("."). We will soon define BindingContext to contain the list of items in the code behind. Typically you'll want to use the XAML ItemTemplate and possibly a ViewModel for binding, but we're starting simple with "." and the page's BindingContext so you can see how ItemsSource works (more on data binding in Chapter 9).

Next, in the main class's constructor, such as ListViewStrings in Listing 6-1, declare your string List class called Items after InitializeComponent();. Populate Items and set it all to the ContextPage's BindingContext.

Listing 6-1. ContentPage Constructor for a ListView Bound to String Items

```
public ListViewStrings()
{
    InitializeComponent();
    List<string> Items = new List<string>
            {
                "First",
                "Second",
                "Third"
            };
    BindingContext = Items;
}
```

Using the default ListView layout, each item in the list will be a single cell using the TextCell template displaying a single line of text. Here's the list in Figure 6-1.

Figure 6-1. *ListView in iOS and Android*

Tip   Create space around the edges of your list using the layout `Padding` property mentioned in Chapter 3:

```
<ContentPage.Padding>
    <OnPlatform x:TypeArguments="Thickness">
        <On Platform="iOS">10,20,10,5</On>
        <On Platform="Android">10,0,10,5</On>
    </OnPlatform>
</ContentPage.Padding>
```

Selecting a list item fires the `ItemSelected` event.

Selecting an Item

There are two events for use in item selection: ItemTapped and ItemSelected. Both can happen when a user taps a cell in the ListView. The difference between them is apparent when a list permits more than just tapping and items can be selected and unselected. In simple lists where there is no unselection of rows (like the example here), there is little difference between them.

ItemTapped is the simplest. It fires as a motion event when the user clicks a list row:

```
<ListView ItemsSource="{Binding Items}" ItemTapped="ListViewItemTapped"/>
```

The ItemTapped event must be implemented in the C# code behind:

```
async void ListViewItemTapped (object sender, ItemTappedEventArgs e)
{
    string item = (string)e.Item;
    await DisplayAlert("Tapped", item + " was selected.", "OK");
}
```

The **ItemSelected** event responds to a change in the state of row selection and happens when a row is selected or unselected by a user or in code:

```
<ListView ItemsSource="{Binding Items}" ItemSelected="ListViewItem
Selected"/>
```

The ItemSelected event must be implemented in the C# code behind:

```
async void ListViewItemSelected(object sender,
SelectedItemChangedEventArgs e)
{
    string item = (string)e.SelectedItem;
    await DisplayAlert("Selected", item + " was selected.", "OK");
}
```

Using async/await isn't mandatory on these event handlers, but it is a good habit when any processing is done, to avoid tying up the UI thread. Use either ItemTapped or ItemSelected to select the first item in Figure 6-2.

Figure 6-2. *The alert displays the selected item*

Clear the selected row (removing the row highlight) by setting the ListView's SelectedItem property to null. The easiest place to do this is inside the ItemTapped handler:

```
async void ListViewItemTapped (object sender, ItemTappedEventArgs e)
{
    string item = (string)e.Item;
    await DisplayAlert("Tapped", item + " was selected.", "OK");
    ((ListView)sender).SelectedItem = null;
}
```

If you're using the ItemSelected event, be aware that changing the SelectedItem value fires the ItemSelected event again. In order to safely clear the selected row, you need to check if e.SelectedItem is null prior to responding to the event:

```
async void ListViewItemSelected (object sender, ItemTappedEventArgs e)
{
    if (e.SelectedItem == null) return;
    string item = (string)e.Item;
    await DisplayAlert("Selected", item + " was selected.", "OK");
    ((ListView)sender).SelectedItem = null;
}
```

The XAML in Listing 6-2 and its code behind in Listing 6-3 show the complete ListView example for binding to a List of Strings, selecting an item using async/await for backgrounding the ItemTapped event handler, and then clearing the selected row when you're done.

Listing 6-2. Binding to a List of Strings in ListViewStrings.xaml

```xml
<?xml version="1.0" encoding="UTF-8"?>
<ContentPage xmlns="http://xamarin.com/schemas/2014/forms" xmlns:x="http://
schemas.microsoft.com/winfx/2009/xaml" x:Class="ListViewExample.Xaml.
ListViewStrings">
<ContentPage.Padding>
    <OnPlatform x:TypeArguments="Thickness">
            <On Platform="Android">10,0,10,5</On>
            <On Platform="iOS">10,20,10,5</On>
    </OnPlatform></ContentPage.Padding>
  <ListView ItemsSource="{Binding .}" ItemTapped="ListViewItemTapped"/>
  <!-- <ListView ItemsSource="{Binding Items}" ItemSelected="ListViewItem
  Selected"/> -->
</ContentPage>
```

Listing 6-3. Binding to a List of Strings in ListViewStrings.cs

```csharp
public partial class ListViewStrings : ContentPage
{
    public ListViewStrings()
    {
        InitializeComponent();
        List<string> Items = new List<string>
        {
            "First",
            "Second",
            "Third"
        };
        BindingContext = Items;
    }

    async void ListViewItemTapped (object sender, ItemTappedEventArgs e)
    {
        string item = (string)e.Item;
        await DisplayAlert("Tapped", item + " was selected.", "OK");
        ((ListView)sender).SelectedItem = null;
    }
```

```
async void ListViewItemSelected(object sender,
SelectedItemChangedEventArgs e)
{
    string item = (string)e.SelectedItem;
    await DisplayAlert("Selected", item + " was selected.", "OK");
}
```
}

Tip   Multiple row selection must be coded manually and is not covered here.

A List<String> is useful for demonstration, but in many real-world scenarios, we bind to a data model.

Binding to a Data Model

Binding ListView to a data model is made easy in Xamarin.Forms through the use of ListView's built-in adapter called ItemTemplate.

Prepare your data model class and assign it to the ListView.ItemsSource property. Then bind each property of your model to the list using the ItemTemplate.SetBinding method.

Create a data model, or custom class, containing the list items. Call it ListItem:

```
public class ListItem {
    public string Title { get; set; }
    public string Description { get; set; }
}
```

Create a List of ListItem and populate the list:

```
List<ListItem> ListItems = new List<ListItem>
{
    new ListItem {Title = "First", Description="1st item"},
    new ListItem {Title = "Second", Description="2nd item"},
    new ListItem {Title = "Third", Description="3rd item"}
};
```

Point the `ListView`'s `ItemsSource` property to `ListItems`. Use the name `DataModelList` for the ListView which you'll declare in XAML in a moment:

```
DataModelList.DataModelList.ItemsSource = ListItems;
```

This is an alternative to setting the `ItemsSource` to `"{Binding .}"` and binds the `ListItems` to the `ListView`.

Next, create a `ListView` in XAML and name it `DataModelList`. Format list rows using the `ListView's` `ItemTemplate` property. Create a `DataTemplate` class and use the standard cell type to display, `TextCell`, which will display a title for each row plus some detail text which you'll add in a minute. Specify the property to display as the main row text by binding it to `TextCell.Text`, in this case `Title`:

```xml
<ListView x:Name="DataModelList" ItemTapped="ListViewItemTapped" >
    <ListView.ItemTemplate>
        <DataTemplate>
            <TextCell Text="{Binding Title}"/>
        </DataTemplate>
    </ListView.ItemTemplate>
</ListView>
```

This will display the same list but from a list of custom class `ListItem` instead of a List of `Strings` (Figure 6-3).

Figure 6-3. *This ListView looks the same as Figure 6-1 but is driven by the ListItem data model*

Add a descriptive line of text to each row by binding the `Detail` property of the `TextCell`:

```xml
<TextCell Text="{Binding Title}" Detail="{Binding Description}"/>
```

This binds the `Description` property of the `ListItem` class to the `Detail` property of the `TextCell`. Figure 6-4 shows the result.

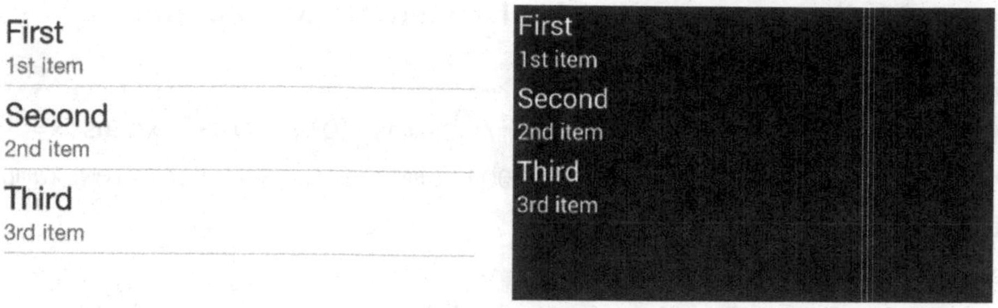

Figure 6-4. *Title and Description properties are bound to each row using properties of TextCell*

Tip   TextCell's font color can be set using its TextColor property

```
<TextCell Text="{Binding Title}" Detail="{Binding
Description}" TextColor="Blue"/>
```

and the detail text color (Description in this example) can be set using the DetailColor property:

```
<TextCell Text="{Binding Title}" Detail="{Binding
Description}" DetailColor="Red"/>
```

When handling the item selection, remember to use the ListItem data model:

```
async void ListViewItemTapped (object sender, ItemTappedEventArgs e)
{
    ListItem item = (ListItem)e.Item;
    await DisplayAlert("Tapped", item.Title + " was selected.", "OK");
    ((ListView)sender).SelectedItem = null;
}
```

CODE COMPLETE: Binding to a Data Model

Listings 6-4 and 6-5 show the complete ListView example where we bind to a data model containing text and detail for each row in the list, found in the ListViewExample solution.

Listing 6-4. Binding to a Data Model in ListViewDataModel.xaml

```xml
<?xml version="1.0" encoding="UTF-8"?>
<ContentPage xmlns="http://xamarin.com/schemas/2014/forms" xmlns:x=
"http://schemas.microsoft.com/winfx/2009/xaml" x:Class="ListViewExample.
Xaml.ListViewDataModel">
    <ContentPage.Padding>
        <OnPlatform x:TypeArguments="Thickness">
            <On Platform="Android">10,0,10,5</On>
            <On Platform="iOS">10,20,10,5</On>
        </OnPlatform>    </ContentPage.Padding>
    <ListView x:Name="DataModelList" ItemTapped="ListViewItemTapped" >
        <ListView.ItemTemplate>
            <DataTemplate>
                <TextCell Text="{Binding Title}" Detail="{Binding
                Description}"/>
            </DataTemplate>
        </ListView.ItemTemplate>
    </ListView>
</ContentPage>
```

Listing 6-5. Binding to a Data Model in ListViewDataModel.cs

```csharp
public partial class ListViewDataModel : ContentPage
{
    public ListViewDataModel()
    {
        InitializeComponent();
        List<ListItem> ListItems = new List<ListItem>
        {
            new ListItem {Title = "First", Description="1st item"},
            new ListItem {Title = "Second", Description="2nd item"},
            new ListItem {Title = "Third", Description="3rd item"}
        };
        DataModelList.ItemsSource = ListItems;
    }
```

```
async void ListViewItemTapped (object sender, ItemTappedEventArgs e)
{
    ListItem item = (ListItem)e.Item;
    await DisplayAlert("Tapped", item.Title + " was selected.", "OK");
    ((ListView)sender).SelectedItem = null;
}

public class ListItem
{
    public string Title { get; set; }
    public string Description { get; set; }
}
}
```

Tip   In Model View ViewModel (MVVM) apps, the data models are typically wrapped inside screen-specific classes called view models (VM). See Chapter 9 for how to create view models that are data-bound to `ListViews`.

Adding an Image

Adding a single image to a `ListView` is easy using the `ImageCell` cell type. Previously, we used the `TextCell` cell type to display text and detail in each row. An `ImageCell` inherits from `TextCell` and adds an `ImageSource` property, which contains the image filename or URI. We use the bindable properties `ImageSource`, `Text`, and `Detail` to bind to our data model. The image is displayed left-justified, as seen in Figure 6-5.

Figure 6-5. *ImageCell in a ListView*

I'll highlight the differences from the previous TextCell data-binding example and then you can see the final result in Listings 6-6 and 6-7. Add a Source property of type String to the ListItem class and populate it with your images (filename or URI):

```
List<ListItem> ListItems = new List<ListItem>
{
    new ListItem {Source = "first.png", Title = "First",
    Description="1st item"},
    new ListItem {Source = "second.png", Title = "Second",
    Description="2nd item"},
    new ListItem {Source = "third.png", Title = "Third",
    Description="3rd item"}
};
```

Create a ListView called ImageList and declare an ItemTemplate with a DataTemplate containing the ImageCell. Bind the ListItem properties to the ImageCell—Title, Description, and Image Source:

```
<ListView x:Name="ImageList" ItemTapped="ListViewItemTapped">
    <ListView.ItemTemplate>
        <DataTemplate>
            <ImageCell ImageSource="{Binding Source}" Text="{Binding
            Title}" Detail="{Binding Description}"/>
        </DataTemplate>
    </ListView.ItemTemplate>
</ListView>
```

Assign the ListItems to the list's ItemsSource property and that's all there is to it:

```
ImageList.ItemsSource = ListItems;
```

Tip   The image folder will be local to each platform project (Android: Resources/ drawable, iOS: /Resources). Remember to set the Build Actions by right-clicking on the image file in your project (Android: AndroidResource, iOS: BundleResource).

Listings 6-6 and 6-7 contain the complete code to add an image to a ListView using ImageCell, as shown in Figure 6-5.

Listing 6-6. Image in a List Row in ListViewImageCell.xaml

```xml
<?xml version="1.0" encoding="UTF-8"?>
<ContentPage xmlns="http://xamarin.com/schemas/2014/forms" xmlns:x="http://
schemas.microsoft.com/winfx/2009/xaml" x:Class="ListViewExample.Xaml.
ListViewImageCell">
    <ContentPage.Padding>
      <OnPlatform x:TypeArguments="Thickness">
            <On Platform="Android">10,0,10,5</On>
            <On Platform="iOS">10,20,10,5</On>
      </OnPlatform>     </ContentPage.Padding>
    <ListView x:Name="ImageList" ItemTapped="ListViewItemTapped">
        <ListView.ItemTemplate>
            <DataTemplate>
                <ImageCell ImageSource="{Binding Source}" Text="{Binding
                Title}" Detail="{Binding Description}"/>
            </DataTemplate>
        </ListView.ItemTemplate>
    </ListView>
</ContentPage>
```

Listing 6-7. Image in a List Row in ListViewImageCell.xaml.cs

```csharp
public partial class ListViewImageCell : ContentPage
{
    public ListViewImageCell()
    {
        InitializeComponent();
        List<ListItem> ListItems = new List<ListItem>
        {
            new ListItem {Source = "first.png", Title = "First",
            Description="1st item"},
            new ListItem {Source = "second.png", Title = "Second",
            Description="2nd item"},
```

```
            new ListItem {Source = "third.png", Title = "Third",
            Description="3rd item"}
        };
        ImageList.ItemsSource = ListItems;
    }

    async void ListViewItemTapped(object sender, ItemTappedEventArgs e)
    {
        ListItem item = (ListItem)e.Item;
        await DisplayAlert("Tapped", item.Title + " was selected.", "OK");
        ((ListView)sender).SelectedItem = null;
    }

    public class ListItem
    {
        public string Source { get; set; }
        public string Title { get; set; }
        public string Description { get; set; }
    }
}
```

Tip   A ListView can contain four built-in cell types: TextCell, ImageCell, SwitchCell, and EntryCell. The most useful here are TextCell and ImageCell. Although cell types can be combined using a TableView, a TableView cannot be data-bound, so TableViews are not useful for building ListViews.

Sooner or later you'll outgrow TextCell and ImageCell and will need greater control over the look of your list rows. So, you'll learn to customize them.

Customizing List Rows

Customize the list rows by creating a *custom row template*, which is basically a custom cell containing a Layout with Views. It begins with a custom class inherited from ViewCell. Then we place a layout on it and add our views. Views are more versatile than the built-in cells like TextCell and expose more properties for layout and design.

With a custom row template, you can customize your labels and add more views to your list, as shown in Figure 6-6. These three labels have their positions, font sizes, attributes, and colors customized.

Figure 6-6. *Custom row template*

Let's walk through the code for this multiline custom row example using three Label Views to display the title, description, and price. Figure 6-6 is an example where more control was needed over fonts and formatting than is provided for by the built-in cells.

Add Price to your ListItem data model:

```
public class ListItem
{
    public string Source { get; set; }
    public string Title { get; set; }
    public string Description { get; set; }
    public string Price { get; set; }
}
```

In the ContentPage's constructor, populate Price with values:

```
List<ListItem> ListItems = new List<ListItem>
{
    new ListItem {Title = "First", Description="1st item", Price="$100.00"},
    new ListItem {Title = "Second", Description="2nd item", Price="$200.00"},
    new ListItem {Title = "Third", Description="3rd item", Price="$300.00"}
};
```

Create a ListView called CustomList, and add a DataTemplate and a row class called ViewCell with a custom template inside it. Place one or more controls or layouts within this custom template. For simple text fields in different-sized fonts, create label controls

and place them on a StackLayout (or AbsoluteLayout or Grid if performance is an
issue). Be careful when using Image views, as images can affect performance, particularly
on older devices.

```xml
<ListView x:Name="CustomList">
<ListView.ItemTemplate>
    <DataTemplate>
        <ViewCell>
            <StackLayout HorizontalOptions="StartAndExpand"
            Orientation="Horizontal" Padding="25,10,55,15">
                <StackLayout HorizontalOptions="StartAndExpand"
                Orientation="Vertical">
                    <Label HorizontalOptions="Start" FontSize="20"
                    FontAttributes="Bold" TextColor="White"
                    Text="{Binding Title}"/>
                    <Label HorizontalOptions="Start" FontSize="12"
                    FontAttributes="Bold" TextColor="White"
                    Text="{Binding Description}"/>
                </StackLayout>
                <Label HorizontalOptions="End" FontSize="25"
                TextColor="Aqua" Text="{Binding Price}"/>
            </StackLayout>
        </ViewCell>
    </DataTemplate>
</ListView.ItemTemplate>
</ListView>
```

Double-bag your StackLayouts for formatting's sake, placing a vertical StackLayout
inside a horizontal one. Inside the inner StackLayout, place two label controls on a
vertical StackLayout and bind them to the ListItem model's Title and Description
fields, respectively. Place the price label after the end of the inner StackLayout and bind
it to the data model's Price property.

Note the use of the main StackLayout's Padding on all four sides to provide proper
positioning of views within the row. LayoutOptions help with alignment (that come
at a performance cost), using Start for left- or top-justified views and End for right- or
bottom-justified ones.

Back in the `ListView` declaration, let's consider `Backgroundcolor` and `RowHeight`. If you're on iOS, we need to set the background color to black so you can see the white text. Also, on all platforms, set the `RowHeight` to accommodate the extra `Views`:

```
<ListView x:Name="CustomList" RowHeight="80" BackgroundColor="Black">
```

Tip   When your list rows vary in height, use `ListView`'s `HasUnevenRows` property instead of `RowHeight` (e.g., `HasUnevenRows` = `"True"`).

As always, bind to the model with your list's `ItemsSource` property:

```
CustomList.ItemsSource = ListItems;
```

Compile and run and you should see Figure 6-6.

Customizing a list can result in a beautiful, highly functional UI feature. It is also one of the best ways to destroy a list's performance, so customize with caution. Use `TextCell` or `ImageCell` as much as you can before deciding to customize. Images and nested layouts are a challenge to optimize in Xamarin.Forms, particularly on older devices. If you're having difficulty with performance as you test your customized list, try the performance tips in the (Xamarin.Forms) "Optimizing Performance" section. If those don't work for you, then consider using a custom renderer with platform-specific controls instead. (See the list views in the Android and iOS sections of this chapter and then turn to Chapter 8 to read about custom renderers.)

Tip   `ListView` row separator lines are customizable using its `SeparatorVisibility` and `SeparatorColor` properties. Set the `ListView`'s `SeparatorVisibility` property to None to hide the lines (the default value is `Default`). Set the color of the separator using `SeparatorColor`.

Headers and footers are supported by `ListView`. Use the `Header` and `Footer` properties for a simple text or view. For more complex layouts, use `HeaderTemplate` and `FooterTemplate`.

CODE COMPLETE: Customizing List Rows

Listings 6-8 and 6-9 contain the complete code for the row customization example shown in Figure 6-6, with the addition of an ItemTapped event.

Listing 6-8. Customizing List Rows in ListViewCustom.xaml

```xml
<?xml version="1.0" encoding="UTF-8"?>
<ContentPage xmlns="http://xamarin.com/schemas/2014/forms" xmlns:x="http://
schemas.microsoft.com/winfx/2009/xaml" x:Class="ListViewExample.Xaml.
ListViewCustom">
  <ContentPage.Padding>
    <OnPlatform x:TypeArguments="Thickness">
        <On Platform="iOS">10,20,10,5</On>
        <On Platform="Android">10,0,10,5</On>
    </OnPlatform>   </ContentPage.Padding>
  <ListView x:Name="CustomList" RowHeight="80" BackgroundColor="Black"
  ItemTapped="ListViewItemTapped" >
    <ListView.ItemTemplate>
      <DataTemplate>
        <ViewCell>
          <StackLayout HorizontalOptions="StartAndExpand"
          Orientation="Horizontal" Padding="25,10,55,15">
            <StackLayout HorizontalOptions="StartAndExpand"
            Orientation="Vertical">
              <Label HorizontalOptions="Start" FontSize="20"
              FontAttributes="Bold" TextColor="White" Text="
              {Binding Title}"/>
              <Label HorizontalOptions="Start" FontSize="12"
              FontAttributes="Bold" TextColor="White" Text="
              {Binding Description}"/>
            </StackLayout>
            <Label HorizontalOptions="End" FontSize="25"
            TextColor="Aqua" Text="{Binding Price}"/>
          </StackLayout>
        </ViewCell>
```

```
        </DataTemplate>
      </ListView.ItemTemplate>
   </ListView>
</ContentPage>
```

Listing 6-9. Customizing List Rows in ListViewCustom.cs

```
public partial class ListViewCustom : ContentPage
{
    public ListViewCustom()
    {
        InitializeComponent();
        List<ListItem> ListItems = new List<ListItem>
        {
            new ListItem {Title = "First", Description="1st item",
            Price="$100.00"},
            new ListItem {Title = "Second", Description="2nd item",
            Price="$200.00"},
            new ListItem {Title = "Third", Description="3rd item",
            Price="$300.00"}
        };
        CustomList.ItemsSource = ListItems;
    }

    async void ListViewItemTapped(object sender, ItemTappedEventArgs e)
    {
        ListItem item = (ListItem)e.Item;
        await DisplayAlert("Tapped", item.Title + " was selected.", "OK");
        ((ListView)sender).SelectedItem = null;
    }

    public class ListItem
    {
        public string Source { get; set; }
        public string Title { get; set; }
```

```
        public string Description { get; set; }
        public string Price { get; set; }
    }
}
```

Tip   Changes to list properties can be reflected in the list in real-time using an implementation of the INotifyPropertyChanged interface. See Chapter 9 for more on editable list data binding.

Among the views that can be added to a list row, Buttons require special attention due to their prevalence and unique qualities.

Adding Buttons

Buttons can be added to a list in one of two ways: as button views and as *Context Actions*. Button views are straightforward views added to the custom template, while Context Actions appear when a row is swiped or long-pressed, such as for buttons hiding behind each row, which are often used for operations on the selected row such as deletion.

Note   Image Views paired with gesture recognizers (manually coded image buttons) contain the list row in their BindingContext, though the property is more cumbersome to retrieve than with a button.

Using Button Views

Add button views to your custom template during the customization of a ListView. Add the Button View onto a layout in a custom ViewCell, and it will display on the list in every row, as shown in Figure 6-7.

Figure 6-7. *Add a Button View to a ListView*

Declare a `Button` view in your custom `ViewCell`. Set up a `Clicked` handler using the `CommandParameter` property to determine which button was clicked. Bind a period (.) to the button's `CommandParameter` property to retrieve the clicked row:

```
<Button x:Name="BuyButton" Text="Buy Now" BackgroundColor="Teal"
HorizontalOptions="EndAndExpand" Clicked="BuyClicked"
CommandParameter="{Binding .}"/>
```

Create a clicked handler called `BuyClicked`. Retrieve the row that was clicked using the `Button`'s `CommandParameter`, which returns the affected `ListItem` object, where you can get the `Title` parameter to display:

```
public async void BuyClicked(object sender, EventArgs e)
{
    var b = (Button)sender;
    var item = (ListItem)b.CommandParameter;
    await DisplayAlert("Clicked", item.Title.ToString() + " button was
    clicked", "OK");
}
```

Listings 6-10 and 6-11 contain the code where we add a `Button` `View` to the `ListView`, as shown in Figure 6-7.

Listing 6-10. Adding a Button to a List Row from ListViewButton.xaml

```
<?xml version="1.0" encoding="UTF-8"?>
<ContentPage xmlns="http://xamarin.com/schemas/2014/forms"
xmlns:x="http://schemas.microsoft.com/winfx/2009/xaml"
x:Class="ListViewExample.Xaml.ListViewButton">
```

```xml
<ContentPage.Padding>
    <OnPlatform x:TypeArguments="Thickness">
            <On Platform="iOS">10,20,10,5</On>
            <On Platform="Android">10,0,10,5</On>
    </OnPlatform>
</ContentPage.Padding>
    <ListView x:Name="ButtonList" RowHeight="100" BackgroundColor="Black"
    HasUnevenRows="true" >
        <ListView.ItemTemplate>
            <DataTemplate>
                <ViewCell>
                    <StackLayout HorizontalOptions="StartAndExpand"
                    Orientation="Horizontal" Padding="5,10,5,15">
                        <StackLayout HorizontalOptions="Start"
                        Orientation="Vertical">
                            <Label HorizontalOptions="Start" FontSize="20"
                            FontAttributes="Bold" TextColor="White"
                            Text="{Binding Title}"/>
                            <Label HorizontalOptions="Start" FontSize="12"
                            FontAttributes="Bold" TextColor="White"
                            Text="{Binding Description}"/>
                        </StackLayout>
                        <StackLayout HorizontalOptions="EndAndExpand"
                        Orientation="Horizontal" WidthRequest="260">
                            <Label HorizontalOptions="Center" FontSize="25"
                            TextColor="Aqua" Text="{Binding Price}"/>
                            <Button x:Name="BuyButton" Text="Buy Now"
                            BackgroundColor="Teal" HorizontalOptions=
                            "EndAndExpand" Clicked="BuyClicked"
                            CommandParameter="{Binding .}"/>
                        </StackLayout>
                    </StackLayout>
                </ViewCell>
            </DataTemplate>
        </ListView.ItemTemplate>
    </ListView>
</ContentPage>
```

Listing 6-11. Adding a Button to a List Row from ListViewButton.xaml.cs

```
public partial class ListViewButton : ContentPage
{
    public ListViewButton()
    {
        InitializeComponent();

        List<ListItem> ListItems = new List<ListItem> {
            new ListItem {Title = "First", Description="1st item",
            Price="$100.00"},
            new ListItem {Title = "Second", Description="2nd item",
            Price="$200.00"},
            new ListItem {Title = "Third", Description="3rd item",
            Price="$300.00"}
        };
        ButtonList.ItemsSource = ListItems;
    }

    public async void BuyClicked(object sender, EventArgs e)
    {
        var b = (Button)sender;
        var item = (ListItem)b.CommandParameter;
        await DisplayAlert("Clicked", item.Title.ToString() + " button was
        clicked", "OK");
    }

    public class ListItem
    {
        public string Title { get; set; }
        public string Description { get; set; }
        public string Price { get; set; }
    }

}
```

> **Tip** On iOS the addition of this button can cause the title text to wrap, so set the FontSize = 20 on `titleLabel`.

An alternative to Button Views are Context Actions.

Using Context Actions

Context Actions are bars of buttons that appear for a particular row when the row is left-swiped on iOS or long-pressed on Android, as shown in Figure 6-8.

Figure 6-8. *The Context Action buttons More and Delete*

In a `ListView`, create a `MenuItem` and place it on your `ViewCell` while customizing your list. Create ContextActions (as `MenuItems`) on the ViewCell, one for each context button you need. Set both `MenuItem's` `Text` property which displays on the contextual button. Set the `Clicked` property to methods `MoreClicked` and `DeleteClicked` which you'll handle in C# in a moment. Bind both `MenuItem`'s `CommandParameter` like a `ListView` button using a period (`.`):

```
<ViewCell.ContextActions>
    <MenuItem Text="More" Clicked="MoreClicked"
    CommandParameter="{Binding .}"/>
    <MenuItem Text="Delete" Clicked="DeleteClicked"
    CommandParameter="{Binding .}" IsDestructive="True" />
</ViewCell.ContextActions>
```

Implement the Clicked events and retrieve the list row data class using CommandParameter, which contains the respective ListItem object with a Title to display:

```
public async void MoreClicked(object sender, EventArgs e)
{
    var mi = ((MenuItem)sender);
    var item = (ListItem)(mi.CommandParameter);
    await DisplayAlert("Clicked", item.Title.ToString() + " More button
    was clicked", "OK");
}
```

Tip   If you're building ViewModels, consider using the Command property instead of Clicked.

For a delete button, do all the same things as the more button except set the IsDestructive flag to true. On iOS this will make the button *red* (not terribly destructive, really). Set IsDestructive flag to true for only one of the buttons:

```
<MenuItem Text="Delete" Clicked="DeleteClicked"
CommandParameter="{Binding .}" IsDestructive="True" />
```

Listings 6-12 and 6-13 contain the relevant excerpts of code for the Context Action example shown in Figure 6-8.

Listing 6-12. Creating Context Actions for a List, from ListViewContextAction.xaml

```
<ListView x:Name="ContextList" RowHeight="100" BackgroundColor="Black"
HasUnevenRows="true">
    <ListView.ItemTemplate>
        <DataTemplate>
            <ViewCell>
                <ViewCell.ContextActions>
                    <MenuItem Text="More" Clicked="MoreClicked"
                    CommandParameter="{Binding .}"/>
                    <MenuItem Text="Delete" Clicked="DeleteClicked"
                    CommandParameter="{Binding .}" IsDestructive="True" />
                </ViewCell.ContextActions>
```

```
                    <StackLayout HorizontalOptions="StartAndExpand"
                    Orientation="Horizontal" Padding="5,10,5,15">
                        <StackLayout HorizontalOptions="StartAndExpand"
                        Orientation="Vertical">
                            <Label HorizontalOptions="Start" FontSize="20"
                            FontAttributes="Bold" TextColor="White"
                            Text="{Binding Title}"/>
                            <Label HorizontalOptions="Start" FontSize="12"
                            FontAttributes="Bold" TextColor="White"
                            Text="{Binding Description}"/>
                        </StackLayout>
                        <Label HorizontalOptions="End" FontSize="25"
                        TextColor="Aqua" Text="{Binding Price}"/>
                    </StackLayout>
                </ViewCell>
            </DataTemplate>
        </ListView.ItemTemplate>
</ListView>
```

Listing 6-13. Creating Context Actions for a List, from ListViewContextAction.
xaml.cs

```
public async void MoreClicked(object sender, EventArgs e)
{
    var mi = ((MenuItem)sender);
    var item = (ListItem)(mi.CommandParameter);
    await DisplayAlert("Clicked", item.Title.ToString() + " More button was
    clicked", "OK");
}

public async void DeleteClicked(object sender, EventArgs e)
{
    var mi = ((MenuItem)sender);
    var item = (ListItem)mi.CommandParameter;
    await DisplayAlert("Clicked", item.Title.ToString() + " Delete button
    was clicked", "OK");
}
```

Tip   Adding and deleting rows from the list can be reflected in the UI using an `ObservableCollection`. See Chapter 9 for more on editable list data binding.

Grouping Headers

Long lists can be difficult to navigate and sometimes sorting just isn't good enough. Grouping headers create categories to help users quickly find what they're looking for. Items can be grouped using the `IsGroupingEnabled` and `GroupDisplayBinding` properties of a `ListView`.

You must first create group titles. A good way to store group headers is to create a static data model that is a collection of groups, each of which contains a collection of data items. That is, a collection of collections is created, with the group header field(s) defined in each group collection.

Create a group class that contains the group-by key and a collection for the items:

```
public class Group : List<ListItem>
{
    public String Key { get; private set; }
    public Group(String key, List<ListItem> items)
    {
        Key = key;
        foreach (var item in items)
            this.Add(item);
    }
}
```

In the `ContentPage` constructor, populate the groups and assign them to a master model. Create as many groups as you need with corresponding keys and their contained items. In this example there are two groups, with keys called "Important" and "Less Important".

```
List<Group> itemsGrouped = new List<Group> {
    new Group ("Important", new List<ListItem>{
        new ListItem {Title = "First", Description="1st item"},
        new ListItem {Title = "Second", Description="2nd item"},
    }),
```

```
        new Group ("Less Important", new List<ListItem>{
            new ListItem {Title = "Third", Description="3rd item"}
        })
    };
```

> **Note** This is a simplified, static data example for demonstration purposes. In the real world, you might use a view model, or populate a sorted data model with LINQ or with a loop, inserting grouped items with their accompanying keys.

Create a `ListView` named `GroupedList`, setting the `IsGroupingEnabled` to `true`. In the `GroupDisplayBinding`, bind the list to your `Group` object's `Key`:

```
<ListView x:Name="GroupedList" IsGroupingEnabled="true"
GroupDisplayBinding="{Binding Key}">
    <ListView.ItemTemplate>
        <DataTemplate>
            <TextCell Text="{Binding Title}" Detail="{Binding
            Description}"/>
        </DataTemplate>
    </ListView.ItemTemplate>
</ListView>
```

> **Note** This `ItemTemplate` happens to contain a `Title` and `Description` for list data, but there is no particular `ItemTemplate` required for the grouping of items.

Assign the group model to the `ListView.ItemsSource` property in your page's constructor:

```
GroupedList.ItemsSource = itemsGrouped;
```

Figure 6-9 shows the grouped list.

Figure 6-9.   *This list of three items is grouped under two headings*

Listings 6-14 and 6-15 contain all code for the ListView with group headers shown in Figure 6-9.

Listing 6-14.   Grouping List Items in ListViewGrouped.xaml

```
<?xml version="1.0" encoding="UTF-8"?>
<ContentPage xmlns="http://xamarin.com/schemas/2014/forms" xmlns:x="http://
schemas.microsoft.com/winfx/2009/xaml" x:Class="ListViewExample.Xaml.
ListViewGrouped">
<ContentPage.Padding>
    <OnPlatform x:TypeArguments="Thickness">
        <On Platform="iOS">10,20,10,5</On>
        <On Platform="Android">10,0,10,5</On>
    </OnPlatform>
```

```
</ContentPage.Padding>
    <ListView x:Name="GroupedList" IsGroupingEnabled="true"
    GroupDisplayBinding="{Binding Key}">
        <ListView.ItemTemplate>
            <DataTemplate>
                <TextCell Text="{Binding Title}" Detail="{Binding
                Description}"/>
            </DataTemplate>
        </ListView.ItemTemplate>
    </ListView>
</ContentPage>
```

Listing 6-15. Grouping List Items in ListViewGrouped.xaml.cs

```
public partial class ListViewGrouped : ContentPage
{
    public ListViewGrouped()
    {
        List<Group> itemsGrouped;
        InitializeComponent();
        itemsGrouped = new List<Group> {
            new Group("Important", new List<ListItem>
                {
                    new ListItem {Title = "First", Description="1st item"},
                    new ListItem {Title = "Second", Description="2nd item"}
                }),
            new Group("Less Important", new List<ListItem>
                {
                    new ListItem {Title = "Third", Description="3rd item"}
                })
        };
        GroupedList.ItemsSource = itemsGrouped;
    }

    public class Group : List<ListItem>
    {
        public string Key
```

```
    {
        get;
        private set;
    }

    public Group(string key, List<ListItem> listItems)
    {
        Key = key;
        foreach (var item in listItems)
            this.Add(item);
    }
    public class ListItem
    {
        public string Title { get; set; }
        public string Description { get; set; }
    }
  }
}
```

Customizing the Group Header

When you're ready for fancier group headers than the default ones, you can create your own in a similar manner to customizing list rows, using a custom template class that implements a layout and controls. Create the custom template using the `ListView's` `GroupHeaderTemplate` property:

```
<ListView x:Name=" CustomGroupedList" IsGroupingEnabled="true"
HasUnevenRows="true">
    <ListView.GroupHeaderTemplate>
```

Tip   The `HasUnevenRows` property helps maintain the formatting when you're handling header and item rows of different heights. On iOS the developer must then calculate (or estimate) the height of each cell manually.

Let us customize the group headers to have a white background with large black text for the header group key. Finish creating your ListView named CustomGroupedList, setting the IsGroupingEnabled to true. Put your group header Label inside the GroupHeaderTemplate and DataTemplate, binding that Label to your Group object's Key:

```
<ListView x:Name="CustomGroupedList" IsGroupingEnabled="true"
HasUnevenRows="true">
    <ListView.GroupHeaderTemplate>
        <DataTemplate>
            <ViewCell Height="40">
                <StackLayout HorizontalOptions="FillAndExpand"
                HeightRequest="40" BackgroundColor="White" Padding="5"
                Orientation="Horizontal">
                    <Label FontSize="16" TextColor="Black"
                    VerticalOptions="Center" Text="{Binding Key}" />
                </StackLayout>
            </ViewCell>
        </DataTemplate>
    </ListView.GroupHeaderTemplate>
    <ListView.ItemTemplate>
        <DataTemplate>
            <TextCell Text="{Binding Title}" Detail="{Binding
            Description}"/>
        </DataTemplate>
    </ListView.ItemTemplate>
 </ListView>
```

Note that your list data, Title and Description, go in the usual ItemTemplate. Figure 6-10 shows the list with custom headers.

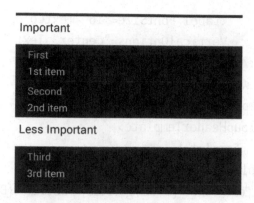

Figure 6-10. *Custom group headings can contain one or more data-bound fields*

Tip   Coding for performance in `Group` `Headers` is the same as when creating custom list row templates. More detail on performance soon.

Listings 6-16 and 6-17 show the `ListView` grouping template code from Figure 6-10.

Listing 6-16. Customizing List Group Headers in ListViewGroupedTemplate.xaml

```xml
<?xml version="1.0" encoding="UTF-8"?>
<ContentPage xmlns="http://xamarin.com/schemas/2014/forms" xmlns:x=
"http://schemas.microsoft.com/winfx/2009/xaml" x:Class="ListViewExample.
Xaml.ListViewGroupedTemplate">
<ContentPage.Padding>
    <OnPlatform x:TypeArguments="Thickness">
            <On Platform="iOS">10,20,10,5</On>
            <On Platform="Android">10,0,10,5</On>
    </OnPlatform>
</ContentPage.Padding>
    <ListView x:Name="CustomGroupedList" IsGroupingEnabled="true"
    HasUnevenRows="true">
        <ListView.GroupHeaderTemplate>
            <DataTemplate>
                <ViewCell Height="40">
                    <StackLayout HorizontalOptions="FillAndExpand"
                    HeightRequest="40" BackgroundColor="White" Padding="5"
                    Orientation="Horizontal">
```

```
                        <Label FontSize="16" TextColor="Black"
                            VerticalOptions="Center" Text="{Binding Key}" />
                    </StackLayout>
                </ViewCell>
            </DataTemplate>
        </ListView.GroupHeaderTemplate>
        <ListView.ItemTemplate>
            <DataTemplate>
                <TextCell Text="{Binding Title}" Detail="{Binding Description}"/>
            </DataTemplate>
        </ListView.ItemTemplate>
    </ListView>
</ContentPage>
```

Listing 6-17. Customizing List Group Headers in ListViewGroupedTemplate. xaml.cs

```
public partial class ListViewGrouped : ContentPage
{
    public ListViewGrouped()
    {
        List<Group> itemsGrouped;
        InitializeComponent();
        itemsGrouped = new List<Group> {
            new Group("Important", new List<ListItem>
                {
                    new ListItem {Title = "First", Description="1st item"},
                    new ListItem {Title = "Second", Description="2nd item"}
                }),
            new Group("Less Important", new List<ListItem>
                {
                    new ListItem {Title = "Third", Description="3rd item"}
                })
        };
        GroupedList.ItemsSource = itemsGrouped;
    }
```

```
public class Group : List<ListItem>
{
    public string Key
    {
        get;
        private set;
    }

    public Group(string key, List<ListItem> listItems)
    {
        Key = key;
        foreach (var item in listItems)
            this.Add(item);
    }

    public class ListItem
    {
        public string Title { get; set; }
        public string Description { get; set; }
    }
}
}
```

Creating a Jump List

Long lists can be unwieldy and require fast scrolling using a jump list, which is a list of keys on the right that permit quick movement through the list. These are often letters corresponding to the first letter of the items.

Assign the jump list values by binding the property in the group model to the ListView.GroupShortNameBinding property. This example binds the Group.Key property to the jump list.

```
<ListView x:Name="JumpList" IsGroupingEnabled="true" HasUnevenRows="true"
GroupShortNameBinding = "{Binding Key}">
```

You'll need a fairly long grouped list to see this in action.

Let's move on to scrolling. Xamarin.Forms ListViews are automatically scrollable when they contain more elements than can fit on the screen at one time.

ListViews Scroll Automatically

No additional coding is required to get a `ListView` to scroll. The `ScrollView` is built-in and the list will scroll if it is longer than the space available on the page.

Add a few more rows to the `ItemsSource` in the original data model binding example:

```
ListItems = new ListItem [] {
new ListItem {Title = "First", Description="1st item"},
new ListItem {Title = "Second", Description="2nd item"},
new ListItem {Title = "Third", Description="3rd item"},
new ListItem {Title = "Fourth", Description="4th item"},
new ListItem {Title = "Fifth", Description="5th item"},
new ListItem {Title = "Sixth", Description="6th item"} ,
new ListItem {Title = "Seventh", Description="7th item"},
new ListItem {Title = "Eighth", Description="8th item"},
new ListItem {Title = "Ninth", Description="9th item"} ,
new ListItem {Title = "Tenth", Description="10th item"},
new ListItem {Title = "Eleventh", Description="11th item"},
new ListItem {Title = "Twelfth", Description="12th item"} ,
new ListItem {Title = "Thirteenth", Description="13th item"},
new ListItem {Title = "Fourteenth", Description="14th item"},
new ListItem {Title = "Fifteenth", Description="15th item"} ,
new ListItem {Title = "Sixteenth", Description="16th item"},
new ListItem {Title = "Seventeenth", Description="17th item"},
new ListItem {Title = "Eighteenth", Description="18th item"}
};
```

Getting a `ListView` to scroll requires only putting enough data/rows into it to make it longer than the space on the screen (Figure 6-11).

Figure 6-11. *ListView scrolls automatically when there are more rows than fit on the screen*

Pull-to-Refresh

ListView supports a pull-to-refresh feature using its IsPullToRefreshEnabled property. Set it:

```
<ListView x:Name="RefreshList" IsPullToRefreshEnabled="True"
RefreshCommand="{Binding RefreshCommand}"
IsRefreshing="{Binding IsRefreshing}" >
```

Implement the RefreshCommand method in order to enact a list refresh (see Chapter 9). Set IsRefreshing to true while you're refreshing and then to false when done for the refresh animation to work correctly.

Optimizing Performance

Cell reuse is built-in with Xamarin.Forms, giving you a leg up over iOS and Android lists. Even so, scrolling lists can become slow, laggy, or janky. This is annoying to the user and makes the app feel unprofessional.

There are two ways to improve ListView performance: use caching and optimize.

ListView Caching

ListView has a built-in caching mechanism to create and retain cells only as needed by the visible screen. Cells that fall offscreen can be recycled to conserve memory. This is largely handled automatically although there are three options:

- RecycleElement—Recycles list cells to minimize memory use. This is the recommended approach but not the default.

- RetainElement—Creates and keeps all list items. This is the default ListView caching behavior.

- RecycleElementAndDataTemplate—Recycles and optimizes for DataTemplateSelector use.

These options are in the ListViewCachingStrategy enumeration used in the CachingStrategy attribute of the ListView:

```
<ListView CachingStrategy="RecycleElement">
```

Caching Tips

- Try RecycleElement first unless you have lots of bindings per cell (20+) or your template changes all the time, in which case use RetainElement.

- If you're using DataTemplateSelectors, opt for RecycleElementAndDataTemplate.

- Sometimes RetainElement is faster than RecycleElement for no apparent reason, so try them both.

There are lots of little improvements and strategies for a faster list.

ListView Optimization

When building ListViews, a few things to watch out for are custom template ViewCells with many views, using images on older devices, and using layouts that require a large amount of measurement calculations.

Here are some recommendations for optimizing ListView performance:

- Enable XAML compilation in your application:

  ```
  [assembly: XamlCompilation(XamlCompilationOptions.Compile)]
  ```

- Use IList<T> instead of IEnumerable<T> in your ItemsSource to employ random access.

- Use the built-in cells whenever you can: TextCell and ImageCell.

- Use custom template ViewCells only when you have to.

- Use images only when necessary and keep images as small as possible. Images typically perform better on iOS than Android.

- Avoid using custom template ViewCells with many views.

- Avoid using images on older devices.

- Avoid using layouts that require a large amount of measurement calculations.

- Use as few elements as possible. For example, consider using a single FormattedString label instead of multiple labels.

- Use AbsoluteLayout when you can, as it does no measurements.

- RelativeLayout can work well if constraints are passed directly.

- Avoid deeply nested layout hierarchies. Use AbsoluteLayout or Grid to help reduce nesting.

- Avoid specific LayoutOptions except Fill (Fill is the cheapest to compute).

As a last resort, with a complex list, use custom renderers to create the list natively (see Chapter 8).

That's it for ListView in Xamarin.Forms!

Summary

In mobile development, lists are the new data grid. (until they're replaced by CollectionViews!)

List views are bound to arrays, `Lists`, or data models and allow scrolling when there are more items than will fit on the screen. They usually contain text string rows, but some contain images or entire layouts of controls.

Selection can be accomplished with a single row or multiple rows. Multiple row selection must be done by hand in Xamarin.Forms.

Cell reuse is a common theme in performant lists and involves the economic use of already populated list rows whenever possible. In Xamarin.Forms, this is built-in.

Grouping is often required for long lists, with *grouping headings* to help guide a user to find what they're looking for.

Built-in list row views give you layout options without having to build them from scratch. These provide a range of control layouts for list rows providing titles, descriptions, and images as well as accessories such as checkboxes and radio buttons.

Custom list rows provide versatility at the risk of slower performance. Beware when creating these, as there are often performance trade-offs. Test for performance and follow the rules of performant customization for each platform when using long lists.

Lists help us navigate an app. Let's now explore other types of navigation in Chapter 7.

CHAPTER 7

Navigation

Navigation gives users what they need to get around an app quickly, moving from screen to screen with confidence and ease. This may include menus, tappable icons, buttons, tabs, and list items, as well as many types of gesture-sensitive screens to display data, information, and options to the user. There are industry-standard ways of doing this called navigation patterns. Each of those patterns provides a template for UI appearance and interaction. These patterns can be combined and stacked and connected like Legos to form the skeleton of an entire app. Once we have a user moving between screens, there is then the consideration of state, or how data is passed back and forth between pages. In this chapter we'll delve into navigation patterns and their ways to manage navigation state.

Navigation Patterns

Navigation patterns are industry-standard templates for tying an app's screens together in an elegant and usable way. The two most common visual design patterns in mobile navigation are hierarchical and modal. An entire family of derivative patterns combine, enhance, and decorate these base navigation patterns to create the full range of mobile UI patterns. Here is an exhaustive list of the most common mobile UI navigation patterns used in Xamarin development:

- *Hierarchical*: A stack-based navigation pattern enabling users to move deeper into a screen hierarchy and then back out again, one screen at a time, by using the Up or Back buttons.

- *Modal*: A screen that interrupts hierarchical navigation, often a pop-up screen with an alert or menu that the user can complete or cancel.

- *Drill-down list*: A list of tappable items selected to display item detail.

© Dan Hermes 2019
D. Hermes and N. Mazloumi, *Building Xamarin.Forms Mobile Apps Using XAML*,
https://doi.org/10.1007/978-1-4842-4030-4_7

- *Navigation drawer*: A navigation menu that slides over from the left side at the tap of an icon, typically three horizontal lines known as the *hamburger* in the upper-left corner of the screen.

- *Tabs*: A bar containing several folder-like buttons at the top or bottom of the screen, each with tappable icons or text invoking new pages.

- *Springboard*: Also referred to as a *dashboard*, this is a grid of tappable icons invoking new pages.

- *Carousel*: Screen-sized panels that slide horizontally and sometimes contain large images.

Let's explore the two most common navigation patterns, hierarchical and modal.

Hierarchical

Hierarchical is a stack-based pattern that allows users to move down into a stack of screens and then pop back out again, one screen at a time. This pattern typically uses a toolbar at the top of the screen to display an Up button (Figure 7-1) in the upper-left corner when a page is selected or "drilled down into" by any means. As the user drills deeper into the menu structure, a stack is maintained, with each page pushed onto it.

Figure 7-1. *Up button*

Two buttons—the Back and the Up button—are used in tandem to navigate backward, popping pages off the stack. The Back button is the curved arrow icon at the bottom of the screen on Android. More powerful than an Up button, the Back button can bring the user out of the app. iOS doesn't have one. The Up button is the less-than icon in the upper-left corner (Figure 7-2).

Figure 7-2. *Back button on Android*

Deep navigation stack can be traversed in this manner, with page selection requiring the use of additional UI navigation patterns such as the navigation drawer, drill-down list, or pop-up menu.

Modal

A *modal* is a single, interruptive pop-up or screen that comes in two flavors. The most common type floats on top of the main page and is usually an alert, dialog box, or menu that the user can respond to or cancel. Navigation reverts back to the originating page when the modal is dismissed. A modal informs users of an important event, such as a saved record, or gives them the opportunity to provide input or direction, such as a menu or whether to commit or cancel a transaction. The second, less common, type of modal replaces the main page entirely, interrupting the hierarchical navigation stack.

The two most common modal menus in the mobile UI are the navigation drawer and the action menu. The *navigation drawer* typically slides in from the left and is triggered by the tapping of an icon (usually the *hamburger*) in the upper-left corner of the screen and displays a list of pages to navigate to. The *action menu* typically slides in or pops up on the right side of the screen, and is invoked by tapping an icon (usually three vertical dots) in the upper-right corner of the screen and contains mostly operations (e.g., Favorite This), though less frequently some navigation pages as well. To follow this established UI pattern, remember this rule: *Nav on the left, Action on the right* (Figure 7-3).

Figure 7-3. *Nav on left, Action on right*

Hierarchical and modal UI navigation patterns are typically used as complementary techniques, with hierarchical providing the skeleton of the navigational structure and modals giving the user choices for what they want to do and where they want to go within the app as well as informational updates along the way.

Before you dive into all the patterns, one cross-cutting navigation topic needs to be addressed: state management. As a user navigates through an app, separate screens must appear to be part of the unified whole application, even though each screen is a separate UI with a separate controller.

State Management

State helps us maintain the illusion of consistency and continuity while the user navigates among screens, through the sharing of data on those screens. We're no longer in the web world of query strings, cookies, and `Session` variables, but we must still maintain state in mobile apps. Most variables are scoped to a particular screen, so state management usually involves the explicit passing of data back and forth between screens. Parameter passing between screens is the encouraged method of state management on all mobile platforms, to minimize the risk of memory abuse and to maximize app performance.

Xamarin.Forms allows us to pass parameters into a `ContentPage` constructor. Android uses a class called `Bundle`, which is a dictionary that contains passed values, housed inside a class called `Intent`, which we use to call new activities. iOS developers favor public properties on the destination view controller, but iOS supports passing parameters into the destination page's constructor.

The static global class is a C# implementation of the singleton pattern. It is available on all platforms but must be used with caution; be mindful of mobile-device memory limitations. Disk persistence is built into Xamarin.Forms by using the `Application` objects' `Properties`, a dictionary using ID/object pairs.

Now that you have a way to pass values between pages, let's begin with Xamarin. Forms navigation.

Xamarin.Forms Navigation

Navigation in Xamarin.Forms is based on the two primary navigation patterns: hierarchical and modal.

The *hierarchical pattern* allows the user to move down through a stack of pages and then pop back up through them by using the Up or Back button. This is sometimes called *drill-down* or *breadcrumb* navigation.

The *modal pattern* is an interruptive screen that requires a particular action from the user but can usually be dismissed with a Cancel button. Examples include notifications, alerts, dialog boxes, and edit or new record pages.

In this chapter, you will explore hierarchical, modal, and the rest of the navigation patterns. Xamarin.Forms provides most of them out of the box:

- Hierarchical navigation using `NavigationPage`

- Modal using `NavigationPage`, alerts, and `ActionSheets`

- Drill-down lists using `NavigationPage`, `ListView`, and `TableView`

- Navigation drawer using `MasterDetailPage`

- Tabs using `TabbedPage`

- Springboard using images with gesture recognizers

- Carousel using `CarouselPage`

The most common Xamarin.Forms navigation component is `NavigationPage`, which is based on the hierarchical pattern but also provides modal functionality.

Hierarchical Navigation Using NavigationPage

`NavigationPage` creates a first-in/last-out stack of pages. Pages can be pushed onto the stack and then popped back off to return to the previous page. `NavigationPage` typically wraps the main, or home, page. It can provide a navigation bar at the top of the screen providing a current page title, icon, and an Up (<) button.

Figure 7-4 shows the navigation bar at the top of the screen for iOS and Android.

Figure 7-4. *NavigationPage*

The default text on the iOS up button is "Back."

Note   Up and Back are different navigation buttons. Up is the less-than arrow in the top-left corner of the navigation page, and the Back button is on the bottom navigation bar provided by the OS (though not in iOS).

To use NavigationPage, in your Application class's constructor, instantiate a NavigationPage object, passing in the home ContentPage as a parameter, and assign it to your MainPage:

```
public class App : Application
{
    public App()
    {
        MainPage = new NavigationPage(new HomePage());
    }
}
```

Tip   Instantiating NavigationPage produces a static object called Navigation that is accessible throughout your app for hierarchical navigation.

As shown in Listing 7-1, create a new XAML page called HomePage that has a label identifying itself as "Home Page" and a button.

Listing 7-1. Hierarchical Navigation Home Page (in NavigationPage1.xaml—See Next Tip)

```
<ContentPage Title="Hierarchical Navigation" xmlns="http://xamarin.com/
schemas/2014/forms" xmlns:x="http://schemas.microsoft.com/winfx/2009/
xaml" x:Class="NavigationExamples. HomePage">
    <ContentPage.Content>
        <StackLayout>
            <Label Text="Home Page" FontSize="40"></Label>
            <Button Clicked="Navigate" Text="Go To Second Page">
            </Button>
        </StackLayout>
    </ContentPage.Content>
</ContentPage>
```

Wire up the button's Clicked event called Navigate to bring us to the second page via the Navigation.PushAsync method as in Listing 7-2.

Listing 7-2. Hierarchical Navigation Home Page (in NavigationPage1.cs—See Next Tip)

```
public partial class HomePage : ContentPage
{
    public HomePage()
    {
        InitializeComponent ();
    }

    protected async void Navigate(object sender, EventArgs args) {
        await Navigation.PushAsync(new secondPage());
    }
}
```

Tip   If you're following along in the online code examples, notice that I simplified this example by renaming `NavigationPage1` to `HomePage` in this text to leave out the super useful but slightly off-topic drill-down `ListView` home page in the downloadable code.

The home page is a simple page with your label and button, waiting to bring you to the second page, as shown in Figure 7-5.

Home Page

Go to Second Page

Figure 7-5. *Home page*

Listing 7-3 contains a simple XAML page called SecondPage that labels itself Second Page. No change is needed in the C# code behind.

Listing 7-3. Second Page in the Hierarchy Similar to NavigationPage2.cs

```
<ContentPage Title="Hierarchical Navigation" xmlns="http://xamarin.com/
schemas/2014/forms" xmlns:x="http://schemas.microsoft.com/winfx/2009/
xaml" x:Class="NavigationExamples.SecondPage">
    <ContentPage.Content>
        <StackLayout>
            <Label Text="Second Page" FontSize="40"></Label>
        </StackLayout>
    </ContentPage.Content>
</ContentPage>
```

Now that a page is pushed onto the navigation stack, the navigation bar becomes visible, as shown in Figure 7-6.

Figure 7-6. *The second page contains a navigation bar with a Back button*

Note that the icon in the navigation bar has been set to a blank image, as described later in the section "Customizing the Navigation Bar."

Note The navigation bar is created by `NavigationPage` automatically. When the Up button (<) is clicked, the page is popped off the stack and control is returned to the previous page.

Pushing and Popping Screens on the Navigation Stack

Three methods are used to move between pages hierarchically:

- PushAsync pushes a page onto the stack and goes there:

  `Navigation.PushAsync(new nextPage());`

  A second parameter can be added to specify whether the navigation is animated:

  `Navigation.PushAsync(new nextPage(), bool animated);`

- PopAsync pops a page off the stack and goes to the previous page:

```
Navigation.PopAsync();
```

- PopToRootAsync pops all pages off the stack and goes to the root page:

```
Navigation.PopToRootAsync();
```

Tip Two more methods, RemovePage and InsertPageBefore, can change the stack without pushing and popping.

RemovePage removes the specified page off the stack:

```
Navigation.RemovePage(page);
```

InsertPageBefore inserts a page into the stack before the specified page:

```
Navigation.InsertPageBefore(insertPage, beforePage);
```

All of these methods are generally executed inside the events of tapped icons or links, either inline, such as on our home page in Listing 7-1:

```
protected async void Navigate(object sender, EventArgs args) {
    await Navigation.PushAsync(new secondPage());
}
```

Setting the Page Title

The ContentPage.Title property displays a title in the navigation bar. This should be settable in the ContentPage.Title property in XAML.

```
<ContentPage Title="Home">
```

However, results can be mixed. If you need better results, set the Title in C# in the ContentPage constructor:

```
Title = "Home";
```

If that doesn't work, try this in XAML:

```
<ContentPage NavigationPage.BackButtonTitle="Home">
```

Customizing the Navigation Bar

NavigationPage has several properties accessible from any child page, all of which give access to the navigation bar's elements. Navigation bar properties such as Title and Icon are set in the child page and not in the page that initiated NavigationPage. This is in keeping with native platform architectures.

In most of these Xamarin.Forms navigation examples, the icon.png file has been replaced with a blank image, so no icon is visible. This is a lean and contemporary look. The icon.png file can also be replaced with an appropriate graphic used to reflect the app, as shown in Figure 7-7.

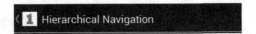

Figure 7-7. *The icon can be changed on the navigation bar*

Tip   The icon.png file is platform-specific and resides in each respective platform project. See Chapter 1 for details on images.

The navigation icon can also be set dynamically to reflect the page or user context, by using SetTitleIcon and the Page.Icon property:

```
var image = "icon.png";
NavigationPage.SetTitleIcon (this, image);
```

Customization of the navigation bar that involves more than a single change should consider use of the newer TitleView property. TitleView is a view defined in the Navigation page either in the XAML (<NavigationPage.TitleView/>) or as a property within the C# page class, NavigationPage.TitleView. It's a view that can contain layouts and other views, such as title and icon.

Further customization of the navigation bar at the top of the screen is accomplished by using these NavigationPage methods:

- SetTitleView exposes TitleView which contains an entire view in the navigation bar for customization.

- SetHasNavigationBar shows/hides the navigation bar on the current page:

For example, NavigationPage.SetHasNavigationBar(this, false);

- SetTitleIcon changes the title icon (Page.Icon property).

- SetHasBackButton shows/hides the Back button.

- SetBackButtonTitle changes the navigation title (the Page.Title property set on the calling page).

- BarBackgroundColor changes the navigation bar's color.

- BarTextColor changes the navigation bar's text color.

Note   Why are we using C# instead of XAML for NavigationPage? Because NavigationPage does not have a property for the root page and the Xamarin-recommended approach is to use C# for NavigationPage.

Handling the Back Button

Popping pages off the stack can be accomplished by either the Up or the Back button. Up is the less-than symbol (<) in the top-left corner of the navigation page, and the Back button is on the bottom navigation bar.

The Back button click event can be explicitly handled by overriding the page's OnBackButtonPressed method:

```
public override void OnBackButtonPressed()
{
    // your code here
    base.OnBackButtonPressed ();
}
```

Creating a Drop-Down Menu

A drop-down menu class called ToolBarItems is built into the Page class and visible when using NavigationPage.

Instantiate NavigationPage to invoke the toolbar ContentPage, as shown in Listing 7-4.

Listing 7-4. Drop-Down Menu in DropdownMenu.xaml

```
<ContentPage Title="Dropdown Using ToolbarItems" xmlns="http://
xamarin.com/schemas/2014/forms" xmlns:x="http://schemas.microsoft.com/
winfx/2009/xaml" x:Class="NavigationExamples.DropdownMenu">
    <ContentPage.ToolbarItems>
        <ToolbarItem Text="Home" Order="Secondary" Clicked="Navigate"
        CommandParameter="NavigationPage1" />
        <ToolbarItem Text="Second" Order="Secondary" Clicked="Navigate"
        CommandParameter="NavigationPage2" />
    </ContentPage.ToolbarItems>
</ContentPage>
```

This is the Navigate method in DropdownMenu.cs which is the implementation of the ToolbarItem's Clicked events. Get the page type from CommandParameter and instantiate a new page using the old .NET trick: (Page)Activator. CreateInstance(pageType). Then navigate there with Navigation.PushAsync.

```
protected async void Navigate(object sender, EventArgs args) {
    string type = (string) ((ToolbarItem)sender).CommandParameter;
    Type pageType = Type.GetType("NavigationExamples." + type + ",
    NavigationExamples");
    Page page = (Page)Activator.CreateInstance(pageType);
    await this.Navigation.PushAsync(page);
}
```

This creates a drop-down menu/toolbar or tab menu with the items Home and Second. Clicking either one navigates to the respective page (see Figure 7-8). On iOS, it looks like a tab menu.

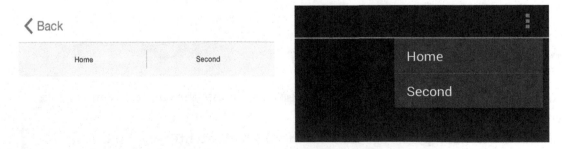

Figure 7-8. *ToolbarItems drop-down menu*

Modal

Xamarin.Forms provides three options for modal navigation:

- NavigationPage for full-page modals

- Alerts for user notifications

- Action sheets for pop-up menus

Full-Page Modal Using NavigationPage

Modal full-screen pages can be created that break the hierarchical pattern. When modal pages are raised, the hierarchy is interrupted and the navigation bar goes away. The navigation bar comes back when the modal is popped off the stack. These two methods are used to move between pages modally:

- PushModalAsync pushes a page on the stack and goes there:

  ```
  Navigation.PushModalAsync(new nextPage());
  ```

- PopModalAsync pops a page off the stack and goes to the previous page:

  ```
  Navigation.PopModalAsync();
  ```

Tip Four events on the Application object can help you manage your modal pages' lifecycles: ModalPushing, ModalPushed, ModalPopping, and ModalPopped.

User Notification Using Alerts

The DisplayAlert method in a ContentPage displays a pop-up alert, as shown in Figure 7-6. This is typically used with async/await so execution will halt until the pop-up is cleared (Listing 7-6).

Create a new XAML page and put a button into a StackLayout. Add a Clicked event containing "ShowAlert".

Listing 7-5. Add Button, from Alerts.xaml

```
<StackLayout>
    <Button Text="Show Alert" Clicked="ShowAlert" />
</StackLayout>
```

Implement the `Clicked` event with a `DisplayAlert` as in Listing 7-6 for the result shown in Figure 7-9.

Figure 7-9. *DisplayAlert pop-up with title, message, and action button*

Listing 7-6. Using DisplayAlert, from Alerts.xaml.cs

```
protected async void ShowAlert(object sender, EventArgs args) {
    await DisplayAlert("Hey", "You really should know about this.", "OK");
}
```

User feedback can be received by returning a value from `DisplayAlert`:

```
Boolean answer = await DisplayAlert("Start",
        "Are you ready to begin?", "Yes", "No");
```

The answer is returned as a `Boolean`, as shown in Figure 7-10.

Figure 7-10. *The DisplayAlert method can return a value*

Pop-Up Menu Using Action Sheets

ActionSheet provides a menu of options in a pop-up and returns a string.

Using DisplayActionSheet, create an action sheet activated by a button click that assigns the result to a label, as shown in Listing 7-7.

Listing 7-7. Add Button and Label, from PopupMenu.xaml

```
<StackLayout>
    <Button Clicked="ShowMenu" Text="Show ActionSheet" />
    <Label FontSize="20" x:Name="Message" />
</StackLayout>
```

Implement the Clicked event with a ShowMenu method containing a DisplayActionSheet with selectable options. The Message.Text property will show the option/action chosen by the user (Listing 7-8).

Listing 7-8. Using DisplayActionSheet from PopupMenu.xaml.cs

```
protected async void ShowMenu(object sender, EventArgs args) {
    String action = await DisplayActionSheet ("Options", "Cancel",
    null, "Here", "There", "Everywhere");
    Message.Text = "Action is :" + action;
}
```

This displays a pop-up menu in the center of the screen containing our options (Figure 7-11).

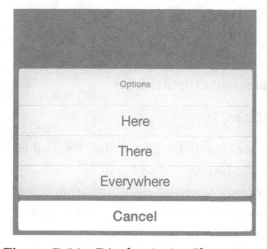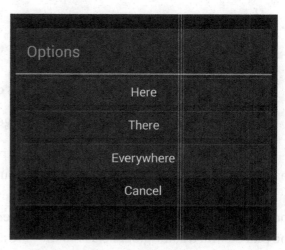

Figure 7-11. *DisplayActionSheet is a method that can return a value*

Managing State

State management is the handling and passing of data *between* pages as the user navigates through the app. There are four main approaches: passing data values directly into a page's constructor, using the static `Properties` dictionary on the `Application` object to persist key/value pairs to disk, a static data instance (*global*) available to all pages, and static properties on the `Application` object. Both the global and `Application` object techniques use the singleton pattern and are useful for app-wide classes such as data access or business objects.

Pass data directly into pages whenever possible to keep the scope of variables narrow and manage memory prudently. The `Properties` dictionary persists when your app is backgrounded and even after your app has restarted!

Let's start with the simplest technique, passing data directly into a page.

Passing Data into Page Parameters

State is typically managed in Xamarin.Forms by passing data directly into a `Page` using its constructor. This approach scopes data objects to a single page, which is ideal from an architecture and memory use standpoint.

When calling a new page with a `Navigation` method, pass in whatever variables were defined in your page's constructor. Define a detail page with a `ListItem` class as a constructor parameter:

```
class DetailPage : ContentPage
{
    public DetailPage(ListItem item)
    {
```

Then pass instances of the `ListItem` class directly into `DetailPage`:

```
Navigation.PushAsync (new detailPage(item));
```

Add all the parameters in your page constructors needed to pass in data from other pages. More details on this example can be found in Listings 7-8 and 7-10.

Data elements are sometimes used on many pages across an entire application, and passing them individually can become cumbersome. Frequently used data elements can be placed into a static global class so they are available app-wide.

Disk Persistence Using the Properties Dictionary

The most persistent state feature built into Xamarin.Forms is the Properties dictionary. Name/value pairs are stored as objects to disk and retrieved on demand from anywhere within the app, even after the app has restarted. Properties works a bit like cookies for your app.

Save a value to the Properties dictionary by using a key value, such as id:

```
Application.Current.Properties["id"] = 12345;
```

Retrieve the value by using a cast from the Properties object type:

```
var id = (int)Application.Current.Properties["id"];
```

Tip   Properties are handy in the Application's OnStart, OnSleep, and OnResume methods for saving data between user sessions. They can also be used in a Page's OnAppearing and OnDisappearing events, which fire when a page is created or right before it is destroyed.

Using a Static Global Class

A static global class, a C# implementation of the singleton pattern, can be used to store data across an entire application.

Important Note   Implementing a singleton is a standard C# technique that can be used across all platforms in Xamarin.Forms.

Create a static class called Global and place properties within it that you desire to use across your app, such as myData, as shown in Listing 7-9.

Listing 7-9. Static Global Class in Global.cs

```
public class Global
{
    private Global () { }

    private static Lazy<Global> _instance = new Lazy<Global>(() => new
    Global());

    public static Global Instance
    {
        get
        {
            return _instance.Value;
        }
    }

    public String myData { get; set; }
}
```

Assign values to your static global class:

```
Global.Instance.myData = "12345";
```

Access the global properties from anywhere in your application:

```
MyData myData = Global.Instance.myData;
```

Caution   Overuse of static global classes can tax memory and affect performance. Pass variables directly between pages whenever you can so they go out of scope when no longer needed.

Using a Static Property on the Application Object

A singleton can be created by using a static property on the Application object:

```
public class App : Application
{
    static Database database;
    public static Database MyDatabase {
        get {
            if (database == null) {
                database = new Database ();
            }
            return database;
        }
    }
}
```

Reference this database object anywhere in your app:

```
App.MyDatabase.DBConnect();
```

You'll use this approach in Chapter 7 for maintaining a database connection. (DBConnect is just an example method on the Database object.)

Drill-Down Lists

A *drill-down list* is a list of tappable items selected to navigate to a new page. There are many ways to build them using Xamarin.Forms, and the following recipes cover the three most common types of drill-down lists: by item, by page, and grouped. A drill-down list *by item* has rows that can be selected to display more information about each item: the traditional master-detail pattern. A drill-down list *by page* is a menu of pages that can be selected to navigate to different ContentPages. Both of these recipes use a ListView to bind to a data model to provide a dynamic list of tappable items. A *grouped* drill-down list built using TableView is useful for creating categorized static menu items.

ListView is one of the most versatile tools for creating drill-down lists. Short lists can, of course, be constructed by hand by using any of the layouts filled with buttons or labels paired with gesture recognizers to handle taps. Longer lists lend themselves to data binding using ListView.

Grouping is the same as it was in Chapter 6 using ListView grouping. Both items and pages can be grouped by using the IsGroupingEnabled and GroupDisplayBinding properties of ListView.

Lists of pages that require grouping can also be built by using TableView. This manual alternative to ListView uses the TextCell Command and CommandParameter properties instead of data binding.

We'll begin with the data-bound ListView menus.

Using ListView by Item

Many lists contain a bunch of items that a user wants to drill down into to reach details about each item. Use ListView to display a list of items data-bound to a data model, and then show a detail page by using PushAsync, all wrapped in NavigationPage so the user can get back to the list.

You can create your ListView by using any of the approaches discussed in Chapter 6. This implementation uses our list item class called DrilldownListViewByItem (see the full Listing 7-11 and 7-12). Instantiate that page in the Application class's constructor wrapped in NavigationPage (see the full Listing 7-13).

```
public class App : Application
{
    public App()
    {
        MainPage = new NavigationPage(new DrilldownListViewByItem ());
    }
}
```

Note that this example must differ slightly from the App.cs found in the downloadable code, so use what you see written here in this example.

This creates the list shown in Figure 7-12, with a navigation bar on iOS and Android.

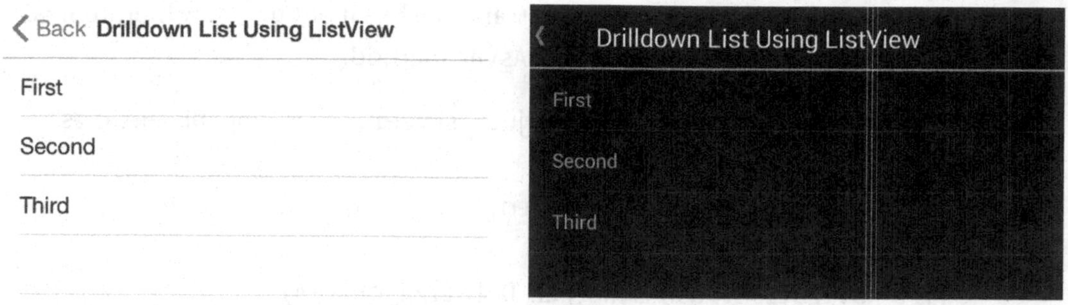

Figure 7-12. *ListView on a page with a navigation bar*

For the drill-down detail page, create a XAML `DetailPage` which displays a `Title` and `Description`.

```
<StackLayout>
    <Label FontSize="40" Text="{Binding Title}" />
    <Label FontSize="40" Text="{Binding Description}" />
</StackLayout>
```

In the `DetailPage` code behind, make a constructor that takes `ListItem` as a parameter (see the full Listing 7-15).

```
public partial class DetailPage : ContentPage
{
    public DetailPage (ListItem item)
    {
        InitializeComponent ();
        this.BindingContext = item;
    }
}
```

The `BindingContext` is set to the incoming `ListItem` parameter from the user tap on the `ListView`.

Back on the list page, when an item row is tapped, the `ItemTapped` event fires. In this case, the event name happens to be named the same thing as the `ItemTapped` property: ItemTapped. Here is the ListView declaration:

```
<ListView x:Name="itemList" ItemTapped="ItemTapped" >
```

The rest of the `ListView` code is in Listing 7-11, `DrilldownListViewByItem.xaml`.

ItemTapped method receives the ListItem and pushes it out to a new hierarchical DetailPage using the NavigationPage's PushAsync method.

```
protected async void ItemTapped(object sender, ItemTappedEventArgs
args) {
    var item = args.Item as ListItem;
    if (item == null) return;
    await Navigation.PushAsync(new DetailPage(item));
    itemList.SelectedItem = null;
}
```

During the Navigation.PushAsync call, the tapped row's ListItem is passed into DetailPage which is then bound to the page's BindingContext, allowing the display of the ListItem's Title and Description, as shown in Figure 7-13.

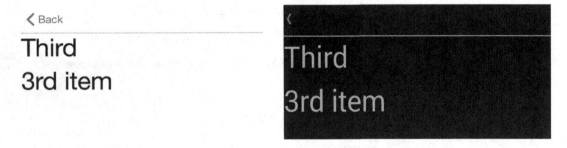

Figure 7-13. *Detail page displaying title and description*

CODE COMPLETE: Drill-Down List

That was a quick summary of a drill-down list by item. Listings 7-10 through 7-15 show the complete code of the drill-down list pattern using NavigationPage.

Listing 7-10. ListItem.cs

```
public class ListItem
{
    public string Title { get; set; }
    public string Description { get; set; }
}
```

Listing 7-11. DrilldownListViewByItem.xaml

```xml
<?xml version="1.0" encoding="UTF-8"?>
<ContentPage Title="Drilldown List Using ListView" xmlns="http://xamarin.
com/schemas/2014/forms" xmlns:x="http://schemas.microsoft.com/winfx/2009/
xaml" x:Class="NavigationExamples.DrilldownListViewByItem">
    <ContentPage.Content>
        <ListView x:Name="itemList" ItemTapped="ItemTapped" >
            <ListView.ItemTemplate>
                <DataTemplate>
                    <TextCell Text="{Binding Title}" />
                </DataTemplate>
            </ListView.ItemTemplate>
        </ListView>
    </ContentPage.Content>
</ContentPage>
```

Listing 7-12. DrilldownListViewByItem.xaml.cs

```csharp
public partial class DrilldownListViewByItem : ContentPage
{
    public DrilldownListViewByItem ()
    {
        InitializeComponent ();

        itemList.ItemsSource = new ListItem [] {
            new ListItem {Title = "First", Description="1st item"},
            new ListItem {Title = "Second", Description="2nd item"},
            new ListItem {Title = "Third", Description="3rd item"}
        };
    }

    protected async void ItemTapped(object sender, ItemTappedEventArgs
    args) {
        var item = args.Item as ListItem;
```

```
        if (item == null) return;
        await Navigation.PushAsync(new DetailPage(item));
        itemList.SelectedItem = null;
    }
}
```

Listing 7-13. App Class for This Example (Differs from Code Download App.cs)

```
public class App : Application
{
    public App()
    {
        MainPage = new NavigationPage(new DrilldownListViewByItem ());
    }
}
```

Listing 7-14. DetailPage.xaml.cs

```
<?xml version="1.0" encoding="UTF-8"?>
<ContentPage xmlns="http://xamarin.com/schemas/2014/forms" xmlns:x="http://
schemas.microsoft.com/winfx/2009/xaml" x:Class="NavigationExamples.
DetailPage">
    <ContentPage.Content>
        <StackLayout>
            <Label FontSize="40" Text="{Binding Title}" />
            <Label FontSize="40" Text="{Binding Description}" />
        </StackLayout>
    </ContentPage.Content>
</ContentPage>
```

Listing 7-15. DetailPage.xaml.cs

```
public partial class DetailPage : ContentPage
{
    public DetailPage (ListItem item)
    {
        InitializeComponent ();
```

```
        this.BindingContext = item;
    }
}
```

Using ListView by Page

Navigating a list of pages is easy with ListView. Build a menu containing a list of distinct pages (e.g., First, Second, Third). Data-bind your ListView to a data model that contains page Titles and ContentPage types. Drill down into each page by using NavigationPage to give the user a way to pop back to the list.

The result of Listing 7-16 looks the same on the screen as Figure 7-9 but navigates to different ContentPage types (FirstPage, SecondPage, ThirdPage) rather than just one (DetailPage).

Listing 7-16. ListView by Page in DrilldownListViewByPage.cs

```
public partial class DrilldownListViewByPage : ContentPage
{
    public DrilldownListViewByPage ()
    {
        InitializeComponent ();

        itemList.ItemsSource = new ListItemPage [] {
            new ListItemPage {Title = "First", PageType=
            typeof(FirstPage)},
            new ListItemPage {Title = "Second", PageType=
            typeof(SecondPage)},
            new ListItemPage {Title = "Third", PageType= typeof(ThirdPage)}
        };

    }

    protected async void ItemTapped(object sender, ItemTappedEventArgs
    args) {
        var item = args.Item as ListItemPage;
        if (item == null) return;
        Page page = (Page)Activator.CreateInstance(item.PageType);
        await Navigation.PushAsync(page);
```

```
        itemList.SelectedItem = null;
    }

    public class ListItemPage
    {
        public string Title { get; set; }
        public Type PageType { get; set; }
    }

}
```

The XAML `ListView` is the same as previous examples, bound to a `Title` field.

Listing 7-17. ListView by Page in DrilldownListViewByPage.xaml.cs

```xml
<?xml version="1.0" encoding="UTF-8"?>
<ContentPage Title="Drilldown List Using ListView" xmlns="http://xamarin.
com/schemas/2014/forms" xmlns:x="http://schemas.microsoft.com/winfx/2009/
xaml" x:Class="NavigationExamples.DrilldownListViewByPage">
    <ContentPage.Content>
        <ListView x:Name="itemList" ItemTapped="ItemTapped" >
            <ListView.ItemTemplate>
                <DataTemplate>
                    <TextCell Text="{Binding Title}" />
                </DataTemplate>
            </ListView.ItemTemplate>
        </ListView>
    </ContentPage.Content>
</ContentPage>
```

Using TableView for Grouping Pages

Perfect for multicategory lists of navigation items, this variation of the drill-down list pattern displays a static list by using a view called `TableView`. When an item is tapped, a detail screen is shown. It also uses the hierarchical pattern, which provides an option to use Back buttons. This hierarchical/drill-down list pattern is used in many of the downloadable code projects throughout the book as the solution home page, allowing selection of the code examples in each chapter.

This recipe looks best when there are multiple categories of items to choose from, because at least one TableSection is required, even if multiple categories aren't needed, as shown in Figure 7-14.

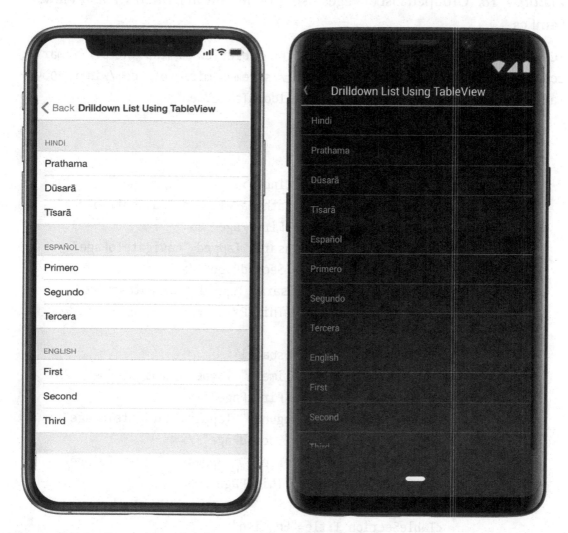

Figure 7-14. *Grouping a list by using TableView*

If you don't want to use categories, you can keep the TableSection title blank, but that leaves a rather large gap at the top of the list. If you don't need categories, consider using ListView by page, as described in the previous section.

TableView isn't technically a layout but works much like one. This view is made up of TextCells arranged in sections, such as Hindi, Español, and English. Each TableSection denotes a different category of item, as shown in Listing 7-18. Set which page the cell should navigate to when tapped by placing `ContentPage` types in the `CommandParameter` of each TextCell. Set the `Tapped` property to the event handling the `TextCell`'s tap.

Listing 7-18. Grouped List of Pages Using TableView in DrilldownTableView. xaml.cs

```
<ContentPage Title="Drilldown List Using TableView" xmlns="http://xamarin.
com/schemas/2014/forms" xmlns:x="http://schemas.microsoft.com/winfx/2009/
xaml" x:Class="NavigationExamples.DrilldownTableView">
    <ContentPage.Content>
        <TableView Intent="Menu">
            <TableView.Root>
                <TableSection Title="Hindi">
                    <TextCell Text="Prathama" Tapped="navigateToPage"
                    CommandParameter="FirstPage" />
                    <TextCell Text="Dūsarā" Tapped="navigateToPage"
                    CommandParameter="SecondPage" />
                    <TextCell Text="Tīsarā" Tapped="navigateToPage"
                    CommandParameter="ThirdPage" />
                </TableSection>
                <TableSection Title="Español">
                    <TextCell Text="Primero" Tapped="navigateToPage"
                    CommandParameter="FirstPage" />
                    <TextCell Text="Segundo" Tapped="navigateToPage"
                    CommandParameter="SecondPage" />
                    <TextCell Text="Tercera" Tapped="navigateToPage"
                    CommandParameter="ThirdPage" />
                </TableSection>
                <TableSection Title="English">
                    <TextCell Text="First" Tapped="navigateToPage"
                    CommandParameter="FirstPage" />
                    <TextCell Text="Second" Tapped="navigateToPage"
                    CommandParameter="SecondPage" />
                    <TextCell Text="Third" Tapped="navigateToPage"
                    CommandParameter="ThirdPage" />
                </TableSection>
```

```
        </TableView.Root>
      </TableView>
    </ContentPage.Content>
</ContentPage>
```

Tip   Using `Binding` may be more elegant in Listing 7-19 than `CommandParameter`, but we don't cover binding until Chapter 9.

When a `TextCell` is tapped, the `navigateToPage` method is called in the C# code behind. There, the `CommandParameter` containing the `ContentPage` type is parsed and the type is instantiated into a `Page using Activator.CreateInstance`. Use `PushAsync` to navigate to this new page, which, in this case, will be `FirstPage`, `SecondPage`, or `ThirdPage`.

Listing 7-19. Grouped List of Pages Using TableView in DrilldownTableView. xaml.cs

```
protected async void navigateToPage(object sender, EventArgs args)
{
    string type = (string) ((TextCell)sender).CommandParameter;
    Type pageType = Type.GetType("NavigationExamples." + type + ",
    NavigationExamples.Xaml");
    Page page = (Page)Activator.CreateInstance(pageType);
    await this.Navigation.PushAsync(page);
}
```

Navigation Drawer Using MasterDetailPage

`MasterDetailPage` implements the navigation drawer pattern, which slides in a menu from the side when an icon, usually the hamburger, is tapped.

In the main page, Listing 7-20, the master and detail pages are defined. The master page is the menu drawer containing a list of menu options. Detail pages are raised when an option is tapped in the menu drawer.

Listing 7-20. Using MasterDetailPage in NavigationDrawer.xaml.cs

```xml
<?xml version="1.0" encoding="UTF-8"?>
<MasterDetailPage Title="Navigation Drawer Using MasterDetailPage"
xmlns="http://xamarin.com/schemas/2014/forms" xmlns:x="http://
schemas.microsoft.com/winfx/2009/xaml" x:Class="NavigationExamples.
NavigationDrawer">
<MasterDetailPage.Master>
        <ContentPage Title="Options" Icon="hamburger.png">
            <ListView x:Name="menu" />
        </ContentPage>
    </MasterDetailPage.Master>
    <MasterDetailPage.Detail>
        <ContentPage>
            <Label Text="Detail"/>
        </ContentPage>
    </MasterDetailPage.Detail>
</MasterDetailPage>
```

Tip   The `Title` property of the `MasterDetailPage` is required.

When a menu item is selected, the `ItemTapped` event fires and sets the `Detail` property to the destination page. `Detail` is set to `HomePage` initially.

Listing 7-21. Using MasterDetailPage in NavigationDrawer.cs

```csharp
public partial class NavigationDrawer : MasterDetailPage
{
    public NavigationDrawer ()
    {
        InitializeComponent ();

        string[] myPageNames = { "Home", "Second", "Third" };
        menu.ItemsSource = myPageNames;
```

```
menu.ItemTapped += (sender, e) =>
{
    ContentPage gotoPage;
    switch (e.Item.ToString())
    {
    case "Home":
        gotoPage = new HomePage();
        break;
    case "Second":
        gotoPage = new SecondPage();
        break;
    case "Third":
        gotoPage = new ThirdPage();
        break;
    default:
        gotoPage = new NavigationPage1();
        break;
    }
    Detail = new NavigationPage(gotoPage);
    ((ListView)sender).SelectedItem = null;
    this.IsPresented = false;
};

    Detail = new NavigationPage(new HomePage());
    }
}
```

A couple of things happen after the Detail page is navigated to. SelectedItem is set to null to remove the highlight over the selected row, and IsPresented is set to false to remove the menu.

Because the navigation drawer already instantiates its own navigation pages, you don't need to create another NavigationPage when you call it. This is how to implement your nav drawer in App.cs, at the root of your navigation.

```
public class App : Application
{
    public App()
    {
        MainPage = new NavigationDrawer ();
    }
}
```

This example begins as the home page set as the detail page, as shown in Figure 7-15. It hard-codes the navigation drawer pages rather than making them dynamic.

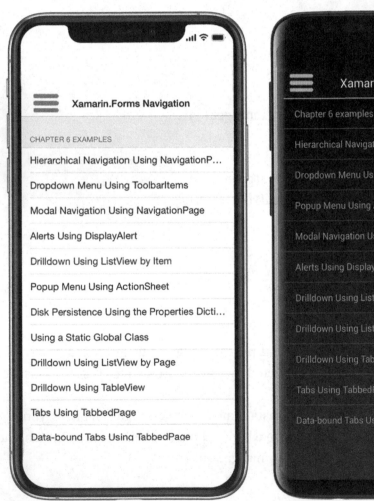
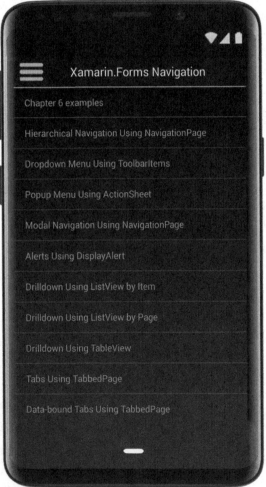

Figure 7-15. *HomePage ContentPage is the initial detail page*

> **Important Note**   HomePage.cs contains the HomePage ContentPage shown
> in Figure 7-12 and is in the downloadable code but is not listed here. Be certain to
> download the code for this chapter and check it out, because it contains some of
> the most project-ready examples in this book.

When the icon is clicked, the master page is shown, containing the menu and the
menu icon in the upper-left corner, as shown in Figure 7-16.

Figure 7-16.   *The fly-in menu is the master page*

Change the menu icon to a hamburger by using the master page's Icon property. The icon file is taken from the local images folder for each platform.

```
<MasterDetailPage.Master>
    <ContentPage Title="Options" Icon="hamburger.png">
```

Clicking a menu item brings you to the specified new detail page.

Note The tablet experience of MasterDetailPage is completely different from the phone experience and is a breath of fresh air. The master list shows on the left and detail page shows on the right-hand portion of the screen. This offers a real-time display of list detail as the user taps on different items in the list. Having the menu and the detail on the screen at the same time takes full advantage of the tablet's ample real estate.

Tabs Using TabbedPage

Having clickable folder-like tabs at the top or bottom of the screen is a common navigation pattern, implemented by TabbedPage, as shown in Figure 7-17. Tabs can be declared in XAML as referenced or inline. Let's begin with references.

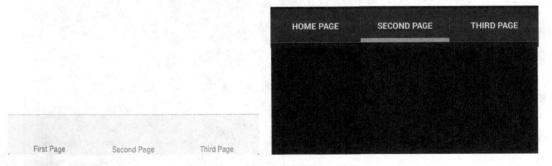

Figure 7-17. TabbedPage makes tabs that navigate to pages

Tip iOS tabs are at the bottom of the screen, and Android tabs are at the top.

Create a TabbedPage, which creates a XAML and code behind. Reference tab pages in the TabbedPage.Children property, as shown in Listing 7-22.

Listing 7-22. Referenced Tabs in TabPage.xaml

```
<TabbedPage Title="Tabs Using TabbedPage" xmlns:local="clr-namespace:
NavigationExamples;assembly=NavigationExamples.Xaml"
    xmlns="http://xamarin.com/schemas/2014/forms" xmlns:x="http://schemas.
    microsoft.com/winfx/2009/xaml" x:Class="NavigationExamples.TabPage">
    <TabbedPage.Children>
        <local:FirstPage />
        <local:SecondPage />
        <local:ThirdPage />
    </TabbedPage.Children>
</TabbedPage>
```

The Title property of each child page is where the tab titles come from. Remember to assign it wherever you create the child page. All of the action happens in the XAML, with no coding needed in the code behind beyond the default constructor. Compile and run this example to see the result in Figure 7-14.

Reference tabs inline by declaring them directly in the TabbedPage XAML tag as shown in Listing 7-23.

Listing 7-23. Inline Tab Declaration in TabbedPage

```
<?xml version="1.0" encoding="utf-8" ?>
    <TabbedPage xmlns="http://xamarin.com/schemas/2014/forms"
        xmlns:x="http://schemas.microsoft.com/winfx/2009/xaml"
        x:Class="NavigationExamples.Xaml.TabbedPageInline">
        <ContentPage Title="FirstPage" />
        <ContentPage Title=" SecondPage" />
        <ContentPage Title="ThirdPage" />
    </TabbedPage>
```

Tip   In iOS, you can place icons on tabs by using the child pages' Icon property. Not so on Android.

Creating Data-Bound Tabs

TabbedPage can be bound to a data source. Use the TabbedPage properties ItemsSource and ItemTemplate to achieve a data-bound tabbed menu.

Create a Tabbed Page, which creates a XAML and code behind. In the XAML, create the DataTemplate page inside the TabbedPage.ItemTemplate property. This is the page you see when a tab is selected, displaying Bind Name and Number properties, as shown in Listing 7-24.

Listing 7-24. TabbedPage Definition in TabPageDatabound.xaml.cs

```
<?xml version="1.0" encoding="utf-8" ?>
<TabbedPage xmlns="http://xamarin.com/schemas/2014/forms"
            xmlns:x="http://schemas.microsoft.com/winfx/2009/xaml"
            x:Class="NavigationExamples.TabPageDatabound"
            Title="Data-bound TabbedPage">
    <TabbedPage.ItemTemplate>
        <DataTemplate>
            <ContentPage Title="{Binding Name}">
                <StackLayout Padding="5, 25">
                    <Label Text="{Binding Number}" Font="Bold,Large"
                    HorizontalOptions="Center" />
                </StackLayout>
            </ContentPage>
        </DataTemplate>
    </TabbedPage.ItemTemplate>
</TabbedPage>
```

Tip   DataTemplate is commonly used for data-binding classes such as ListView and TableView. Read more about it in Chapter 6.

Create a list of tabs by declaring a TabItem class and building an array of them. Name and Number are the properties of TabItem, as shown in Listing 7-25.

Listing 7-25. TabItem Class from TabPageDatabound.cs

```
class TabItem
{
    public TabItem(string name, int number)
    {
        this.Name = name;
        this.Number = number;
    }

    public string Name { private set; get; }
    public int Number { private set; get; }

}
```

The binding in Listing 7-24 ties the TabItem.Name property to the page's Title, and the TabItem.Number property to the label's Text property. Build the TabItem array and assign to the TabbedPage's ItemsSource property (Listing 7-26).

Listing 7-26. Data-Bound Tabs in TabPageDatabound.xaml.cs

```
public TabPageDatabound()
{
    InitializeComponent();
    this.ItemsSource = new TabItem[] {
        new TabItem ("First", 1),
        new TabItem ("Second", 2),
        new TabItem ("Third", 3),
        new TabItem ("Fourth", 4),
        new TabItem ("Fifth", 5),
        new TabItem ("Sixth", 6)
    };
}
```

ItemsSource exposes the properties of TabItem array binding in the ItemTemplate, TabItem.Name as ContentPage.Title and TabItem.Number as Label.Text.

> **Tip** Remember InitializeComponent(); in your TabbedPage constructor. Cryptic errors can occur otherwise.

The result is six named tabs, as shown in Figure 7-18.

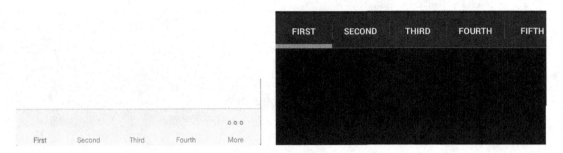

Figure 7-18. *TabbedPage with data-bound tabs*

Scroll the tab bar vertically on Android or tap "More" on iOS to see the sixth tab.

When a tab is tapped, the corresponding NumberPage is created and navigated to, displaying the bound Number.

Putting NavigationPages Inside a TabbedPage

Navigation pages are used within a tabbed page by assigning them as children, creating a navigation bar when the tab is selected (Listing 7-27). Remember to assign a Title to NavigationPage to specify the name of the tab.

Listing 7-27. NavigationPage as a Child of a TabbedPage

```
<TabbedPage Title="Tabs Using TabbedPage" xmlns:local="clr-namespace:
NavigationExamples;assembly=NavigationExamples.Xaml"
    xmlns="http://xamarin.com/schemas/2014/forms" xmlns:x="http://
    schemas.microsoft.com/winfx/2009/xaml" x:Class="NavigationExamples.
    TabPage">
    <local:FirstPage />
    <NavigationPage Title="Second Page" Icon="Navigation.png">
        <x:Arguments>
            <local:SecondPage />
```

Figure 7-19. *Springboard using tap-gesture recognizers added to the images*

```
        </x:Arguments>
      </NavigationPage>
  </TabbedPage>
```

This example will display two tabs, First Page and Second Page. Second Page is wrapped within a NavigationPage.

Springboard

A *springboard* is a grid of tappable images on a home screen menu, sometimes referred to as a *dashboard*, as shown in Figure 7-19.

This springboard is implemented with a Grid layout, as shown in Listing 7-28. This code places three images on the grid.

Listing 7-28. Grid in Springboard.xaml

```
<Grid VerticalOptions="FillAndExpand" RowSpacing="65" ColumnSpacing="65"
Padding="60" >
    <Grid.RowDefinitions>
        <RowDefinition Height="*" />
        <RowDefinition Height="*" />
        <RowDefinition Height="*" />
    </Grid.RowDefinitions>
    <Grid.ColumnDefinitions>
        <ColumnDefinition Width="*" />
    </Grid.ColumnDefinitions>
    <Image x:Name="FirstImage" Grid.Column="0" Grid.Row="0" Source="first.
    png" Aspect="AspectFit" HorizontalOptions="FillAndExpand"
    VerticalOptions="FillAndExpand" />
    <Image x:Name="SecondImage" Grid.Column="0" Grid.Row="1"
    Source="second.png" Aspect="AspectFit" HorizontalOptions="FillAndExpand
    " VerticalOptions="FillAndExpand" />
    <Image x:Name="ThirdImage" Grid.Column="0" Grid.Row="2" Source="third.
    png" Aspect="AspectFit" HorizontalOptions="FillAndExpand"
    VerticalOptions="FillAndExpand" />
</Grid>
```

Each of the three Images is provisioned with tap-gesture recognizers, as shown in Listing 7-29. The Tapped event of each gesture handler contains a PushAsync to the requested page. I'll talk more about the TapGestureRecognizers shortly.

Listing 7-29. TapGestureRecognizers in Springboard.xaml.cs

```
public partial class Springboard : ContentPage
{
    public Springboard ()
    {
        InitializeComponent ();

        var tapFirst = new TapGestureRecognizer();
        tapFirst.Tapped += async (s, e) =>
        {
            await this.Navigation.PushAsync(new FirstPage());
        };
        FirstImage.GestureRecognizers.Add(tapFirst);

        var tapSecond = new TapGestureRecognizer();
        tapSecond.Tapped += async (s, e) =>
        {
            await this.Navigation.PushAsync(new SecondPage());
        };
        SecondImage.GestureRecognizers.Add(tapSecond);

        var tapThird = new TapGestureRecognizer();
        tapThird.Tapped += async (s, e) =>
        {
            await this.Navigation.PushAsync(new ThirdPage());
        };
        ThirdImage.GestureRecognizers.Add(tapThird);
    }
}
```

Making Icons Tappable by Using Gesture Recognizers

The gesture recognizers added to each image in Listing 7-28 handle taps in the TapGestureRecognizer Tapped event, using PushAsync to push the specified page onto the navigation stack. Here a tap-gesture recognizer is added to firstImage:

```
var tapFirst = new TapGestureRecognizer();
tapFirst.Tapped += async (s, e) =>
{
    await this.Navigation.PushAsync(new FirstPage());
};
FirstImage.GestureRecognizers.Add(tapFirst);
```

Tappable images should be visually responsive to touch. Use the opacity trick covered back in Chapter 1 (Listing 1-6):

```
var tapFirst = new TapGestureRecognizer();
tapFirst.Tapped +=  async (sender, e) =>
{
    image.Opacity = .5;
    await Task.Delay(100);
    image.Opacity = 1;
    await this.Navigation.PushAsync(new FirstPage());
};
firstImage.GestureRecognizers.Add(tapFirst);
```

This dims the image slightly for an instant when touched to provide user feedback and let them know that their gesture did something. When using the Task class, remember to add the using statement:

```
using System.Threading.Tasks;
```

Carousel Using CarouselPage

Carousel pages scroll off the screen to reveal another page when a user slides left or right. Create a carousel page and add child pages, as shown in Listing 7-30.

Listing 7-30. Carousel.xaml

Figure 7-20. *Sliding to the left shows the second page*

```xml
<?xml version="1.0" encoding="UTF-8"?>
<CarouselPage Title="Carousel Using CarouselPage"
    xmlns:local="clr-namespace:NavigationExamples;assembly=NavigationExamples"
    xmlns="http://xamarin.com/schemas/2014/forms" xmlns:x="http://schemas.
    microsoft.com/winfx/2009/xaml" x:Class="NavigationExamples.Carousel">
    <CarouselPage.Children>
        <local:FirstPage />
        <local:SecondPage />
        <local:ThirdPage />
    </CarouselPage.Children>
</CarouselPage>
```

This allows horizontal scrolling between child pages. Figure 7-20 shows that the home page, when slid to the left, reveals the second page.

When using `CarouselPage` as a detail page in `MasterDetailPage`, set `MasterDetailPage.IsGestureEnabled` to `false` to prevent gesture conflicts between `CarouselPage` and `MasterDetailPage`.

Tip   The CarouselView community project is considered more up-to-date than CarouselPage by some. `https://github.com/alexrainman/CarouselView`

You are now equipped to build the navigation outline for just about any Xamarin. Forms app you can imagine!

Summary

Navigation is a key topic in the creation of mobile apps. In web and desktop apps, single screens are so large and hold so much of the user workflow that navigation is often a small part of the user experience and is even sometimes added as an afterthought. Because of the economy of screen real estate in mobile apps, we must enable users to easily get around in an app in as short a time as possible. Consumer apps can engage a user for a long period of time, but success in business apps is not measured in the amount of time a user spends in the app but in the answer to this question: Did they find the information they were looking for? Menus can't be a catchall parking lot of drop-downs at the top of the page or (just as bad) a navigation drawer bursting with disorganized features.

The criticality of navigation in mobile apps leads us to this tenet: *Mobile navigation must closely match the user workflow.* If it doesn't, we risk confused and frustrated users.

In most of our apps, especially business apps, it is useful to try and match our user stories and use cases with these key navigation patterns: hierarchical, modal, drill-down list, navigation drawer, and tabs.

Hopefully, this chapter provides you with the ideas and patterns to map out the skeleton of just about any app you can imagine. The downloadable code samples can be mixed and matched to help you sketch out your app.

In the next chapter, we will return to the mobile UI for the final and catalyzing topic in Xamarin.Forms development: customization using effects, native controls, and custom renderers. Custom renderers allow you to use *almost all* of Xamarin's platform-specific UI functionality within the context of a Xamarin.Forms app. You can include platform-specific code, which employs Xamarin.iOS and Xamarin.Android, in your Xamarin.Forms pages by using effects, native views, and custom renderers.

Please navigate to the next chapter.

Custom Renderers, Effects, and Native Views

When you're ready to extend the capability of Xamarin.Forms views beyond their out-of-the-box functionality, then it's time to start customizing them using custom renderers, effects, and native views. Platform-specific controls and layouts have scores of features inaccessible using only the Xamarin.Forms abstraction. There are three ways to access those features and extend the functionality of your application. The custom renderer gives full control over a Xamarin.Forms control by allowing you to gain access to all of its native functionality. It allows you to override the methods of the default renderers provided by Xamarin.Forms or even replace the platform-specific control Xamarin. Forms used with another control. Xamarin.Forms developers' customization approach of choice is effects, a milder form of customization. Use effects if you need to change properties or use event listeners. Finally, Xamarin.Forms supports the use of the native views directly in XAML. This provides full access to the power of native controls along with the full responsibility of managing their lifecycle and behavior.

Custom Renderer

Xamarin.Forms exposes the mechanism whereby cross-platform views are made into platform-specific views, called *renderers*. By creating your own custom renderers, you get full access to platform-specific features buried deep within each view! *Custom renderers* are a bridge between Xamarin.Forms and Xamarin platform-specific libraries, Xamarin. iOS as well as Xamarin.Android.

© Dan Hermes 2019

D. Hermes and N. Mazloumi, *Building Xamarin.Forms Mobile Apps Using XAML*,
https://doi.org/10.1007/978-1-4842-4030-4_8

Note   Custom renderers are the most powerful option for Xamarin.Forms view customization, so we'll explore it first before moving onto a milder but more popular approach: Effects. Xamarin.Forms controls are drawn on the screen using two primary components: *elements* and renderers. Throughout this book you've been working with the elements: views, pages, or cells defined within Xamarin. Forms. The renderers take a cross-platform element and draw it on the screen using the platform-specific UI library. All Xamarin screens use renderers! For example, if you create a Label view using Xamarin.Forms, this element is rendered in iOS using `UILabel` and in Android using `TextView`. However, Xamarin.Forms provides only a partial binding to these platform-specific views. If you want to gain access to all of the properties and methods within platform-specific elements (such as `UILabel`, `TextView`, and `TextBlock`), then you need to create a custom renderer (or an Effect, but we'll get to that later).

Think of a custom renderer as a way to access and extend your use of the platform-specific elements.

Tip   You can create custom renderers for these elements: `Views`, `Cells`, and `Pages`.

At the end of this topic, I'll list most of the Xamarin.Forms elements covered in this book, their platform-specific equivalents, and which renderers to use when customizing them.

When to Use a Custom Renderer

When might you want to use a custom renderer?

You may want a view to behave differently and Xamarin.Forms isn't obliging you. For example, you know for a fact that iOS does text decorations or shadows on a particular view and this isn't available in Xamarin.Forms, so you create a custom renderer to access a Xamarin.iOS control. Use a custom control when you need direct access to an element's platform-specific properties and methods, when you need to override platform-specific control methods, or when you need to replace a Xamarin.Forms element with your own custom platform-specific element.

Tip   A Xamarin.Forms *customized control* uses a custom renderer to access native functionality in a single control. A *custom control* is typically a group of controls composited into a single reusable component using `ContentView` (Chapter 5) (but you can also create a custom control using a custom renderer and replace the view with a group of views). Sometimes developers will say "custom control" to refer to a customized control.

Let's explore how to create a custom renderer for Android and iOS.

Creating and Using a Custom Renderer

A custom renderer is created to implement the visual representation of a custom element. You create a custom element class that inherits from a standard Xamarin. Forms element, such as `Button`. Then you use that custom element in the UI. You can implement the custom renderer for each platform to use platform-specific members of that element, such as Android's `SetBackgroundColor` method or the iOS `BackgroundColor` property.

Note   `Button Backgroundcolor` is the example used in this chapter. It's a simple function that lends itself well to demonstrating how to create custom renderers. In the real world, outside of a teaching context, you would not customize this particular element because there is an easy way to do this in Xamarin.Forms:

```
View.BackgroundColor = Color.FromRGB(50,205,50);
```

or

```
<Button Text="Press Me" HorizontalOptions="FillAndExpand"
BackgroundColor="#32cd32" />
```

Custom renderers should only be written for functionality that cannot be achieved using regular Xamarin.Forms views and their elements.

There are several steps in the creation and implementation of a custom renderer, but I'll break them into two tasks: preparing the custom element in the Xamarin.Forms project and creating a custom renderer in each platform-specific project.

Prepare the custom element in your Xamarin.Forms project by creating an element subclass and then using it in your UI. The following steps only happen once.

1. Create an element subclass. Create a custom element that is a subclass of the element you want to customize, such as Button, in your Xamarin.Forms project.

    ```
    <Button FontSize="Large" HorizontalOptions="Center"
    VerticalOptions="Fill" xmlns="http://xamarin.com/schemas/2014/
    forms" xmlns:x="http://schemas.microsoft.com/winfx/2009/xaml"
    x:Class="CustomRendererExample.CustomButton"/>
    ```

2. Create the C# partial class implementation of your custom element (code behind).

    ```
    public partial class CustomButton : Button
    {
        public CustomButton()
        {
          InitializeComponent();
        }
    }
    ```

3. Use the element. Use the subclassed element, such as this CustomButton, in a layout in your Xamarin.Forms project.

Create a custom renderer in each of your platform-specific projects (iOS, Android) using these three steps. The following steps occur *once for each platform*.

1. Create a custom renderer. Add a custom renderer class to each platform-specific project where you want to make customizations.

    ```
    public class CustomButtonRenderer : ButtonRenderer
    ```

2. Add [assembly]. Add the [assembly] attribute outside of the namespace declaration to declare the new renderer.

3. Add using. Add using statements to the renderer class so that the renderer types are resolved.

That's the upshot for creating a custom renderer.

In the next example, you will create a custom button that has custom renderers for each platform. Start by preparing your custom view in the Xamarin.Forms project before moving onto the renderers.

Creating the Custom Element

A custom renderer first requires a custom Xamarin.Forms element, which can be a View, a Cell, or a Page. In this example, you will use custom renderers to change the background color of a button view to some variant of green. The custom view will be called CustomButton and inherit from the Button view and is defined in XAML file. You need to provide two files for every custom element you are creating: the XAML file and the associated code behind file.

Now, to make your CustomButton green, create a Xamarin.Forms solution called CustomRenderer; then I'll go through these steps in more detail.

1. Create an element subclass. Create a new XAML document called CustomButton.xaml, and replace the root element ContentPage that Visual Studio created with Button both in the XAML and the code behind and assign some default values.

```
<Button xmlns="http://xamarin.com/schemas/2014/forms"
xmlns:x="http://schemas.microsoft.com/winfx/2009/xaml"
x:Class="CustomRendererExample.CustomButton" FontSize="Large"
HorizontalOptions="Center" TextColor="Black"
VerticalOptions=="Fill" />
```

2. Create the C# partial class implementation of your custom element (code behind).

```
public partial class CustomButton : Button
{
    public CustomButton()
    {
```

```
        InitializeComponent();
    }
}
```

3. Use the element. Use the subclassed element, such as this
    CustomButton, in a layout in your Xamarin.Forms project.

Create a new ContentPage in a file called CustomRendererExamplePage.xaml. Declare
the namespace of your CustomButton using the xmlns directive; provide a prefix for this
namespace, e.g., local; declare an instance of the CustomButton view; provide a name for
a click handler; and place the button on a Stacklayout, as shown in Listing 8-1.

Listing 8-1. Use the CustomButton in CustomRendererExamplePage.xaml
(in the Forms Project)

```
<ContentPage xmlns="http://xamarin.com/schemas/2014/forms"
xmlns:x="http://schemas.microsoft.com/winfx/2009/xaml"
xmlns:local="clr-namespace:CustomRendererExample"
x:Class="CustomRendererExample.CustomRendererExamplePage">
    <StackLayout VerticalOptions="Center">
        <local:CustomButton Text="Custom Button" Clicked=
        "ButtonClicked" />
    </StackLayout>
</ContentPage>
```

The CustomRendererExamplePage also requires a partial class implementation
in the code behind CustomRendererExamplePage.xaml.cs, which includes a
default constructor that calls the InitializeComponent method and provides an
implementation of the event hander ButtonClicked, as shown in Listing 8-2.

Listing 8-2. Use the CustomButton in CustomRendererExamplePage.xaml
(in the Forms Project)

```
public partial class CustomRendererExamplePage : ContentPage {
    public CustomRendererExamplePage() {
        InitializeComponent();
    }
```

```
public void ButtonClicked(object sender, EventArgs args) {
    DisplayAlert("Congratulations",
    "This button was rendered in a platform-specific class.", "OK");
}
}
```

Remember to assign this `CustomRendererExamplePage` class to the `MainPage` property of your `Application` constructor. In the `StackLayout`, your use of the custom view, `CustomButton`, is exactly the same as the use of a regular Xamarin.Forms `Button` view.

Creating the Custom Renderer

Now that you have created a custom element and used it in your UI, you'll need to create the custom renderer. You'll need to determine the name of the renderer for your element, and I'll show you how to do that later in this chapter in the section "Which Renderer and View Do You Customize?" In this example, you'll use `ButtonRenderer`.

There are two main ways to customize a control: by property or by replacing the entire control. Customizing a control's properties involves accessing platform-specific properties unavailable via the Xamarin.Forms view (such as a button's background color). A Xamarin.Forms control can also be *completely replaced* by a platform-specific control of the developer's choice. I'll cover property customization in depth in this chapter and touch upon control replacement in the notes.

Here are the custom renderer's key methods:

- `OnElementChanged`: This main method fires upon changes to the element and is used for control initialization. Set the initial control value and its properties. This is also where to replace the entire control with your own customized platform-specific control.

- `OnElementPropertyChanged`: This method fires upon changes to element and attached properties and is useful for data binding.

- `SetNativeControl`: Call this method manually to replace the entire element with a custom platform-specific control (such as `SetNativeControl(new YourCustomizedControl());`).

Here are the custom renderer's important properties:

- *Control*: A reference to the platform-specific element (such as UIButton) displayed by the renderer. Platform-specific properties are available here. This object can also be replaced with an entirely new (and customized) platform-specific control.

- *Element*: A reference to the Xamarin.Forms subclassed element (such as CustomButton). Xamarin.Forms element properties are available here.

- Customize controls and their properties by using the Control property within the OnElementChanged method.

Implement data-bound customized controls by assigning Control properties from their corresponding Element properties in the OnElementPropertyChanged method.

Now create a custom renderer on each platform. Begin with the Android platform, then do iOS.

Android Custom Renderer

Renderers realize a view on the native platform. Create your own renderer by inheriting from the standard renderer, such as ButtonRenderer. Then call into the native view's platform-specific API to customize the view using the renderer's Control property. In OnElementChanged, you'll assign your Control's background color property.

Do the first of three platform-specific steps.

1. Create a custom renderer. Add a custom renderer class to the platform-specific project, which is ButtonRenderer in this case.

Tip   Refer to the section "Which Renderer and View Do You Customize?" at the end of this chapter to help you determine the renderer and platform-specific control(s) to use for the element you want to customize.

Create CustomButtonRenderer.cs as a class in the Droid project. Inherit from the ButtonRenderer class and modify the Control property to affect your button as needed. The platform-specific view is assigned to the Control property, in this case an Android Button control, and its native properties and methods are made available. Listing 8-3 shows an Android renderer where the background color is set using the SetBackgroundColor method.

Listing 8-3. Customized ButtonRenderer in CustomButtonRenderer.cs (in the Droid Project)

```
public class CustomButtonRenderer : ButtonRenderer {
    public CustomButtonRenderer(Context context) : base(context) {
        AutoPackage = false;
    }

    protected override void OnElementChanged
    (ElementChangedEventArgs<Button> e) {
        base.OnElementChanged (e);

        if (Control != null) {
            Control.SetBackgroundColor (global::Android.Graphics.Color.
            LimeGreen);
            }
        }
    }
}
```

Note   If you don't add a platform-specific renderer, the default Xamarin.Forms renderer will be used.

Complete the final two platform-specific steps. In order to make the custom renderer visible to the Xamarin.Forms project, an attribute on the class is required. Then add the using statements.

2. Add the [assembly] attribute outside of the namespace declaration to declare the new renderer.

    ```
    [assembly: ExportRenderer (typeof (CustomButton), typeof
    (CustomButtonRenderer))]
    ```

3. Add using statements to the renderer class so that the renderer
    types are resolved.

```
using Xamarin.Forms.Platform.Android;
using Xamarin.Forms;
using CustomRendererExample;
using CustomRendererExample.Droid;
using Android.Content;
```

Figure 8-1 shows the result: a "lime green"-colored button. Setting a button's
background color is only possible using a custom renderer with the current version of
Xamarin.Forms.

Figure 8-1. *Lime green CustomButton via an Android custom renderer*

Tip   Color is close-captioned in this chapter for all of you black-and-white print readers.

CODE COMPLETE: Android Custom Renderer

Listings 8-4, 8-5, 8-6, 8-7, and 8-8 contain the complete code listing for the Android custom button renderer. Listing 8-4, `CustomButton.xaml`; Listing 8-5, `CustomButton.xaml.cs`; Listing 8-6, `CustomRendererExamplePage.xaml`; and Listing 8-7 are in the Xamarin.Forms project, and Listing 8-8, `CustomButtonRenderer.cs`, is from the Droid project in the same solution, `CustomRendererExample`.

Listing 8-4. CustomButton.xaml (in the Forms Project)

```
<?xml version="1.0" encoding="UTF-8"?>
<Button FontSize="Large" HorizontalOptions="Center" VerticalOptions=
"Fill"
x:Class="CustomRendererExample.CustomButton"/>
```

Listing 8-5. CustomButton Code Behind in CustomButton.xaml.cs (in the Forms Project)

```
using Xamarin.Forms;

namespace CustomRendererExample {
    public partial class CustomButton : Button {
        public CustomButton()
        {
            InitializeComponent();
        }
    }
}
```

Listing 8-6. Use the CustomButton in CustomRendererExamplePage.xaml (in the Forms Project)

```
<ContentPage xmlns="http://xamarin.com/schemas/2014/forms"
xmlns:x="http://schemas.microsoft.com/winfx/2009/xaml"
xmlns:local="clr-namespace:CustomRendererExample"
x:Class="CustomRendererExample.CustomRendererExamplePage">
    <StackLayout VerticalOptions="Center">
        <local:CustomButton Text="Custom Button" Clicked=
        "ButtonClicked" />
    </StackLayout>
</ContentPage>
```

Listing 8-7. Use the CustomButton in CustomRendererExamplePage.xaml (in the Forms Project)

```
using Xamarin.Forms
namespace mynamespace {
public partial class MainPage : ContentPage {
    public XAMLBookPage() {
        InitializeComponent();
    }
    void Handle_Clicked(object sender, EventArgs e) {
        DisplayAlert("Congratulations",
                "This button was rendered in a platform-specific class.",
                "OK");
    }
  }
}
```

Listing 8-8. CustomButtonRenderer.cs (Droid Project)

```
using Xamarin.Forms.Platform.Android;
using Xamarin.Forms;
using CustomRendererExample;
using CustomRendererExample.Droid;
using Android.Content;
```

```
[assembly: ExportRenderer (typeof (CustomButton), typeof
(CustomButtonRenderer))]

namespace CustomRendererExample.Droid {
    public class CustomButtonRenderer : ButtonRenderer {
        public CustomButtonRenderer(Context context) : base(context) {
            AutoPackage = false;
        }

        protected override void OnElementChanged
        (ElementChangedEventArgs<Button> e) {
            base.OnElementChanged (e);

            if (Control != null) {
                Control.SetBackgroundColor (global::Android.Graphics.
                Color.LimeGreen);
            }
        }
    }
}
```

Now we'll do a green button in iOS.

iOS Custom Renderer

Creating an iOS renderer for the Button view is similar to making the Android one. Create a custom renderer that inherits from a standard renderer, such as ButtonRenderer. Then call into the native view's platform-specific API to customize it using the renderer's Control property. In OnElementChanged, you'll assign your Control's background color property.

Begin with the first platform-specific step.

1. Create a custom renderer. Create CustomButtonRenderer.cs as a class in the iOS project. Inherit from the ButtonRenderer class and modify the Control property to affect your button as needed. The platform-specific view is assigned to the Control property, in this case an iOS UIButton control, and its native properties and methods are available. Listing 8-9 shows an iOS renderer where the background color is set using the UIButton's BackgroundColor property.

Listing 8-9. Customized ButtonRenderer in CustomButtonRenderer.cs (iOS Project)

```
public class CustomButtonRenderer : ButtonRenderer {
    protected override void OnElementChanged
    (ElementChangedEventArgs<Button> e) {
        base.OnElementChanged (e);
        if (Control != null) {
            Control.BackgroundColor = UIColor.FromRGB(50,205,50);
        }
    }
}
```

Next, do the final two steps. In order to make the custom renderer visible to the Xamarin.Forms project, you need to add an attribute on the class and the two using statements.

2. Add [assembly]. Add the [assembly] attribute outside of the namespace declaration to declare the new renderer.

    ```
    [assembly: ExportRenderer (typeof (CustomButton), typeof
    (CustomButtonRenderer))]
    ```

3. Add using statements to the renderer class so that the renderer types are resolved.

    ```
    using Xamarin.Forms.Platform.iOS;
    using Xamarin.Forms;
    using UIKit;
    using CustomRenderer;
    using CustomRenderer.iOS;
    ```

Figure 8-2 displays the result: another lime green button, using a custom renderer with the current version of Xamarin.Forms.

Figure 8-2. *Lime green CustomButton via an iOS custom renderer*

CODE COMPLETE: iOS Custom Renderer

Listing 8-10 shows the complete code listing for the iOS custom button renderer, which goes in the iOS project in the solution, `CustomRendererExample`.

Listing 8-10. CustomButtonRenderer.cs for the iOS Project

```
using Xamarin.Forms.Platform.iOS;
using Xamarin.Forms;
using UIKit;
using CustomRendererExample;
using CustomRendererExample.iOS;

[assembly: ExportRenderer (typeof (CustomButton), typeof
(CustomButtonRenderer))]
```

```
namespace CustomRendererExample.iOS {
    public class CustomButtonRenderer : ButtonRenderer {
        protected override void OnElementChanged
        (ElementChangedEventArgs<Button> e) {
            base.OnElementChanged (e);

            if (Control != null) {
                Control.BackgroundColor = UIColor.Brown;
            }
        }
    }
}
```

That's how to build a custom renderer on both mobile platforms!

The first trick in building a custom renderer is figuring out what the renderer is called and the native element name. Here's a quick guide to help with that.

Which Renderer and View Do You Customize?

Table 8-1 shows most of the Xamarin.Forms elements covered in this book, their renderers, and their platform-specific equivalents that can be customized.

Table 8-1. *Elements, Their Renderers, and Platform-Specific Elements*

Xamarin.Forms	Renderer	Android	iOS
Chapter 1: Views			
ContentPage	PageRenderer	ViewGroup	UIViewController
Label	LabelRenderer	TextView	UILabel
Button	ButtonRenderer	Button	UIButton
Entry	EntryRenderer	EditText	UITextField
Image	ImageRenderer	ImageView	UIImageView
BoxView	BoxRenderer	ViewGroup	UIView
ScrollView	ScrollViewRenderer	ScrollView	UIScrollView

(continued)

Table 8-1. (*continued*)

Xamarin.Forms	Renderer	Android	iOS
ActivityInidcator	ActivityIndicator Renderer	ProgressBar	UIActivityIndicator
SearchBar	SearchBarRenderer	SearchView	UISearchBar
Map	MapRenderer	MapView	MKMapView
WebView	WebViewRenderer	WebView	UIWebView
Chapter 3: Layouts			
StackLayout	ViewRenderer	View	UIView
RelativeLayout	ViewRenderer	View	UIView
AbsoluteLayout	ViewRenderer	View	UIView
Grid	ViewRenderer	View	UIView
ContentView	ViewRenderer	View	UIView
Frame	FrameRenderer	ViewGroup	UIView
Chapter 4			
Editor	EditorRenderer	EditText	UITextView
Chapter 5: Controls			
Picker	PickerRenderer	TextView, AlertDialog, NumberPicker EditText	UIPickerView, UIPickerViewModel, UIToolBar, UIBarButtonItems, UITextField
DatePicker	DatePickerRenderer	TextView, AlertDialog	UIDatePicker, UIToolbar, UITextField, UIBarButtonItems

(*continued*)

Table 8-1. (*continued*)

Xamarin.Forms	Renderer	Android	iOS
TimePicker	TimePickerRenderer	TextView, AlertDialog EditText	UIDatePicker, UIToolbar, UITextField, UIBarButtonItems
Stepper	StepperRenderer	LinearLayout, Button	UIStepper
Slider	SliderRenderer	SeekBar	UISlider
Switch	SwitchRenderer	Switch	UISwitch
TemplatedPage	PageRenderer	ViewGroup	UIViewController
TemplatedView	ViewRenderer	View	UIView
ContentPresenter	ViewRenderer	View	UIView
Chapter 6: Lists			
ListView	ListViewRenderer	ListView	UITableView
TextCell	TextCellRenderer	LinearLayout, TextView, ImageView	UITableViewCell
EntryCell	EntryCellRenderer	LinearLayout, TextView, EditText	UITableViewCell, UITextField
ViewCell	ViewCellRenderer	View	UITableViewCell
SwitchCell	SwitchCellRenderer	Switch	UITableViewCell, UISwitch
ImageCell	ImageCellRenderer	LinearLayout, TextView, ImageView	UITableViewCell, UIImage

(*continued*)

Table 8-1. (*continued*)

Xamarin.Forms	Renderer	Android	iOS
Chapter 7: Navigation			
NavigationPage	NavigationRenderer	ViewGroup	UINavigation Controller, UIToolbar
MasterDetailPage	MasterDetailRenderer, PhoneMasterDetail Renderer (iPhone) TabletMasterDetail Renderer(iPad)	DrawerLayout	UIViewController (iPhone), UISplitView Controller(iPad)
TableView	TableViewRenderer	ListView	UITableView
TabbedPage	TabbedRenderer	ViewPager	UIView
CarouselPage	CarouselPageRenderer	ViewPager	UIScrollView

That should be sufficient to get you started with custom renderers. Now that you've seen the complete implementation of a renderer, it's time for a subtler approach.

Effects

What do you do when Xamarin.Forms view you want to use is just shy of perfect? If you could just change one or two properties or its behavior, the view would meet your requirements. This is where effects come into play.

Effects allow access to the platform-specific control and container Xamarin.Forms uses to access the Xamarin.Android or Xamarin.iOS layer. Effects can be added to any page, layout, and view in Xamarin.Forms. Effects offer a reusable and lightweight approach to extend the capability of a Xamarin.Forms view compared to a custom renderer. Use effects if you only need to change a small number of the properties or behaviors of the underlying platform-specific control that Xamarin.Forms uses.

Tip   Fast renderers on view have increased performance over containers. Fast renderers are available only for certain controls on certain platforms (e.g., Button, Image, Label on Android, and more every release).

An effect is created by deriving from PlatformEffect in each platform-specific project to access the native control and then registering the effect with a unique identifier and organization-wide name. To use the effect, subclass the RoutingEffect in the shared project, resolving the effect by the organization-wide name and identifier. All Xamarin.Forms views have an Effects member that accepts one or more effects. Use the Effects property in XAML to add an effect.

Creating and Using Effects

An *Effect* gives access to the native control and container used by the Xamarin. Forms view through the platform-specific PlatformEffect class. The cross-platform RoutingEffect class is used to resolve the platform-specific effect in the Forms project. Both classes need to be subclassed to create and use an effect.

Creating an effect is simpler than creating a custom renderer primarily because you don't have to determine and implement the native renderer. There is only one class PlatformEffect that gives direct access to a generic Container, Control, and the Xamarin.Forms Element. This simplicity comes with a greater responsibility. The developer needs to ensure that an effect is not accidentally added to a view that the effect does not support.

PlatformEffect

PlatformEffect gives direct access to the native control, its container, and the Xamarin. Forms element. Here are the PlatformEffect properties that reference those three classes:

- Control—references the platform-specific control Xamarin.Forms uses to implement its view

- Container—references the platform-specific control used to implement the layout

- Element—references the Xamarin.Forms view itself

Create an effect by subclassing `PlatformEffect` in each platform-specific project and registering a unique organization-wide namespace using `ResolutionGroupName` and a unique identifier using `ExportEffect` assembly attributes, e.g.:

```
[assembly: ResolutionGroupName("my.company")]
[assembly: ExportEffect(typeof(DroidEffect), "MyEffect")]
```

Override the `OnAttached` and `OnDetached` methods as needed for initialization and cleanup:

- `OnAttached`—called on initialization of your effect on the Xamarin.
  Forms view. Use this method to implement your effect.

- `OnDetached`—called when the effect is detached from your Xamarin.
  Forms view for cleanup. This method is used less frequently.

To listen to changes to the bindable properties of the Xamarin.Forms view, override the `OnElementPropertyChanged` method of `PlatformEffect`.

Listing 8-11 shows the basic structure of the platform-specific effect.

Listing 8-11. Platform-Specific Effect

```
public class MyEffect : PlatformEffect
{
    protected override void OnAttached() { ... }
    protected override void OnDetached() { ... }
    protected override void
    OnElementPropertyChanged(PropertyChangedEventArgs args) { ... }
}
```

RoutingEffect

The `RoutingEffect` class abstracts from the platform-specific `PlatformEffect` implementation and is there to resolve the effect in the Forms project by its resolution group name and identifier. Subclass `RoutingEffect` and provide a default constructor that passes the resolution name group and identifier to the base class to initialize the effect, as shown in Listing 8-12.

Listing 8-12. MyEffect RoutingEffect (in the Forms Project)

```
public class MyEffect : RoutingEffect
{
    public MyEffect() : base("my.company.MyEffect") { }
}
```

Routing effects can have auto-implemented properties that can be used in the XAML to parameterize the effect, e.g.,

```
public bool MyProperty {get;set;};
```

Note   Attached properties are often used in the context of customizing Xamarin. Forms views. An attached property is a particular kind of bindable property, coded in XAML as an attribute that contains a `class.property`. Details in the upcoming section, Adding Effects via Attached Properties.

Using the Effect

To use the effect, first register its namespace in XAML, e.g.:

```
xmlns:local="clr-namespace:my.company"
```

Next you add the effect to the `Effects` property of the target view, as `YourEffect` is added to `Entry.Effects` in Listing 8-13.

Listing 8-13. Applying the Effect to a Xamarin.Forms View (in the Forms Project)

```
<Entry>
    <Entry.Effects>
        <local:MyEffect MyProperty="some value"/>
    </Entry.Effects>
</Entry>
```

Let's create an effect that validates the Text entered in an Entry view.

Text Validator Effect

Imagine the following scenario: You want to give visual feedback to a user if the text he or she enters exceeds a maximum length! Wouldn't it be nice if a Xamarin.Forms Entry would allow this type of validation? Unfortunately, this is not possible out of the box. You can use an effect to implement this behavior.

Let's create an effect that allows you to validate the length of the text.

Create in your Forms library the TextValidatorEffect class that inherits from RoutingEffect and add an auto-implemented property MaxLength of type int and the default value 5, as shown in Listing 8-14.

Listing 8-14. Custom RoutingEffect (in the Forms Project)

```
public class TextValidatorEffect : RoutingEffect {
    public int MaxLength {get;set;} = 5;
    public TextValidatorEffect() : base("EffectExample.TextValidator
    Effect") { }
}
```

The empty default constructor passes our namespace EffectExample as the resolution group name and the name of the class TextValidatorEffect as the identifier to the base class RoutingEffect.

Create a page called TextValidatorPage.xaml and add the effect namespace to the ContentPage. Define two Entry controls and register the effect with the Effects property of the Entry controls. The first Entry uses the TextValidatorEffect without explicitly setting the MaxLength property, which defaults to 5. The second control sets MaxLength explicitly to 10, as demonstrated in Listing 8-15.

Listing 8-15. Registering an Effect in XAML (in the Forms Project)

```
<Entry Text="Good">
    <Entry.Effects>
        <local:TextValidatorEffect/>
    </Entry.Effects>
</Entry>
```

```
<Entry Text="Not so good">
    <Entry.Effects>
        <local:TextValidatorEffect MaxLength="10"/>
    </Entry.Effects>
</Entry>
```

Xamarin.Forms uses EditText in Android and UITextField in iOS as the native control to render an Entry. Both platform-specific views provide the ability to set the background color. Begin with the Android platform, then do iOS.

Android Platform Effect

The Android platform-specific control Android.Widget.EditText has the method SetBackgroundColor that expects an Android.Graphics.Color.

Create in the platform-specific Android project the DroidTextValidatorEffect class that derives from PlatformEffect. Register the effect with the namespace EffectExample using the assembly attribute ResolutionGroupName and export the effect with the identifier TextValidatorEffect. Override the OnAttached and OnDetached methods of PlatformEffect. The OnDetached method can be empty. In the OnAttached method, call a Validate method that we will implement next, as shown in Listing 8-16.

Listing 8-16. Android Platform-Specific TextValidatorEffect (in the Droid Project)

```
[assembly: ResolutionGroupName("EffectExample")]
[assembly: ExportEffect(typeof(DroidTextValidatorEffect),
"TextValidatorEffect")]
namespace EffectExample.Droid {
    public class DroidTextValidatorEffect : PlatformEffect {

        protected override void OnAttached() {
            Validate();
        }
        protected override void OnDetached() {}
    }
}
```

Create a private `Validate` method that casts `Element` view to `Entry` and `Control` to the `EditText` view, retrieves the `TextValidatorEffect` effect, and evaluates the length of the `Entry.Text` property to determine if it exceeded the `MaxLength` value of the effect and changes the background color of `EditText,` respectively, as shown in Listing 8-17.

Listing 8-17. Android Platform-Specific TextValidatorEffect (in the Droid Project)

```
private void Validate() {
    var entry = Element as Entry;
    var view = Control as EditText;
    var effect = (TextValidatorEffect)Element.Effects.FirstOrDefault(
    e => e is TextValidatorEffect);
    if (entry.Text.Length > effect.MaxLength) {
        view.SetBackgroundColor = Color.Maroon.ToAndroid();
    } else {
        view.SetBackgroundColor = Color.Lime.ToAndroid();
    }
}
```

Figure 8-3 shows the text validation effect on Android. The first `Entry` has a `Lime` background, and the second has a `Maroon` background.

327

Figure 8-3. *TextValidatorEffect on Android*

Now create the platform-specific IOSTextValidatorEffect for iOS.

iOS Platform Effect

The iOS platform-specific control UIKit.UITextField has the property
BackgroundColor that can be set using a UIColor.

Create in the platform-specific iOS project the ITextValidatorEffect class that
derives from PlatformEffect. Similarly, register the effect by its namespace and
identifier and override the OnAttached and OnDetached methods. The OnDetached
method can be empty. In the OnAttached method, call a Validate method, as shown in
Listing 8-18.

Listing 8-18. iOS Platform-Specific TextValidatorEffect (in the iOS Project)

```
[assembly: ResolutionGroupName("EffectExample")]
[assembly: ExportEffect(typeof(IOSTextValidatorEffect),
"TextValidatorEffect")]
namespace EffectExample.iOS {
    public class IOSTextValidatorEffect : PlatformEffect {

        protected override void OnAttached() {
            Validate();
        }
        protected override void OnDetached() {}
    }
}
```

Create a private `Validate` method that casts `Element` view to `Entry` and `Control` to the `UITextField` view, retrieves the `TextValidatorEffect` effect, and evaluates the length of the `Entry.Text` property to determine if it exceeded the `MaxLength` value of the effect and changes the background color of `UITextField,` respectively, as shown in Listing 8-19.

Listing 8-19. iOS Platform-Specific TextValidatorEffect (in the iOS Project)

```
private void Validate() {
    var entry = Element as Entry;
    var view = Control as UITextField;
    var effect = (TextValidatorEffect)Element.Effects.FirstOrDefault(
    e => e is TextValidatorEffect);
    if (entry.Text.Length > effect.MaxLength) {
        view.BackgroundColor = Color.Maroon.ToUIColor();
    } else {
        view.BackgroundColor = Color.Lime.ToUIColor();
    }
}
```

Figure 8-4 shows the text validation effect on iOS. The first `Entry` has a `Lime` background, and the second has a `Maroon` background.

Figure 8-4. *TextValidatorEffect on iOS*

Tip   Attached Behaviors are often used in the context of Effects, removing extra code from code behind files. Details here: `https://docs.microsoft.com/en-us/xamarin/xamarin-forms/app-fundamentals/behaviors/reusable/effect-behavior`

The effect does not listen to changes to the `Text` property of `Entry` and will not re-validate it. Let's change that.

Handling Events

Effects can override the `OnElementPropertyChanged` of `PlatformEffect` to listen to property changes of the Xamarin.Forms `Element`. This is useful when the effect needs to change the behavior of the native view depending on what has changed.

Let's listen to what the user is writing in the `Entry` and re-validate the `Text`.

The `PlatformEffect`'s `OnElementPropertyChanged` method has the argument `PropertyChangedEventArgs` with the member `PropertyName` that contains the name of the bindable property of the Xamarin.Forms Element that was changed. Check if the property that has changed is `Text` and call the `Validate` method to re-validate the entry, e.g.:

```
if (args.PropertyName == "Text") Validate();
```

The implementation of the `OnElementPropertyChanged` method is identical for both iOS and Android, shown in Listings 8-22 and 8-23.

Tip   You can also register event handlers for the `PlatformEffect`'s `Container` and `Control` members. These are platform-specific and require familiarity with the underlying platform.

CODE COMPLETE: TextValidatorEffect

Listings 8-20, 8-21, 8-22, and 8-23 show the complete code listing for the iOS and Android `TextValidatorEffect`. Listing 8-20, `TextValidatorEffect.cs`, and Listing 8-21, `TextValidatorPage.xaml`, are in the Forms project, and Listing 8-22, `DroidTextValidatorEffect.cs`, and Listing 8-23, `IOSTextValidatorEffect.cs`, are in the respective platform-specific Droid and iOS projects of the solution `EffectExample`.

Listing 8-20. Custom RoutingEffect (in the Forms Project)

```
using System;
using Xamarin.Forms;

namespace EffectExample {
public class TextValidatorEffect : RoutingEffect {
    public bool IsActive { get; set; } = true;
```

```
    public TextValidatorEffect() : base("EffectExample.TextValidator
    Effect") { }
  }
}
```

Listing 8-21. Registering and Using an Effect in XAML (in the Forms Project)

```
<ContentPage xmlns="http://xamarin.com/schemas/2014/forms"
xmlns:x="http://schemas.microsoft.com/winfx/2009/xaml"
xmlns:local="clr-namespace:EffectExample"
x:Class="EffectExample.EffectExamplePage">
    <StackLayout Padding="30">
        <Entry Text="Good">
            <Entry.Effects>
                <local:TextValidatorEffect />
            </Entry.Effects>
        </Entry>
        <Entry Text="Not so good">
            <Entry.Effects>
                <local:TextValidatorEffect MaxLength="10" />
            </Entry.Effects>
        </Entry>
    </StackLayout>
</ContentPage>
```

Listing 8-22. Android Platform-Specific TextValidatorEffect (in the Droid Project)

```
using System;
using System.ComponentModel;
using System.Linq;
using Android.Text;
using Android.Widget;
using EffectExample.Droid;
using Xamarin.Forms;
using Xamarin.Forms.Platform.Android;
```

```
[assembly: ResolutionGroupName("EffectExample")]
[assembly: ExportEffect(typeof(DroidTextValidatorEffect),
"TextValidatorEffect")]
namespace EffectExample.Droid {
    public class DroidTextValidatorEffect : PlatformEffect {
        protected override void OnAttached() {
            Validate();
        }

        protected override void OnDetached() { }

        protected override void
        OnElementPropertyChanged(PropertyChangedEventArgs args) {
            base.OnElementPropertyChanged(args);
            if (args.PropertyName == "Text") Validate();
        }

        private void Validate() {
            var entry = Element as Entry;
            var view = Control as EditText;
            var effect = (TextValidatorEffect)Element.Effects.
            FirstOrDefault(
            e => e is TextValidatorEffect);
            if (entry.Text.Length > effect.MaxLength) {
                view.SetBackgroundColor(Color.FromHex("#f9c5c9").
                ToAndroid());
        } else {
            view.SetBackgroundColor(Color.FromHex("#c5f9e1").
            ToAndroid());
        }
    }
  }
}
```

Listing 8-23.   iOS Platform-Specific TextValidatorEffect (in the iOS Project)

```
using System;
using System.ComponentModel;
using System.Linq;
using EffectExample.iOS;
using UIKit;
using Xamarin.Forms;
using Xamarin.Forms.Platform.iOS;

[assembly: ResolutionGroupName("EffectExample")]
[assembly: ExportEffect(typeof(IOSTextValidatorEffect),
"TextValidatorEffect")]
namespace EffectExample.iOS {
    public class IOSTextValidatorEffect : PlatformEffect {
        protected override void OnAttached() {
            Validate();
        }

        protected override void OnDetached() {}

        protected override void
        OnElementPropertyChanged(PropertyChangedEventArgs args) {
            base.OnElementPropertyChanged(args);
            if (args.PropertyName == "Text") Validate();
        }

        private void Validate() {
            var entry = Element as Entry;
            var view = Control as UITextField;
            var effect = (TextValidatorEffect)Element.Effects.
            FirstOrDefault(
            e => e is TextValidatorEffect);
            if (entry.Text.Length > effect.MaxLength) {
                view.BackgroundColor = Color.FromHex("#f9c5c9").
                ToUIColor();
```

```
        } else {
            view.BackgroundColor = Color.FromHex("#c5f9e1").ToUIColor();
        }
    }
}
```

You can pass an effect as an attached property instead of adding it in XAML using the view's Effects property. Let's see how.

Adding Effects via Attached Properties

Chapter 5 explained the concept of attached properties. Attached properties allow you to associate properties to elements that do not have the property defined themselves. Attached properties can also be used as wrappers to assign triggers, commands, behaviors, and effects programmatically through C# instead of using XAML. Currently, assigning an effect to a view is a multiline process, as shown in Listing 8-24.

Listing 8-24. Adding an Effect Using the Effects Property (in the Forms Project)

```
<Entry Text="Not so good">
    <Entry.Effects>
        <local:TextValidatorEffect MaxLength="10" />
    </Entry.Effects>
</Entry>
```

Create a new static class called TextValidatorEffect2 with a bindable attached property called MaxLengthProperty and its static accessor methods GetMaxLength and SetMaxLength, as shown in Listing 8-25.

Listing 8-25. Static Class with Attached Property (in the Forms Project)

```
public class TextValidatorEffect2 {
    public static readonly BindableProperty MaxLengthProperty =
    BindableProperty.CreateAttached("MaxLength", typeof(int),
    typeof(TextValidatorEffect2), 5, propertyChanged:
    ValidatorChanged);
```

```
public static int GetMaxLength(BindableObject view) {
    return (int)view.GetValue(MaxLengthProperty);
}

public static void SetMaxLength(BindableObject view, int value) {
    view.SetValue(MaxLengthProperty, value);
}
}
```

Add a MaxLengthPropertyChanged method that is fired when the MaxLength property is attached to a view or is changed. Check if the view is not null. Remove any existing TextValidatorEffect, and then add a new one to ensure that MaxLength property has the most recent value, as shown in Listing 8-26.

Listing 8-26. MaxLengthPropertyChanged Method (in the Forms Project)

```
private static void MaxLengthPropertyChanged(BindableObject bindable,
object oldValue, object newValue) {
    var view = bindable as View;
    if (view == null) return;

    var effect = view.Effects.FirstOrDefault(e => e is TextValidator
    Effect);
    if (effect != null) {
        view.Effects.Remove(effect);
    } else {
        effect = new TextValidatorEffect {MaxLength = GetMaxLength
        (view)};
        view.Effects.Add(effect);
    }
}
```

Internally, the previously defined routing effect TextValidatorEffect is used, which references the platform-specific implementation at runtime.

Create a new page called UsingAttachedPropertyPage.xaml, add the local namespace, and assign the effect to an Entry view, as shown in Listing 8-27.

Listing 8-27. MaxLengthPropertyChanged Method (in the Forms Project)

```
<ContentPage xmlns:local="clr-namespace:EffectExample" ...>
        <Entry Text="Looks Good" local:TextValidatorEffect2.MaxLength="10"/>
</ContentPage>
```

Tip   Attached properties can also be used to attach commands, behaviors, triggers, and other functionality to XAML elements.

This covers the building blocks to create cross-platform effects for Xamarin. Forms controls. Up until now the platform-specific (sometimes we call these "native") control's role was behind the scenes, either encapsulated within the custom renderer or concealed by an effect. The final section of this chapter will present native controls as the headliner on the Xamarin.Forms XAML stage.

Native Views

Native views give you the power of platform-specific controls such as those found in Xamarin.iOS and Xamarin.Android directly within your XAML.

Custom renderers and effects leave the plumbing to Xamarin.Forms, which provides over 40 cross-platform visual elements and views and takes care of the mapping to platform-specific controls using custom renderers. The last topic in this chapter shows you how to use native (platform-specific) controls directly in a XAML page and handling their details manually, such as instantiating them and setting their properties.

Note   Using native views will quickly become advanced as you will find yourself having to take care of all aspects of the controls. This technique requires knowledge of the platform-specific APIs, Xamarin.iOS and Xamarin.Android.

Adding native views to your XAML file is easy. As with any other C# class, you need to declare the namespace in the root element of your XAML file, and you are ready to declare the class in your XAML. For native views this process is called *Native View Declaration*.

Create a XAML page called `NativeViewsPage.xaml`.

Next, declare all the namespaces that are intended to be used in the root element of the page. For a page that is supposed to work both on iOS and Android, these are the namespaces `UIKit` for iOS and `Android.Widget` and `Xamarin.Forms` for Android, as shown in Listing 8-28.

Listing 8-28. Registering the Namespaces for Native Views in XAML (in the Forms Project)

```
xmlns:ios="clr-namespace:UIKit;assembly=Xamarin.iOS;targetPlatform=iOS"
xmlns:droid="clr-namespace:Android.Widget;assembly=Mono.Android;
targetPlatform=Android"
xmlns:formsdroid="clr-namespace:Xamarin.Forms;
assembly=Xamarin.Forms.Platform.Android;targetPlatform=Android"
x:Class="NativeViewsExample.NativeViewsPage">
```

The `xmlns` declaration accepts the directive `targetPlatform` followed by the name of the platform `Android` or `iOS`. This tells XAML parser to ignore any namespace declaration not relevant for the platform the application is currently running on. This is very nice, because it allows you to create one XAML file for all platforms.

Add the iOS `UITextField` view to the XAML, e.g.:

```
<ios:UITextField Text="iOS UITextField"/>
```

Figure 8-5 shows the iOS result.

Figure 8-5. *Native View Declaration on iOS*

Most `Android.Widget` views require that you pass in the `Activity` within which they are used as their Android `Context` in the constructor. Xamarin.Forms provides the `Forms.Context` member that represents the `Activity`. Use the XAML directive `x:Arguments` to pass required parameters.

Add the Android `EditText` view to the XAML, e.g.:

```
<droid:EditText Text="Android EditText" x:Arguments="{x:Static
formsdroid:Forms.Context}"/>
```

Figure 8-6 shows the result for Android.

Figure 8-6. *Native View Declaration on Android*

CODE COMPLETE: Native View Declaration

Listing 8-29 shows the complete XAML listing for declaring native views in the
NativeViewsPage.xaml in the solution NativeViewsExample.

Listing 8-29. Native View Declaration (in the Forms Project)

```
<ContentPage Title="Native View Declaration"
xmlns="http://xamarin.com/schemas/2014/forms"
xmlns:x="http://schemas.microsoft.com/winfx/2009/xaml"
xmlns:ios="clr-namespace:UIKit;assembly=Xamarin.iOS;targetPlatform=iOS"
xmlns:droid="clr-namespace:Android.Widget;assembly=Mono.Android;
targetPlatform=Android"
xmlns:formsdroid="clr-
```

```
namespace:Xamarin.Forms;assembly=Xamarin.Forms.Platform.Android;
targetPlatform=Android"
x:Class="NativeViewsExample.NativeViewsPage">
    <ios:UITextField Text="iOS UITextField"/>
    <droid:EditText Text="Android EditText"
    x:Arguments="{x:Static formsdroid:Forms.Context}"/>
</ContentPage>
```

Tip   There are some limitations to consider when working with native views.
You cannot use the `Style` element because the properties of the native view are
not bindable properties, and you cannot use the `x:Name` directive. If you want to
reference them in your code behind, create a custom control as a wrapper using
`ContentView` that has a name.

In Listing 8-29, a non-default constructor for the Android `EditText` view was used
to pass the `Context` as an argument to its constructor using the `x:Static` markup
extension, that is:

```
<droid:EditText x:Arguments="{x:Static formsdroid:Forms.Context}"/>
```

Properties of native views often require instances of other native classes that may
require a factory method to construct the object. Let's use some factory methods to
assign properties to a native view next.

Using Factory Methods

Some native classes have in addition to default constructors and non-default
constructors factory methods for instantiation. In Chapter 2, you learned to instantiate
objects using factory methods and the `x:Arguments` keyword in the XAML syntax to pass
the arguments.

Create a new XAML page called `FactoryMethodsPage.xaml`.

Both `EditText` in Android and `UITextField` on iOS have factory methods that
specify a platform-specific font. In iOS the `UIFont` class is used to specify a font. In
Android the `TypeFace` class is used. Listing 8-30 and 8-31 extend the example provided
in Listing 8-29 to specify fonts for the `UITextField` and `EditText` views.

UIFont has the static factory method FromName that expects two arguments, the name of the font as a string and the font size as a single, that is:

```
<x:Arguments><x:String>Papyrus</x:String><x:Single>24</x:Single>
</x:Arguments>
```

Declare a UITextField with the font Papyrus and the size 24, as shown in Listing 8-30.

Listing 8-30. Passing Arguments to Native Views (in the Forms Project)

```
<ios:UITextField>
    <ios:UITextField.Font>
        <ios:UIFont x:FactoryMethod="FromName">
            <x:Arguments>
                <x:String>Papyrus</x:String>
                <x:Single>24</x:Single>
            </x:Arguments>
        </ios:UIFont>
    </ios:UITextField.Font>
</ios:UITextField>
```

In Android, the Typeface property of EditText expects an Android.Graphics. TypeFace object. Likewise, the factory method Create of TypeFace can be used to create an object by passing in a string argument with the font family name as well as providing the name of the enumeration value of TypefaceStyle. The arguments for a Serif font with an Italic font style are:

```
<x:Arguments><x:String>Serif</x:String>
    <androidGraphics:TypefaceStyle>Italic</
    androidGraphics:TypefaceStyle>
</x:Arguments>
```

To use TypeFace in the XAML, add the namepace Android.Graphics to the page, e.g.:

```
xmlns:androidGraphics="clr-namespace:Android.Graphics;assembly=Mono.
Android;
targetPlatform=Android"
```

Define an EditText with the size 24, a Serif font with an Italic font style, as shown in Listing 8-31.

Listing 8-31. Passing Arguments to Native Views (in the Forms Project)

```
<droid:EditText TextSize="24">
    <droid:EditText.Typeface>
        <androidGraphics:Typeface x:FactoryMethod="Create">
            <x:Arguments>
                <x:String>Serif</x:String>
                <androidGraphics:TypefaceStyle>Italic</android
                Graphics:TypefaceStyle>
            </x:Arguments>
        </androidGraphics:Typeface>
    </droid:EditText.Typeface>
</droid:EditText>
```

Figure 8-7 shows the result for both platforms.

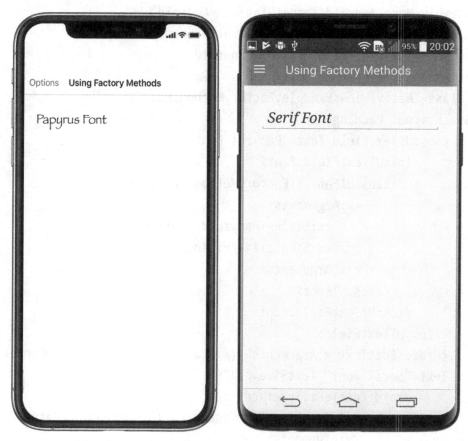

Figure 8-7. *Using Factory Methods*

CODE COMPLETE: Non-Default Constructors and Factory Methods

Listing 8-32 shows the complete XAML listing for declaring native views in the FactorMethodsPage.xaml in the solution NativeViewsExample.

Listing 8-32. Passing Arguments to Native Views (in the Forms Project)

```
<ContentPage Title="Using Factory Methods"
xmlns="http://xamarin.com/schemas/2014/forms"
xmlns:x="http://schemas.microsoft.com/winfx/2009/xaml"
xmlns:ios="clr-namespace:UIKit;assembly=Xamarin.iOS;targetPlatform=iOS"
xmlns:droid="clr-namespace:Android.Widget;assembly=Mono.Android;
targetPlatform=Android"
xmlns:androidGraphics="clr-namespace:Android.Graphics;
assembly=Mono.Android;targetPlatform=Android"
xmlns:formdroid="clr-namespace:Xamarin.Forms;
assembly=Xamarin.Forms.Platform.Android;
targetPlatform=Android"
x:Class="NativeViewsExample.FactoryMethodsPage">
<StackLayout Padding="30">
    <ios:UITextField Text="Papyrus Font">
        <ios:UITextField.Font>
            <ios:UIFont x:FactoryMethod="FromName">
                <x:Arguments>
                    <x:String>Papyrus</x:String>
                    <x:Single>24</x:Single>
                </x:Arguments>
            </ios:UIFont>
        </ios:UITextField.Font>
    </ios:UITextField>
    <droid:EditText x:Arguments="{x:Static formdroid:Forms.Context}"
    Text="Serif Font" TextSize="24">
        <droid:EditText.Typeface>
            <androidGraphics:Typeface x:FactoryMethod="Create">
                <x:Arguments>
```

```
            <x:String>Serif</x:String>
                <androidGraphics:TypefaceStyle>Italic
                </androidGraphics:TypefaceStyle>
            </x:Arguments>
        </androidGraphics:Typeface>
      </droid:EditText.Typeface>
    </droid:EditText>
  </StackLayout>
</ContentPage>
```

This covers the basics of declaring native views. Refer to Chapter 9 to create user interfaces that use data bindings to allow native views and Xamarin.Forms views to interact in harmony.

Summary

Custom renderers, effects, and native views complete the Xamarin.Forms picture, extending the reach of Xamarin.Forms deep into the platform-specific APIs using Xamarin.iOS and Xamarin.Android. The Xamarin.Forms abstraction provides immeasurable value as a cross-platform tool, but the platforms differ, and developers need a way to bridge the gap. These platform-specific techniques, custom renderer, effects, and native views are that bridge.

Now it's time for the foundation beneath all of our UI technique: the data. Let's explore data access and data binding in depth.

CHAPTER 9

Data Access with SQLite and Data Binding

Data access in Xamarin apps often involves a local database and a remote data server accessed via web services. Local data access can be handled in many ways with many products, both open source and proprietary, but the most popular mobile database is SQLite, which is built into iOS and Android. Data can be queried from a SQLite database and manually populated into the UI, but a more sophisticated approach is to use data binding to transfer information automatically between the UI and your data models. In this chapter, you'll learn how to employ SQLite in your Xamarin apps as well as how to use data binding in your Xamarin.Forms apps.

What Is SQLite?

SQLite is a C-based relational database designed in the spring of 2000 by D. Richard Hipp for use in US Navy guided-missile warships. It is now a standby database engine included in many operating systems, including iOS and Android. SQLite implements most of the SQL standard and has no standalone database server process but instead is linked as a library-accessed datastore, providing an on-demand, app-specific database.

You will typically use SQLite with Xamarin in one of two ways:

- *SQLite.NET*: Using the SQLite.NET object-relational mapping (ORM) to form CRUD transactions with `Insert`, `Get`, `Delete`, `Table`, and `Query`

- *Third-party MVVM libraries*: Data binding views to fields in the SQLite database by using a third-party MVVM framework such as MvvmCross or MVVM Light Toolkit

© Dan Hermes 2019
D. Hermes and N. Mazloumi, *Building Xamarin.Forms Mobile Apps Using XAML*,
https://doi.org/10.1007/978-1-4842-4030-4_9

Third-party MVVM libraries are beyond the scope of this book. SQLite-NET is a popular choice with developers.

What Is SQLite.NET?

To use C-based SQLite in C#, a binding library is required, which is why Frank Krueger founded SQLite.NET, an open-source SQLite library in C# founded upon Eric Sink's C# libraries. SQLite.NET is an object-relational mapping (ORM) library. ORMs allow you to manipulate database objects instead of working with fields and tables. SQLite.NET provides both options. We can do data-object manipulations by using methods such as Insert, Get, and Delete acting on data classes that map to tables. We can also use SQL to query a table with the Query method and use LINQ to operate on a table's contents using the Table method. SQLite using SQLite.NET gives you everything you need from a local mobile database to build consumer, business, and enterprise native mobile apps.

DATA STORAGE OPTIONS

Many successful mobile apps use non-database storage options. You can use file-based data storage in addition to or even instead of using a SQLite database for data storage. This can involve serialized data in XML or JSON, HTML, or comma-delimited fields in text files stored in local folders on the device. *Preferences* is another data storage option. iOS and Android provide ways to store preferences as key/value pairs typically used to record user settings or other small bits of data. This chapter focuses on local database access and does not explore these or other non-database data storage techniques, but I encourage you to do so in the Xamarin online docs. Also, Chapter 7 touches on disk storage techniques involving XML serialization in the "Managing State" section.

Data Binding

Keeping your UI in sync with your data model can be a lot of work if you do it by hand in code. Every time the user makes a change in the UI, you can implement event handlers (such as TextChanged) that update the contents of the data model, and each time the data model changes in code, you can notify the UI to refresh (by implementing PropertyChanged).

Data binding handles all of that for you by providing a framework to sync the views with a data model. Data binding manages views that need to modify the contents of their accompanying data model and the refresh of the UI from changes in the data model.

Data binding is built into Xamarin.Forms.

This real-time connection between the data layer and presentation layer is available to us in mobile development, because the presentation layer and data layer reside together on a single physical tier, the mobile device. Many similarities exist with the development of Windows Presentation Foundation (WPF) desktop apps. The design pattern used frequently in WPF development is *MVVM* (Model-View-ViewModel). MVVM and data binding combine the presentation and data layers to create a rich, responsive user experience.

Xamarin apps can use third-party data-binding libraries such as MvvmCross or MVVM Light. This chapter delves into cross-platform SQLite techniques and data binding using Xamarin.Forms.

Xamarin.Forms Data Binding

Xamarin.Forms has data binding built in, allowing you to bind views to models easily and elegantly. XAML is often used to implement data binding in Xamarin.Forms. Xamarin.Forms data binding supports the binding of one view to another as well as a view to a variable. This section focuses primarily on the most common business app use case: binding a view to a data model.

Xamarin.Forms data binding is done by binding a data source property to a target UI element property. The target property must be a bindable property (derived from `BindableObject`), which can be specified by using the view's `SetBinding` method. Bindable properties are indicated in the online Xamarin.Forms API documentation for each class. The data source can be a variable or data model class property and may be set by using the `BindingContext` and `Binding.Path` property on a page or view.

The `Binding` property for view fields is `Path`, but the `"Path="` part of the markup extension can be omitted if the path is the first item in the `Binding` markup extension. This

```
<Entry HorizontalOptions="FillAndExpand" Text="{Binding Title}" />
```

is the same as

```
<Entry HorizontalOptions="FillAndExpand" Text="{Binding Path=Title}" />
```

Path is frequently omitted for convenience, so we use the shorthand approach with no explicit Path throughout this book.

It's worth noting that data binding can be done manually by using a view's PropertyChanged or TextChanged event to synchronize with the source.

However, Xamarin.Forms data binding is largely automatic after the setup is complete. You need to create and configure the target view and pair it with a source. You also need to prepare that source by implementing the INotifyPropertyChanged interface to make changes to that source observable via PropertyChanged event handlers. Xamarin.Forms lays in the remaining event handlers under the covers to carry out the transfer of data to and from the source and target. The following examples focus on this automatic approach, using the BindingContext property and SetBinding method.

Trivial data binding involves views that contain initial values from the data model (source), and changes to the UI (target) are reflected in the model. However, no refresh of the UI occurs to reflect changes to the data model. Refreshing of the UI requires *nontrivial data binding*, covered later, in "Using INotifyPropertyChanged."

Let's walk through a few examples of automatic data binding in Xamarin.Forms. You will begin with a trivial example, in which the UI updates a data model. Next you'll proceed into nontrivial examples, in which changes to the data model are refreshed in the view. You'll explore the MVVM design pattern, wrapping your data model in a view model (or ViewModel). Then you will revisit data-bound lists, except you will make them editable instead of read-only.

In trivial, automatic data binding, changes to the UI are reflected in the data model in real time. Here is a common way (but not the only way) to approach trivial data binding in C#:

1. Specify the source data model by using the BindingContext page (or view) property in C#:

    ```
    this.BindingContext = listItem;
    ```

2. Pair the source property with the target view property by using the SetBinding method in XAML:

    ```
    <Entry Text="{Binding Title}"/>
    ```

These two steps bind the Entry view to the Title property of the Item model (listItem is an instance of Item).

Nontrivial data binding, in which the target must be refreshed to reflect changes made to the contents of the source in real time, requires an implementation of the INotifyPropertyChanged interface's observer event called PropertyChanged, which fires when the view model detects a change to the data (in a property's Set accessor method).

Tip   Do you want third-party options for binding? Check out the third-party MVVM data-binding libraries such as MvvmCross, MVVM Light, or ReactiveUI.

Let's look at a trivial Xamarin.Forms data-binding example.

Binding to a Data Model

Using the two-step data-binding approach in the preceding section, bind an Entry view to the Title property of a data model called Item. This is trivial binding: changes to the view result in an update to the data model.

Create a new C# class called Item and build a data model called Item with a Title and Description string property, as shown in Listing 9-1.

Listing 9-1. Item Data Model in Item.cs

```
public class Item
{
    public string Title { get; set; }
    public string Description { get; set; }
}
```

Create a XAML page called ItemPage and, in the C# ContentPage constructor, instantiate and populate an Item (Listing 9-2). Set the BindingContext property of the page to the item object.

Listing 9-2. Bind a View to a Model in ItemPage.xaml.cs

```
public ItemPage ()
{
    InitializeComponent ();
    item = new Item { Title = "First", Description = "1st item" };
    this.BindingContext = item;
}
```

Create the Entry view, and then bind the Text property to the Title property in Item, as shown in Listing 9-3.

Listing 9-3. Bind a View to a Model in ItemPage.xaml

```
<ContentPage Title="Trivial Data Binding" xmlns="http://xamarin.com/
schemas/2014/forms" xmlns:x="http://schemas.microsoft.com/winfx/2009/
xaml" x:Class="DataBindingExamples.ItemPage">
    <ContentPage.Content>
        <StackLayout>
            <Entry HorizontalOptions="FillAndExpand" Text="{Binding
                Title}" />
        </StackLayout>
    </ContentPage.Content>
</ContentPage>
```

BindingContext can be set at the page or view level. In most cases, the page-level property will suffice, but be certain to set BindingContext at the view level if you are using more than one source. In MVVM apps, a single source (the ViewModel) is typical. More on this in a moment.

Note   Setting BindingContext to a ViewModel can lead to a mature data-binding architecture.

Any value that you type into the Entry view is populated into the item.Title property because of the binding. Prove this by adding a button view to the StackLayout with an event handler that shows the value of the item object, as shown in Listing 9-3.

Listing 9-4. Button Click Displays the Value of the Title Property

```
<StackLayout>
    <Entry HorizontalOptions="FillAndExpand" Text="{Binding Title}" />
    <Button Text="Display Item Value" FontSize="Large"
    HorizontalOptions="Center" VerticalOptions="Fill"
    Clicked="ButtonClicked" />
</StackLayout>
public async void ButtonClicked(object sender, EventArgs args)
{
```

```
    await DisplayAlert("Item Object", "Title property:" +  item.Title.
    ToString(), "OK");
}
```

Fire up the app and you'll see your Entry view with data prepopulated (Figure 9-1).

Figure 9-1. *Trivial data binding populates the target with an initial source value*

Change the entry value to something else, and click the button to see the data binding in action, as shown in Figure 9-2.

Figure 9-2. *The data-bound Entry view changes the Item property when edited*

The data model was automatically updated by the user's change to the Entry view's Text property.

The BindingContext used here is at the page level. This could just as easily have been set at the view level:

```
titleEntry.BindingContext = item;
```

On pages with multiple views that require separate bindings, set BindingContext at the view level.

Tip   If you want to see the limitations of trivial binding firsthand (not using INotifyPropertyChanged), put the following line of code into your button. Clicked event. When you click the button, you'll see that the UI is *not* updated by this change to the data model.

```
item.Title = "Trivial binding";
```

All of the previous examples are trivial data-binding examples; the data model and variables will reflect changes to the UI. In order for the UI to be refreshed from the data model, you will need to use the INotifyPropertyChanged interface to implement nontrivial data binding.

Using INotifyPropertyChanged

INotifyPropertyChanged is a .NET interface used to notify binding clients that a property value has changed. Use INotifyPropertyChanged when your data-bound UI must refresh to reflect changes to the data model in real time (above and beyond just displaying the initial data in the UI).

Here is the definition of the INotifyPropertyChanged interface:

```
public interface INotifyPropertyChanged
{
    event PropertyChangedEventHandler PropertyChanged;
}
```

Implement INotifyPropertyChanged in a view model (or ViewModel), a class built to serve data to a particular screen. The INotifyPropertyChanged interface is found in the System.ComponentModel namespace, and the CallerMemberName attribute resides in the System.Runtime.CompilerServices namespace, so remember to add them to your class:

```
using System.ComponentModel;
using System.Runtime.CompilerServices;
```

Implement INotifyPropertyChanged to create a simple view model with one property called Title, as shown in Listing 9-4. The Set accessor on the Title property invokes the OnPropertyChanged event to notify the UI of a data change so it can refresh.

Listing 9-4. INotifyPropertyChanged Implementation in a View Model in TitleViewModel.cs

```
public class TitleViewModel : INotifyPropertyChanged
{
    public event PropertyChangedEventHandler PropertyChanged;
    String title;

    public string Title
    {
        set
        {
            if (!value.Equals(title, StringComparison.Ordinal))
            {
                title = value;
                OnPropertyChanged("Title");
            }
        }
        get
        {
            return title;
        }
    }
```

```
void OnPropertyChanged([CallerMemberName] string property
Name = null)
{
    var handler = PropertyChanged;
    if (handler != null)
    {
        handler(this, new PropertyChangedEventArgs(propertyName));
    }
}
}
```

When the `Title` property is set, a call is made to the `OnPropertyChanged` event to fire, with the calling property passed in by the `[CallerMemberName]` attribute. The `PropertyChangedEventHandler` event is the Xamarin.Forms mechanism for notifying the view that is bound to that property to refresh and reflect the updated data model.

Note that this simplified approach does not use the `Item` data model. You'll do that soon.

Back in your `ContentPage`, update the binding:

```
var titleViewModel = new TitleViewModel();
titleViewModel.Title = "First";
this.BindingContext = titleViewModel;
```

In the `Entry` declaration, since the property name (`Title`) hasn't changed, the `Text` property's binding remains the same as the previous example.

```
<Entry HorizontalOptions="FillAndExpand" Text="{Binding Title}" />
```

In your `buttonDisplay.Clicked` event, change the display property to `titleViewModel.Title`.

```
public async void DisplayButtonClicked(object sender, EventArgs args)
{
    await DisplayAlert("Item Object", "Title property:" +
    titleViewModel.Title, "OK");
}
```

Add a new button to click when you're ready to update your data model and witness nontrivial data binding.

```
<Button Text="Update the Data Model" FontSize="Large" Horizontal
Options="Center" VerticalOptions="Fill" Clicked="UpdateButtonClicked" />
```

Handle the UpdateButtonClicked event to modify the titleViewModel's Title property and displaying the updated value:

```
public async void UpdateButtonClicked(object sender, EventArgs args)
{
    titleViewModel.Title = "Data Model Updated";
    await DisplayAlert("Item Object", "Title property:" +
    titleViewModel.Title, "OK");
}
```

Figure 9-3 shows the updated ContentPage.

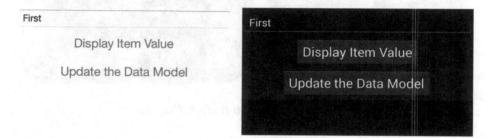

Figure 9-3. *ContentPage for nontrivial data binding*

Click buttonUpdate to change the Title property and see that change propagated back into the Entry view (Figure 9-4). This is nontrivial binding.

Figure 9-4. *The Entry view has refreshed to match the model*

CODE COMPLETE: Using INotifyPropertyChanged

Listings 9-5 and 9-6 are the complete code for the INotifyPropertyChanged
implementation against TitleViewModel.

Listing 9-5. ItemPageUsingTitleViewModel.xaml

```
<?xml version="1.0" encoding="UTF-8"?>
<ContentPage xmlns="http://xamarin.com/schemas/2014/forms" xmlns:x="http://
schemas.microsoft.com/winfx/2009/xaml" x:Class="DataBindingExamples.
ItemPageUsingTitleViewModel">
    <ContentPage.Content>
    <StackLayout>
```

```
        <Entry HorizontalOptions="FillAndExpand" Text="{Binding Title}" />
        <Button Text="Display Item Value" FontSize="Large" Horizontal
        Options="Center" VerticalOptions="Fill" Clicked="Display
        ButtonClicked" />
        <Button Text="Update the Data Model" FontSize="Large" Horizontal
        Options="Center" VerticalOptions="Fill" Clicked="UpdateButton
        Clicked" />
    </StackLayout>
    </ContentPage.Content>
</ContentPage>
```

Listing 9-6. ItemPageUsingTitleViewModel.xaml.cs

```
public partial class ItemPageUsingTitleViewModel : ContentPage
{
    TitleViewModel titleViewModel;

    public ItemPageUsingTitleViewModel ()
    {
        InitializeComponent ();

        titleViewModel = new TitleViewModel ();
        titleViewModel.Title = "First";
        this.BindingContext = titleViewModel;
    }

    public async void DisplayButtonClicked(object sender, EventArgs args)
    {
        await DisplayAlert("Item Object", "Title property:" + titleView
        Model.Title.ToString(), "OK");
    }

    public async void UpdateButtonClicked(object sender, EventArgs args)
    {
        titleViewModel.Title = "Data Model Updated";
        await DisplayAlert("Item Object", "Title property:" + titleView
        Model.Title.ToString(), "OK");
    }
}
```

Tip Avoid repeating boilerplate `PropertyChanged` code by creating a `BindableBase` class that implements `INotifyPropertyChanged`. Then you can subclass `BindableBase` in your models or view models to make them ready for nontrivial binding.

```
public abstract class BindableBase :
INotifyPropertyChanged
{
    public event PropertyChangedEventHandler
    PropertyChanged;
    void OnPropertyChanged([CallerMemberName] string
    propertyName = null)
    {
        var handler = PropertyChanged;
        if (handler != null)
        {
            handler(this, new PropertyChangedEventArgs
            (propertyName));
        }
    }
}
```

With your implementation of `INotifyPropertyChanged`, your app can now notify the UI when data has changed, and Xamarin.Forms will refresh the UI. By creating a class that serves data to a particular view (`TitleViewModel`), you have just created a view model.

Understanding ViewModels and MVVM

A ViewModel (the VM in MVVM) is a class built to serve data to a particular screen by using one or more models (the M in MVVM, or data models). The ViewModel is decorated with view-specific properties and bound to the view (the V in MVVM, referring to the presentation layer, or UI, not to be confused with a Xamarin.Forms `View` class). A ViewModel is like a data model except that it is customized to a particular view (or screen) by using helper classes and handler events necessary to populate the data on that page or manage changes to the data model. In a traditional MVVM app, you create a view model for each view (screen), imbuing your view model with the constructors and helper methods needed to serve up and save data on each screen.

MVVM apps typically use data models (not just a few variables added as properties to a view model). This requires wrapping the data models within the view models with the notion that views should not use models directly but should interact only with view models.

MVVM: WHAT'S THE BIG DEAL?

What's the big deal with MVVM and why use it? MVVM provides true separation between the View and Model which means decoupled development where your model doesn't get perverted by UI needs and the View page doesn't sport a bunch of data access and data processing code.

MVVM is lauded for its structure, testability, and ability to adapt to different presentation layers. Use ViewModel to aggregate data models and business logic spread throughout separate classes/libraries to facilitate a more succinct and flexible interface for the View.

Binding to ViewModels and Data Models

ViewModels can implement INotifyPropertyChanged, as discussed earlier, but data models can also implement INotifyPropertyChanged. These are the two standard approaches for implementing INotifyPropertyChanged for nontrivial data binding, in order of popularity. There are heated arguments for why one or the other is the only way to do things, but I'll show you both ways and let you decide. I'll also show a third way that avoids some of the problems of the other two. Here are the three approaches I'll cover:

- *Create a view model that implements INotifyPropertyChanged.*
  Implement from INotifyPropertyChanged and encapsulate the necessary variables and data models within your view model class, and, within each editable property Set accessor, raise the OnPropertyChanged event. This approach is strict MVVM.

- *Implement INotifyPropertyChanged in your data model.* Every time you use your model in a data-binding context, it will be ready for nontrivial binding and provide notifications to the bound UI via its OnPropertyChanged events.

- *Wrap your data model in an observable class.* More on this in a moment.

The first two approaches are functionally similar but architecturally different.

The first approach, creating a view model that implements INotifyPropertyChanged, means including an instance of the data model in the view model and wrapping the top-level model class as a property as well as all of the data model's properties that must be exposed in the view model. This gives complete control to the view for instantiating, assigning, and changing the encapsulated data model and all of its relevant properties. If the view model implements INotifyPropertyChanged, and OnPropertyChanged is called in the Set method of each public property, this class can provide nontrivial binding. (See Listing 9-7.)

The second approach to implementing INotifyPropertyChanged happens in your data model even before you use it in the view model. See Listing 9-8 for an example of implementing INotifyPropertyChanged in the Item class to create an observable collection of items. For MVVM apps, this approach still requires the extra step of embedding the resulting data model in a view model.

Some developers don't like the first approach because it can lead to code duplication with multiple INotifyPropertyChanged implementations of the same properties in different view models, and some developers don't like the second approach because it clutters up the data model and increases the number of notifications sent, which can impact performance for large data objects.

A *third* approach avoids both of those problems, and that is to wrap your data model in a class that implements INotifyPropertyChanged to make it observable (at the cost of creating yet another subclass). This is done for us in .NET for classes such as ObservableCollection, and you'll do it in a moment for your Item model to create an ObservableItem. It's a little extra work but keeps your models clean. We'll get to the third approach in the section "Binding an Editable ListView," in Listing 9-11.

Here are examples of each of the first two approaches:

Create a ViewModel That Implements INotifyPropertyChanged

Implement INotifyPropertyChanged in your ViewModel by using an encapsulated data model for a straightforward MVVM approach.

Create a view model based on the Item data model, as shown in Listing 9-7. It's basically the same as the TitleViewModel view model in Listing 9-4 except that an Item class is instantiated and used to hold the Title property value instead of a string. (This is an architectural change, not a functional one.)

Listing 9-7. View Model Based on the Item Data Model (ItemViewModel.cs)

```
class ItemViewModel : INotifyPropertyChanged
{
    public event PropertyChangedEventHandler PropertyChanged;

    Item item;

    public ItemViewModel ()
    {
        item = new Item();
    }

    public string Title
    {
        get
        {
            return item.Title;
        }
        set
        {
            if (!value.Equals(item.Title, StringComparison.Ordinal))
            {
                item.Title = value;
                OnPropertyChanged("Title");
            }
        }
    }
}
```

```
    void OnPropertyChanged([CallerMemberName] string propertyName = null)
    {
        var handler = PropertyChanged;
        if (handler != null)
        {
            handler(this, new PropertyChangedEventArgs(propertyName));
        }
    }
}
```

Note that you didn't wrap the Description property, since that was not needed by the view in this case. View models typically contain only what is needed by their view.

Implement the view model as before by using ItemViewModel:

```
var itemViewModel = new ItemViewModel();
itemViewModel.Title = "First";
this.BindingContext = itemViewModel;
```

Even the Entry view is bound the same way as before:

```
<Entry HorizontalOptions="FillAndExpand" Text="{Binding Title}" />
```

The rest of the ContentPage is the same as the previous example ItemPageUsingTitleViewModel, in Listing 9-5, with renaming to use itemViewModel instead of titleViewModel. See the downloadable code ItemPageUsingItemViewModel. xaml.cs for details.

The functionality of the app is exactly the same as the previous example except that instead of using the Title string variable, you're using the Item data model, which is a more real-world implementation (and MVVM).

Now for the second approach to INotifyPropertyChanged.

Implement INotifyPropertyChanged in Your Data Model

INotifyPropertyChanged can be implemented in your data model instead of in your view model. This data model can then be bound directly to the view, as in the following example, or you can include the data model in a view model in an MVVM app.

Create a class called ItemBindable.cs, as shown in Listing 9-8. Implementing the OnPropertyChanged event and calling it in the Set method of each property, Title and Description, ensures that changes to the list data are reflected in the UI in real time.

Listing 9-8. Implementing INotifyPropertyChanged in a Data Model

```
class ItemBindable: INotifyPropertyChanged
{
    public event PropertyChangedEventHandler PropertyChanged;

    string title;
    string description;

    public string Title
    {
        set
        {
            if (!value.Equals(title, StringComparison.Ordinal))
            {
                title = value;
                OnPropertyChanged("Title");
            }
        }
        get
        {
            return title;
        }
    }

    public string Description
    {
        set
        {
            if (!value.Equals(description, StringComparison.Ordinal))
            {
                description = value;
                OnPropertyChanged("Description");
            }
        }
```

```
            }
        get
        {
            return description;
        }
    }

    void OnPropertyChanged([CallerMemberName] string propertyName = null)
    {
        var handler = PropertyChanged;
        if (handler != null)
        {
            handler(this, new PropertyChangedEventArgs(propertyName));
        }
    }
}
```

This `ItemBindable` class can now be implemented to bind its properties to any view:

```
var itemBindable = new ItemBindable();
itemBindable.Title = "First";
this.BindingContext = itemBindable;
```

Use the `Entry` view binding once again with the `Title` property:

```
<Entry HorizontalOptions="FillAndExpand" Text="{Binding Title}" />
```

This direct use of the model in the view (which I've used to simplify the demonstration) is not consistent with the MVVM pattern, which encourages a separation between the model and the view. Include `ItemBindable` within a view model to utilize the MVVM pattern.

Those are some techniques for building view models and data models for nontrivial, two-way binding in Xamarin.Forms. Now let's explore data binding as it applies to lists.

Binding a Read-Only ListView

Binding to a `ListView` was covered extensively in Chapter 6, but we did only trivial, read-only binding. That means that the initial values of the data model are displayed in the list for viewing or selection, but no changes to the UI or model take place. Nontrivial, editable list binding means that the initial values of the data model are displayed in the list, and controls are provided to allow the user to add or delete rows or change row properties displayed in the list.

I'll begin with a review of trivial binding to a ListView before moving on to nontrivial binding.

In the ContentPage's constructor, instantiate and populate the data model as shown in Listing 9-9. Assigning the model to the list's ItemsSource property is the equivalent of setting BindingContext.

Listing 9-9. Trivial, Read-Only ListView Binding from Listing 6-5 in Chapter 6

```
public partial class ListViewDataModel : ContentPage
{
    public ListViewDataModel()
    {
        InitializeComponent();
        List<ListItem> ListItems = new List<ListItem>
        {
            new ListItem {Title = "First", Description="1st item"},
            new ListItem {Title = "Second", Description="2nd item"},
            new ListItem {Title = "Third", Description="3rd item"}
        };
        DataModelList.ItemsSource = ListItems;
    }

    async void ListViewItemTapped (object sender, ItemTappedEventArgs e)
    {
        ListItem item = (ListItem)e.Item;
        await DisplayAlert("Tapped", item.Title + " was selected.", "OK");
        ((ListView)sender).SelectedItem = null;
    }

    public class ListItem
    {
        public string Title { get; set; }
        public string Description { get; set; }
    }
}
```

Tip   This example, `ListViewDataModel`, is a `ListView` using a `DataModel` and is not a data model or a view model. Some of the main pages and filenames in this chapter are meant to convey the purpose of the example rather than the class.

In the XAML, create an `ItemTemplate` in the `ListView` with a `DataTemplate` and bind `Title` and `Description` properties in your `TextCell` as shown in Listing 9-10.

Listing 9-10. XAML for Trivial, Read-Only ListView Binding from Listing 6-4 in Chapter 6

```
<?xml version="1.0" encoding="UTF-8"?>
<ContentPage xmlns="http://xamarin.com/schemas/2014/forms" xmlns:x="http://
schemas.microsoft.com/winfx/2009/xaml" x:Class="ListViewExample.Xaml.
ListViewDataModel">
    <ContentPage.Padding>
        <OnPlatform x:TypeArguments="Thickness">

            <On Platform="Android">10,0,10,5</On>

            <On Platform="iOS">10,20,10,5</On>

    </OnPlatform></ContentPage.Padding>
    </ContentPage.Padding>
    <ListView x:Name="DataModelList" ItemTapped="ListViewItemTapped" >
        <ListView.ItemTemplate>
            <DataTemplate>
                <TextCell Text="{Binding Title}" Detail="{Binding
                Description}"/>
            </DataTemplate>
        </ListView.ItemTemplate>
    </ListView>
</ContentPage>
```

This approach works well for read-only, selectable lists (and can even be extended to include editing of data model properties in the list UI, such as `Entry` views, though that is beyond the scope of this book). If you want to read more about building and customizing read-only lists by using Xamarin.Forms, turn to the beginning of Chapter 6.

If your list needs to change dynamically, with rows added or deleted or properties changed in real time in the code, then nontrivial data binding may be required.

Binding an Editable ListView

The standard ways that a user can edit a list are to add or delete list rows, or modify properties of list rows. These types of list edits require nontrivial data binding, when list rows are added or deleted from an array or collection, or when changes to list properties take place in code. We need those data model changes to be reflected in the UI.

Nontrivial list binding requires the implementation of an INotify interface to notify the UI to refresh when changes to the model take place. There are two ways to do this: using a manual implementation of INotifyPropertyChanged and using an ObservableCollection. ObservableCollection *already* implements the INotifyCollectionChanged interface. Which approach you use (either or both) should depend on the types of changes to the list that you want to reflect in the list UI.

Here are the two main list-editing scenarios and a standard way to handle them:

- *Adding and deleting rows*: Use an ObservableCollection as the list data source.

- *Editing properties in the ListView*: Create a view model implementing INotifyPropertyChanged that exposes the editable properties in the list data model (such as Title).

Tip   If you need to replace the entire list, you'll likely need to rebind the list by reassigning ItemsSource to get the UI to refresh.

Let's begin with adding and deleting rows.

Adding and Deleting Rows

Nontrivial data binding while adding and deleting rows from ListView can be handled using ObservableCollection, which has a built-in implementation of INotifyCollectionChanged. Any class, such as ListView, that is bound to an ObservableCollection will automatically install a handler for the CollectionChanged event.

Using ObservableCollection as the bound data type for ListItem ensures that changes to the list rows are reflected in the UI in real time.

Create and populate ObservableCollection, as shown in Listing 9-11. Declare BindingContext instead of ItemsSource this time, just to show they're interchangeable, although you'll also need to set the ListView's ItemsSource in the XAML in just a moment.

Listing 9-11. List Binding Using an ObservableCollection (ListObservablePage.cs)

```
items = new ObservableCollection<Item> {
    new Item {Title = "First", Description="1st item"},
    new Item {Title = "Second", Description="2nd item"},
    new Item {Title = "Third", Description="3rd item"}
};

this.BindingContext = items;
```

Earlier in ContentPage, I declared items in class scope so I can use it across methods in the class:

```
ObservableCollection<Item> items;
```

In the ListView, assign the ItemsSource to "{Binding .}". This defaults to whatever the BindingContext is set to, which is the items collection in this case.

```
<ListView ItemsSource="{Binding .}" ItemTapped="ListItemTapped" >
```

The ListView's ItemTemplate implementation is the same as in the previous example in Listing 9-10:

```
<TextCell Text="{Binding Title}" Detail="{Binding Description}"/>
```

The complete code can be found in the downloadable code file ListObservablePage.cs.

Test this approach by adding a button that adds or deletes rows in the ObservableCollection called items, and you'll see your model changes reflected immediately in the list UI.

```
items.RemoveAt(0);
```

Upon execution of our RemoveAt method, the first list row is immediately deleted in the UI, as shown in Figure 9-5. Note that without an items.Count > 0 check, our simple demo code can break with multiple deletes.

Figure 9-5. *The deleted first item disappears from the list*

This approach does not use a view model, so it is not an MVVM implementation. We'll get serious about MVVM for editable lists soon.

Tip   Adding and deleting list rows by using ObservableCollection works especially well with Context Actions, the Xamarin.Forms approach for providing a Delete and/or More button on each list row. Turn to Chapter 6 for more on Context Actions.

An ObservableCollection tracks only the addition or removal of rows. Reflecting changes to properties within those rows is another matter.

Editing Properties

Editing list properties in code and reflecting those changes in the list UI can be handled in any of the three ways discussed earlier, binding the list to one of the following:

- Create a view model that implements INotifyPropertyChanged.

- Implement INotifyPropertyChanged in your data model.

- Wrap your data model in a class that implements INotifyPropertyChanged.

The first approach is a popular choice, but since you already saw that earlier in Listing 9-7, and the second approach in Listing 9-8, here you'll use the third approach: wrapping your data model in an observable item class using INotifyPropertyChanged. Then bind this observable class to your list (directly or via a view model).

Create a class called ObservableItem.cs, as shown in Listing 9-12. Implementing the OnPropertyChanged event and calling it in the Set method of ListItem properties ensures that changes to the list data are reflected in the UI in real time. Note that this class alone isn't MVVM unless you encapsulate it in a view model, which you'll do in a moment.

Listing 9-12. Wrap Your Data Model in an Observable Class (ObservableItem.cs)

```
class ObservableItem: INotifyPropertyChanged
{
    public event PropertyChangedEventHandler PropertyChanged;
    Item item;

    public ObservableItem()
    {
        item = new Item();
    }

    public string Title
    {
        set
        {
            if (!value.Equals(item.Title, StringComparison.Ordinal))
            {
                item.Title = value;
                OnPropertyChanged("Title");
            }
        }
        get
        {
            return item.Title;
        }
    }

    public string Description
    {
        set
        {
```

```
            if (!value.Equals(item.Description, StringComparison.Ordinal))
            {
                item.Description = value;
                OnPropertyChanged("Description");
            }
        }
        get
        {
            return item.Description;
        }
    }
    void OnPropertyChanged([CallerMemberName] string propertyName = null)
    {
        var handler = PropertyChanged;
        if (handler != null)
        {
            handler(this, new PropertyChangedEventArgs(propertyName));
        }
    }
}
```

This ObservableItem class can now be implemented to create a nontrivial data-bound list:

```
items = new List<ObservableItem> {
    new ObservableItem {Title = "First", Description="1st item"},
    new ObservableItem {Title = "Second", Description="2nd item"},
    new ObservableItem {Title = "Third", Description="3rd item"}
};
```

```
this.BindingContext = items;
```

Again, I declared items in the class scope for use in multiple methods:

```
ObservableCollection<Item> items;
```

In the ListView as before, assign the ItemsSource to "{Binding .}".

```
<ListView ItemsSource="{Binding .}" ItemTapped="ListItemTapped" >
```

The `ListView`'s `ItemTemplate` implementation is the same as in the (two) previous examples covered in Listing 9-10:

```
<ListView.ItemTemplate>
    <DataTemplate>
        <TextCell Text="{Binding Title}" Detail="{Binding
        Description}"/>
    </DataTemplate>
</ListView.ItemTemplate>
```

See the downloadable file `ListPropertiesPage.xaml.cs` for the complete `ListView` code listing.

Changes to any of the properties in code will be reflected in the list UI in real time. You can see this for yourself by creating a button or Context Action that edits a property in the items list—the `Title`, for example:

```
items[0].Title = "First Edited";
```

Upon execution of this single statement, the first list row is immediately updated in the UI, as shown in Figure 9-6. That's a bound list with an observable data model!

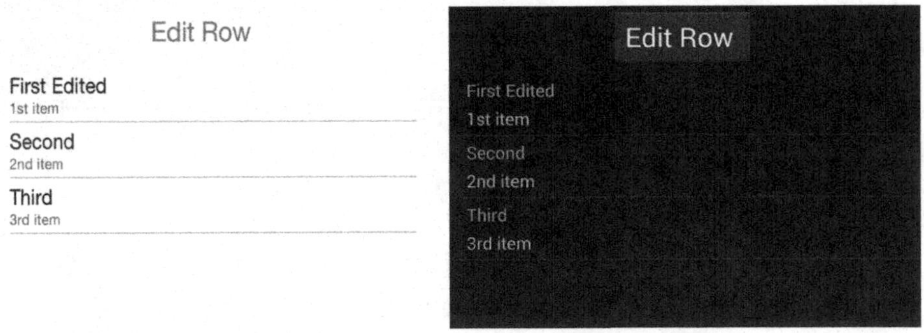

Figure 9-6. *The first row is edited in code, and the UI is refreshed automatically*

Note   If editable views in your list rows, such as `Entry` views, are bound to properties in your data model, then trivial data binding described earlier may be sufficient, and this `INotifyPropertyChanged` approach may not be needed.

Binding `List<ObservableItem>` directly to the list didn't use a view model either, so it's still not MVVM.

Next you will see how to use the observable item class in tandem with the observable collection to create a view model for an editable list.

Binding to a View Model

Building MVVM apps requires some attention to structure as you build your view models. When using MVVM, it's an antipattern to implement data models directly in your view. You'll need to create a view model, create your data models, and then employ your models in your view model to bind them to your editable list.

Create a ListViewModel class that includes all the features in the previous list-binding examples. The Items property is an ObservableCollection, so the UI can reflect rows that are added or deleted, and the base item class is ObservableItem, so property changes can also be reflected in the list UI. See Listing 9-11.

Note   Listing 9-13 is an unusual example of a view model, as there is no explicit implementation of INotifyPropertyChanged. INotifyPropertyChanged was already implemented in all the encapsulated models: ObservableCollection and ObservableItem. Additional implementation of INotifyPropertyChanged in this view model would be redundant or extraneous.

Listing 9-13. ListViewModel for an Editable List in ListViewModel.cs

```
class ListViewModel
{
    ObservableCollection<ObservableItem> items;

    public ListViewModel()
    {
        items = new ObservableCollection<ObservableItem> {
        new ObservableItem {Title = "First", Description="1st item"},
        new ObservableItem {Title = "Second", Description="2nd item"},
        new ObservableItem {Title = "Third", Description="3rd item"}
        };
    }
```

```
    public ObservableCollection<ObservableItem> Items
    {
        set
        {
            if ( value != items)
            {
                items = value;
            }
        }
        get
        {
            return items;
        }
    }
}
```

Bind the Items property in your view model to your list source:

```
var items = new ListViewModel();
this.BindingContext = items.Items;
```

In the ListView as before, assign the ItemsSource property to "{Binding .}".

```
<ListView ItemsSource="{Binding .}" ItemTapped="ListItemTapped" >
```

The ListView's ItemTemplate implementation is the same as in the (two) previous examples covered in Listing 9-10:

```
<ListView.ItemTemplate>
    <DataTemplate>
        <TextCell Text="{Binding Title}" Detail="{Binding
        Description}"/>
    </DataTemplate>
</ListView.ItemTemplate>
```

And *that* is a nontrivial, fully editable list using MVVM. Add and delete rows from the list, edit properties in code, and all will be reflected in the list UI in real time.

Create a ContentPage demo app that includes row editing, property editing, and replacing the entire list. Bind it to your ListViewModel. Figure 9-7 shows how this listing data-binding demo app might look.

Figure 9-7.   *Editable ListView data binding to a view model*

This basic example of editable list binding is for demo purposes only. For a professional-looking UI, consider using Context Actions, the Xamarin.Forms approach to providing a Delete and/or More button on each list row. Turn to Chapter 5 for more on Context Actions.

See the ContentPage for this example, called ListPageUsingListViewModel.cs, in Listing 9-14.

Tip   Replacing the entire list requires the list to be rebound (this example is a Replace method in the ListViewModel).

```
public void Replace()
{
    Items = new ObservableCollection<ObservableItem> {
        new ObservableItem {Title = "Primero",
        Description="First"},
        new ObservableItem {Title = "Segundo",
        Description="Second"},
        new ObservableItem {Title = "Tercero",
        Description="Third"}
    };
}
```

CODE COMPLETE: Binding an Editable ListView

Listings 9-14 and 9-15 show the complete ListView implementation that binds to the view model ListViewModel in Listing 9-13. This example demonstrates row editing, property editing, and replacing the entire list. It's a nontrivial, fully editable list using MVVM.

Listing 9-14.   ListPageUsingListViewModel.xaml

```
<?xml version="1.0" encoding="UTF-8"?>
<ContentPage xmlns="http://xamarin.com/schemas/2014/forms" xmlns:x="http://
schemas.microsoft.com/winfx/2009/xaml" x:Class="DataBindingExamples.
ListPageUsingListViewModel">
    <ContentPage.Content>
        <StackLayout>
            <Button Text="Edit Row" FontSize="Large" HorizontalOptions=
            "Center" VerticalOptions="Fill" Clicked="EditClicked" />
            <Button Text="Delete Row" FontSize="Large" HorizontalOptions=
            "Center" VerticalOptions="Fill" Clicked="DeleteClicked" />
```

```
        <Button Text="Replace List" FontSize="Large" HorizontalOptions=
        "Center" VerticalOptions="Fill" Clicked="ReplaceClicked" />
        <ListView ItemsSource="{Binding .}" ItemTapped="ListItemTapped" >
            <ListView.ItemTemplate>
                <DataTemplate>
                    <TextCell Text="{Binding Title}" Detail="{Binding
                    Description}"/>
                </DataTemplate>
            </ListView.ItemTemplate>
        </ListView>
    </StackLayout>
    </ContentPage.Content>
</ContentPage>
```

Tip   A reminder that the following Listing 9-15 is not the ViewModel but merely has ViewModel in the name to define the purpose of the example. ListViewModel in Listing 9-13 is the ViewModel.

Listing 9-15. ListPageUsingListViewModel.xaml.cs

```
public partial class ListPageUsingListViewModel : ContentPage
{
    ListViewModel items;

    public ListPageUsingListViewModel ()
    {
        InitializeComponent ();

        items = new ListViewModel();
        this.BindingContext = items.Items;
    }

    public async void EditClicked(object sender, EventArgs e) {
        items.Items[0].Title = "First Edited";
        await DisplayAlert("Item Object", "First row edited", "OK");
    }
```

```
    public async void DeleteClicked(object sender, EventArgs e) {
        items.Items.RemoveAt(0);
        await DisplayAlert("Delete", "Row deleted", "OK");
    }

    public async void ReplaceClicked(object sender, EventArgs e) {
        items.Replace();
        await DisplayAlert("Replace", "List replaced con Español", "OK");
        this.BindingContext = items.Items;
    }

    public async void ListItemTapped(object sender, ItemTappedEventArgs e)
    {
        ObservableItem item = (ObservableItem)e.Item;
        await DisplayAlert("Tapped", item.Title.ToString() + " was
        selected.", "OK");
        ((ListView)sender).SelectedItem = null;
    }

}
```

The "Replace List" Button invokes Replace(), a method added to ListViewModel
that is shown in the previous tip and is viewable in the downloadable code
ListViewModel.cs. Replace() swaps out the list with Spanish translations of the row
titles before the list is rebound to reflect the changes.

Views can also be bound to other views.

Binding a View to Another View

The focus of this book is data-driven applications, which means binding views to models
and view models. However, views can be bound to one another. A slider can be bound to
a label. A switch can be bound to an entry view, and so forth.

The target of a data binding must be backed by a BindableProperty object, and
most Xamarin.Forms views have many properties that fit this requirement. Explore
the Xamarin API documentation to learn about these. Many view properties are also
bindable as sources.

Single views are easily bound, as each view must have one BindingContext. Multiple views require mapping using the BindingModes OneWayToSource and TwoWay, which are beyond the scope of this book. Refer to the Xamarin online docs for details.

String Formatting

Format your data using the StringFormat property on bound data fields, just like .NET always has. Apply a string format template using System.String.Format() to your value before it is passed to the target property. C# has a lot of useful format templates for numbers and dates. We can pretty print the result of System.DateTime.Now using <Label Text="{Binding .,Source={x:Static sys:DateTime.Now},StringFormat='Time: {0:t}'}"/>. The 0 represents the value returned by DateTime.Now, which is then converted using the short time format t, which results in 11:59 PM.

Value Converter

Bound data often needs to be converted to another data type before use. Convert a value from one data type to another by implementing the two methods Convert or ConvertBack from IValueConverter. If you need to support two-way updates, implement both methods.

Create a value converter that receives ticks and converts it to DateTime and vice versa.

Listing 9-16. Ticks to DateTime Value Converter

```
class TicksToDateTimeConverter : IValueConverter {
    public object Convert(object value, Type targetType, object
    parameter, CultureInfo culture) {
        return new DateTime((long)value);
    }
    public object ConvertBack(object value, Type targetType, object
    parameter, CultureInfo culture) {
        return ((DateTime)value).Ticks;
    }
}
```

The converter `TicksToDateTimeConverter` in Listing 9-15 has a `Convert` method that expects a number of type `long` and uses the `DateTime(long)` constructor to return a `DateTime` object. The `ConvertBack` method does the opposite. It receives a value object of type `DateTime` and returns a `long` value representing the ticks. Assuming that you have added the namespace of your converter to your XAML page and assigned the prefix `my` to your namespace, you can use this converter in a Label:

```
<Label Text="{Binding .,Source={x:Static sys:DateTime.Now},Converter=
{my:TicksToDateTimeConverter}}"/>.
```

You can also register converters as a resource in your dictionary if you want to use them application-wide or in your page.

```
<ResourceDictionary>
    <local:TicksToDateTimeConverter x:Key="TicksConverter" />
</ResourceDictionary>
```

Then use the converter name in the `ResourceDictionary` Key.

```
<Label Text="{Binding .,Source={x:Static sys:DateTime.Now},Converter=
{TicksConverter}}"/>.
```

Always consider before you opt for a converter whether a matching bindable property is not the better choice. These perform better and are easier to test.

Database access is truly cross-platform in Xamarin development. Using SQLite is basically the same regardless of what platform you're developing for.

Using SQLite.NET

Data models are often populated from and synchronized with a local database. SQLite. NET is the mobile, cross-platform database library of choice for many Xamarin developers using Xamarin.Forms, Xamarin.Android, or Xamarin.iOS.

How you install SQLite.NET in your solution depends on the solution type. A .NET Standard setup differs from a shared project setup:

> *NET Standard*: The best option for using SQLite-NET with .NET
> Standard is the NuGet package called SQLite-Net PCL. There are
> a few of these with similar names, so be certain to use the package
> with these attributes:

- Name: **SQLite-Net PCL**

- Created by: Frank A. Krueger

- ID: SQLite-net-pcl

- NuGet link: SQLite-net-pcl

  Install SQLite-Net PCL in the projects where you'll need it, usually most if not all of them in your solution. Do *not* manually add the SQLite.cs file to your project(s). See the downloadable code solution SQLiteNetPCL.

Note   SQLite-net-PCL works for .NET Standard. Yes, the library has PCL in it and will also work for obsolete PCL. Ignore all the PCLs and focus on using the SQLite-Net PCL library for your .NET Standard projects.

Shared project setup: Add a file to your shared project called SQLite.cs from the SQLite-net GitHub project by downloading it and then clicking your application solution and selecting Add File. See the downloadable code solution SQLiteNETSharedProject.

Many of the SQLite.NET examples in this section use a PCL because it's clearer in a demonstration, but I'll cover shared projects too. PCL and shared project SQLite.NET implementations are similar except for how they handle platform-specific implementations of the database path and connection. More about that in the section "Building the Database Path."

Now that you have SQLite.NET installed in your solution, reference the library in your data access layer classes with a using statement:

```
using SQLite;
```

Constructing a data access layer using SQLite.NET requires the creation of a database connection, a locking object, and CRUD transaction methods (get, insert, update, and delete) that are specific to your table data.

Locking Is Key

Inserting, getting, updating, and deleting rows should be done using locks in order to avoid conflicts. The following examples exclude the lock for simplicity until the section "Locking Rows." There are two ways to achieve locking with SQLite:

1. **Synchronous SQLite calls and explicit locking**. This is described in Listing 9-19 or Listing 9-22.

2. **Asynchronous SQLite calls with implicit locking**. Async calls *do the locking for you*.

Your architecture will determine which approach is best for you. Authorities on this are increasingly recommending number 2, asynchronous calls with built-in locking. More details here from Frank Kreuger: `https://github.com/praeclarum/sqlite-net#asynchronous-api`. We'll be working with synchronous calls with no locking (tsk tsk) in this entire chapter so the database commands are readable and the concepts clear. Be certain to take the next step after this and learn about the SQLite asynchronous API.

Now that SQLite.NET is installed, let's create a SQLite database.

Creating a Database

Create a new SQLite database by establishing a database connection to a database filename that includes the folder path. You can open a SQLite connection and use it throughout your app without closing it.

First locate the folder that the database should go into and create the database folder path:

```
string folder = Environment.GetFolderPath (Environment.SpecialFolder.
Personal);
databasePath = Path.Combine(documents, "ItemsSQLite.db3");
```

Create a database connection by specifying the database path and name:

```
var database = new SQLite.SQLiteConnection(databasePath);
```

No check is needed to see if the file already exists. It will be created if it does not yet exist; otherwise, it will simply be opened.

Tip   Avoid using a single connection on different threads. Using locks helps avoid conflicts, as described in the section "Locking Rows."

In real apps, building database paths is often the only platform-specific code in the data access layer.

Tip   Explore the Xamarin.Essentials solutions for building paths, starting with `FileSystem.AppDataDirectory`.

Building the Database Path

The database path is typically platform-specific, requiring an implementation for each platform to retrieve it. The implementation of the database path and database connection is the primary difference between the PCL approach and shared project approach to building a data access layer. In PCLs, use dependency injection (DI) to create platform-specific implementations of the database path and connection. In shared projects, create the database path by using *conditional compilation*, which is a way to implement platform-specific code at compile time.

Let's begin with the shared projects database connection implementation before moving on to .NET Standard.

Connect by Using Shared Projects

The trick with SQLite database connections in Xamarin apps is that the database path is usually platform-specific. For example, iOS iCloud requirements specify that files not created by the user should not reside in the personal documents folder but can reside in a subfolder such as `/Library`.

In a shared project, use conditional compilation as in Listing 9-16 to specify platform-specific folders.

Listing 9-17. Database Path in a Shared Project

```
string databasePath {
    get {
        var dbName = "ItemsSQLite.db3";
        #if __IOS__
        string folder = Environment.GetFolderPath (Environment.
        SpecialFolder.Personal);
        folder = Path.Combine (folder, "..", "Library");
        var databasePath = Path.Combine(folder, dbName);
        #else
        #if __ANDROID__
        string folder = Environment.GetFolderPath (Environment.
        SpecialFolder.Personal);
        var databasePath = Path.Combine(folder, dbName);
        #else
        // WinPhone
        var databasePath = Path.Combine(Windows.Storage.
        ApplicationData.Current.LocalFolder.Path, dbName);;
        #endif
        #endif

        return databasePath;
    }
}
```

Tip   Shared projects can't have references added to them, so you'll need to add the `SQLite.cs` code from GitHub.

Connect by Using .NET Standard

In .NET Standard, acquiring a connection to your SQLite database will require dependency injection (DI), which can be done using the Xamarin.Forms DependencyService.

In the Xamarin.Forms project, create an interface for platform-specific database functionality called IDatabase containing a connection method, DBConnect:

```
public interface IDatabase {
    SQLiteConnection DBConnect();
}
```

To connect to the SQLite database, call out to the connection method, DBConnect, using DependencyService:

```
database = DependencyService.Get< IDatabase > ().DBConnect ();
```

Tip   The Asynchronous API version of the call is this: `database = new SQLit eAsyncConnection(dbPath);`

The rest of the examples in this section on SQLite will use this database connection type in .NET Standard.

Next you need to implement the IDatabase interface on each platform.

Tip   .NET Standard solutions require a special SQLite.NET NuGet library installed called SQLite-NET PCL that was created by Frank A. Krueger with an ID of SQLite-net-pcl. Do *not* manually add the SQLite.cs file to your project(s).

Connect in Android

Create a database path for Android in the Android project by implementing the IDatabase interface in a class called Database_ Android (Listing 9-17). Begin the class with an [assembly] attribute declaring the class as a dependency injection for use in a DependencyService back in the .NET Standard project. Set the folder name to System. Environment.GetFolderPath (System.Environment.SpecialFolder.Personal).

Listing 9-18. Database Path in the Android Project of a .NET Standard Solution

```
[assembly: Dependency(typeof(Database_Android))]
namespace SQLiteNetPCL.Android
```

```
    {
        public class Database_Android : IDatabase
        {
            public Database_Android() { }
            public SQLiteConnection DBConnect()
            {
                var filename = "ItemsSQLite.db3";
                string folder =
                    System.Environment.GetFolderPath(System.Environment.
                    SpecialFolder.Personal);
                var path = Path.Combine(folder, filename);
                var connection = new SQLiteConnection(path);
                return connection;
            }
        }
    }
}
```

Connect in iOS

Create a database path for iOS in the iOS project by implementing the IDatabase interface in a class called Database_iOS (Listing 9-18). Meet iCloud requirements of not placing files directly in the user's personal folder by finding the user's /Library folder. Start with the user's personal folder at System.Environment.GetFolderPath (System. Environment.SpecialFolder.Personal) and locate /Library.

Listing 9-19. Database Path in the iOS Project of a .NET Standard Solution

```
[assembly: Dependency(typeof(Database_iOS))]
namespace SQLiteNetPCL.iOS
{
    public class Database_iOS : IDatabase
    {
        public Database_iOS() { }
        public SQLiteConnection DBConnect()
        {
            var filename = "ItemsSQLite.db3";
            string folder =
```

```
        Environment.GetFolderPath (Environment.SpecialFolder.
        Personal);
      string libraryFolder = Path.Combine (folder, "..",
      "Library");
      var path = Path.Combine(libraryFolder, filename);
      var connection = new SQLiteConnection(path);
      return connection;
    }
  }
}
```

Once you get your implementations of IDatabase wired up correctly, your call to retrieve the SQLite database connection will work: DependencyService.Get< IDatabase > ().DBConnect (). If you're running into difficulty, check your references and using statements. Platform-specific solutions need to reference the .NET Standard project containing your data access layer, and using statements (or direct namespace references) are needed when referring to those libraries. Once in a while, Visual Studio appears to fail when adding new libraries, and it's then helpful to close and reopen the solution.

The rest of this chapter uses .NET Standard instead of a shared project, for simplicity of demonstration only, but the code is basically the same between these approaches except for the database path and initial connection. If you want to understand the basic differences in a SQLite.NET implementation between .NET Standard and shared project, refer back to the section "Building the Database Path."

Once the connection to your SQLite database is made, you can add tables to our new database and start inserting, getting, updating, and deleting rows.

Creating a Table

Create a new table in a database by defining the table in a data model and then using the database's CreateTable method. Use attributes such as [PrimaryKey, AutoIncrement] to specify keys, max lengths, and other properties of the table and its fields (Listing 9-19).

Define the Item data model. Using the PrimaryKey and AutoIncrement attributes, specify an integer primary key to help facilitate queries. Unless specified otherwise (using attributes), SQLite will use the class name as the table name and the property names as column names.

Listing 9-20. Table Class Declaration Using SQLite Attributes (Item.cs)

```
public class Item {
    [PrimaryKey, AutoIncrement]
    public int ID { get; set; }
    [MaxLength(15)]
    public string Name { get; set; }
    [MaxLength(50)]
    public string Description { get; set; }
}
```

Create the table by using the `CreateTable` method:

```
database.CreateTable<Item>();
```

The table now exists and is ready for rows to be inserted. `CreateTable` won't overwrite an existing table (use `DropTable` to drop a table).

The bracketed attributes tell SQLite.NET how to regard the properties in the data model in relation to the database table.

Using Attributes

The following commonly used attributes for SQLite data models help you define the table in the database:

- `[PrimaryKey]`: Specifies the table's primary key when applied to an integer property (no composite keys).

- `[AutoIncrement]`: Automatically increments an integer property when each object is inserted into the database.

- `[Column(name)]`: Specifies the column name. Useful for when it should differ from the property name.

- `[Table(name)]`: Specifies the table name. Useful for when it should differ from the data model class name.

- `[Ignore]`: SQLite.NET will disregard this property. Useful for properties that cannot be stored in the database.

- [MaxLength(value)]: Limit the size of a text field on inserts and
  updates by rejecting longer text objects. Remember to validate the
  length in your own code before committing text to this field. SQLite
  itself has no limits on string length.

Once the table is created and fields defined, you can add data to the database.

Inserting and Deleting Rows

Insert a new row into a table by populating the data model and then calling the Insert
method.

Populate the Item data model with data:

```
var item = new Item { Name = "First" , Description = "This is the first
item"};
```

Call the database connection's Insert method to attempt to add a row to the table:

```
database.Insert (item);
```

Delete rows by using the Delete method:

```
database.Delete<Item>(id);
```

Tip   SQLite supports transactions using the SQLiteTransaction object with
the BeginTransaction, Commit, and Rollback methods. SQLite expects
operations to be performed in a transaction. If one is not supplied, then each
operation will be wrapped in a transaction. If you can batch them, you will get a
performance boost.

Getting Rows

Retrieve rows from a table by using the Get, Table, or Query methods. Get returns a
single row, Table returns the entire table, and Query returns multiple rows using SQL.

Pass the integer key ID into the Get method to return a row from the Item table:

```
var item = database.Get<Item>(1);
```

Return the entire table by using the Table method:

```
var itemList = database.Table<Item>();
```

Use SQL to filter the table's contents by using the Query method, a performant option:

```
var firstItem = database.Query<Item>("SELECT * FROM Item WHERE Name = 'First' ");
```

Use LINQ to filter the table's contents, less quickly than SQL:

```
var firstItem = from i in database.Table<Item>()
    where i.Name == "First"
    select i;
```

Or to specify parameters in the FirstOrDefault method to filter:

```
var itemList = database.Table<Item>().FirstOrDefault(x => x.ID == id);
```

Updating Rows

Update rows in the table by using the Update method. This changes data on an existing row.

First populate the Item data model with data:

```
var item = new Item { Name = "First" , Description = "This is the first item"};
```

Call the Update method to populate the new data in the existing row:

```
database.Update(item);
```

Check whether the ID exists so you know whether you should update or insert a new row:

```
if (item.ID != 0) {
    database.Update(item);
    return item.ID;
} else {
    return database.Insert(item);
}
```

If you're not sure that the row exists, use a combination Insert/Update. The Insert method will return a nonzero value if it fails, allowing the Update to proceed.

```
if (database.Insert(item) != 0)
    database.Update(item);
```

Locking Rows

To avoid database collisions, all transactions should be locked. Use the lock keyword against a static object.

Here's a locking example using the Delete method:

```
static object locker = new object ();
lock (locker) {
    database.Delete<Item>(id);
}
```

To avoid a deadlock, do not lock a method that calls another method that creates a lock.

Note   The SQLite Asynchronous API takes care of locks for you, implicitly! The entire SQLite.NET section in this book keeps SQLite calls as simple as possible for demonstration purposes. That means with no concurrency. Best practice with SQLite.NET typically involves the extensive use of async await, on connection, query, and SQL execution. Read all about it from Frank Kreuger himself here: `https://github.com/praeclarum/sqlite-net#asynchronous-api`.

Those are all the basic techniques you need to use the SQLite.NET ORM! Now you're ready to build a data access layer (DAL) for your app by using these techniques. Since it's not good architectural form to use SQLite.NET inside your UI layer, you can encapsulate SQLite.NET calls in the repository pattern to create a more elegant and decoupled architecture.

Creating the Data Access Layer

The *data access layer* (DAL) is an industry-standard architecture for data access in a C# app. This group of classes encapsulates the data layer and includes the database connection, the database path, and the CRUD transactions, exposing data access methods that reflect the specific data in a particular app (e.g., GetItem and SaveItem methods). Depending on the level of architectural rigor, the data access layer can offer a simple group of loosely arrayed access classes and methods to a highly structured and decoupled layer with limited access points (which often uses the repository pattern). This approach decouples the data layer implementation from the business and presentation layer of your app.

Note   Create, read, update, and delete (CRUD) transactions running against a local database typically make up the foundation of mobile application data. Some apps don't require local database access and run entirely using web services, but I'm not covering those in this book.

Creating a Repository

At the heart of many enterprise-grade Xamarin data access layers is an implementation of the repository pattern. This abstraction placed between the business layer and the data layer (the SQLite.NET ORM) provides app-specific CRUD methods using object collections, without exposing details of data source implementations (databases, XML, JSON, flat files, etc.). Use this pattern to abstract away the details of SQLite implementation, including locking. Later you can couple your repository with the singleton pattern to maintain the database connection.

Note   The definition of the repository pattern has evolved since its inception. It was originally intended as an abstraction to decouple the data layer implementation (e.g., SQLite) from the rest of the app with the added benefit of providing in-memory data-object collections. Over the years, many C# apps needed the decoupling but not the in-memory data objects, so those collections have evolved to become data objects returned by methods in many cases, not kept in repository properties. This is true in most Xamarin apps as well.

Create table-specific data access methods (GetItems, SaveItem, etc.) that encapsulate and employ the generalized SQLite CRUD methods described earlier (Get, Insert, Update, etc.):

```
public IEnumerable<Item> GetItems ()
public IEnumerable<Item> GetFirstItems ()
public Item GetItem(int id)
public int SaveItem(Item item)
public int DeleteItem(int id)
public void DeleteAllItems()
```

Make methods that are specific to the kind of data you're using, the Item table in this case. Avoid generic methods like Get and Insert and instead employ data-specific methods like GetItem and InsertItem (generic-sounding but specific to your Item table). There is a place for generic repository components, and we'll get to that soon.

A basic repository that represents a single database with a single table will typically look like the class outline in Listing 9-21.

Listing 9-21. Repository Class Outline (ItemDatabaseBasic.cs)

```
Public Class ItemDatabaseBasic
    {
        protected static object locker = new object ();
        protected SQLiteConnection database;

        public ItemDatabaseBasic()
        {
            database = DependencyService.Get<IDatabase>().DBConnect();
            database.CreateTable<Item>();
        }

        public IEnumerable<Item> GetItems () { ... }
        public IEnumerable<Item> GetFirstItems () { ... }
        public Item GetItem(int id) { ... }
        public int SaveItem(Item item) { ... }
        public int DeleteItem(int id) { ... }
        public void DeleteAllItems() { ... }

    }
```

Create a .NET Standard solution for this example called `SQLiteNetStd`. See the earlier section "Connect by Using Portable Class Libraries" for implementations of `DBConnect()` and `IDatabase`.

Tip   If you want to create a repository using a shared project, virtually everything is identical to what you would do with a .NET Standard project except the initial connection. For details on shared project implementations, see the earlier section "Connect by Using .NET Standard" and the downloadable solution example `SQLiteNETSharedProject`.

Listing 9-22 shows the full code for this basic repository based on the outline in Listing 9-21. Create a static `locker` object that is used within the data access methods for avoiding concurrency issues on different threads, as discussed earlier. Encapsulate the `SQLiteConnection` object and instantiate it in the constructor. The `databasePath` is created using the method described earlier in "Connect by Using Portable Class Libraries."

Listing 9-22. Single-Table Repository in ItemDatabaseBasic.cs

```
public class ItemDatabaseBasic
{
    protected static object locker = new object ();
    protected SQLiteConnection database;

    public ItemDatabaseBasic()
    {
        database = DependencyService.Get<IDatabase>().DBConnect();
        database.CreateTable<Item>();
    }

    public IEnumerable<Item> GetItems ()
    {
        lock (locker) {
            return (from i in database.Table<Item>() select i).ToList();
        }
    }
```

```csharp
public IEnumerable<Item> GetFirstItems ()
{
    lock (locker) {
        return database.Query<Item>("SELECT * FROM Item WHERE Name
        = 'First'");
    }
}

public Item GetItem(int id)
{
    lock (locker) {
        return database.Table<Item>().FirstOrDefault(x => x.ID == id);
    }
}

public int SaveItem(Item item)
{
    lock (locker) {
        if (item.ID != 0) {
            database.Update(item);
            return item.ID;
        } else {
            return database.Insert(item);
        }
    }
}

public int DeleteItem(int id)
{
    lock (locker) {
        return database.Delete<Item>(id);
    }
}

public void DeleteAllItems()
{
    lock (locker) {
```

```
            database.DropTable<Item>();
            database.CreateTable<Item>();
        }
    }
}
```

Important Tip   This basic repository works for only a single table: Item. You can access additional tables either by adding more methods to this repository or by refactoring the class using generics, both of which you'll do in a moment in the section "Adding Methods to the Repository."

Let's get back to the database connection.

Managing the Repository

In Xamarin apps using SQLite, the database connection is often kept in memory so it can be reused throughout the user session. Because static classes remain in memory, they are a likely candidate for helping to build a repository and store the connection. You can also open and close the connection for each transaction, but because SQLite is a serverless database, there is less of a need, and keeping a single connection open is common practice.

The connection is typically handled in one of two ways, either encapsulated in the repository or passed in as a parameter. In these examples, the SQLite database connection is encapsulated in the repository. (You may want to move the connection out of the repository and pass it in as a parameter if you wish to have more control over the connection instance, for testability, for example.) Since the connection resides in our repository in this example, we need to keep the repository in memory.

A common location to maintain a repository is in a static property on the Application class, as shown in Listing 9-23. The following code references the earlier ItemDatabaseBasic repository in Listing 9-22.

Listing 9-23. Static Database Property Declared in the Application Object

```
public class App : Application
{

    static ItemDatabaseBasic database;

    public static ItemDatabaseBasic Database {
        get {
            if (database == null) {
                database = new ItemDatabaseBasic ();
            }
            return database;
        }
    }

    ...


}
```

Use this self-instantiating repository by referring to it via the `Application` object:

```
App.Database.SaveItem (item);
```

The `ContentPage` UI is found in downloadable code files `App.cs` and `DataAccessPageDatabase.cs`.

Often, you have to access more than one table in your database, or you have multiple data sources, such as files, XML, JSON, or multiple databases. These situations warrant a more advanced repository approach.

Adding Methods to the Repository

Accessing multiple tables or multiple data sources requires some thinking about how the DAL architecture should grow to accommodate that. Here are the two common options for multisource repositories:

- Add data access methods directly to your repository class.

- Refactor your repository into a repository class and a generic database access class.

The first option is quick and dirty, whereas the second option is more suitable for enterprise-grade business apps. Let's look at each option.

Add data access methods directly to your repository class. If you want to access a new table, a Person table, for example, you need to create GetPerson and SavePerson methods somewhere. You could just add these methods to your repository.

```
public Person GetPerson (int id) { ... }
public IEnumerable<Person> GetPeople () { ... }
public int SavePerson(Person person) { ... }
public int DeletePerson(int id) { ... }
public int DeleteAllPeople() { ... }
```

That will work just fine. It's even moderately testable. Use it if it works for you.

The problem with this approach is all the code that's not shown: the implementation of these methods is virtually identical for every table. This approach smells of code duplication. If you need to access a third or fourth table, you'll wind up with dozens of methods that look more or less like this:

```
public int GetOrSaveOrDeleteSomething(int id)
{
    lock (locker) {
        return database.GetOrSaveOrDelete<TableName>(id);
    }
}
```

Very smelly, indeed. If you're lucky, that's all that will be in there. In some cases, a mash-up of table-specific logic and SQLite implementation will provide additional smells. It's time for a refactoring, and the second option is the obvious choice.

Refactor your repository into a repository class and a generic database access class.

A more advanced approach to the repository pattern separates the repository class from the DAL implementations. This approach is useful if you have multiple tables, or mixed types of data access, such as file-based, XML, and JSON, as well as a SQLite data layer, or multiple databases (rare). Each data source can have its own implementation; then the repository ties them all together with one interface. SQLite implementations can all be encapsulated into a single generic database class.

Create a generic database class that handles the SQLite data layer, and then create an advanced repository class that handles all the data access calls to that generic database and to other sources.

Begin with the generic database class, as shown in Listing 9-24. Take your original ItemDatabaseBasic class, make a copy, and call it ItemDatabaseGeneric.cs. Replace all references to specific tables, data models, and data classes such as Item or Person with T. In a liberal use of generics, create methods that could transact with *any* table, depending on the data type passed into them.

Listing 9-24. Generic Database Class (ItemDatabaseGeneric.cs)

```
public class ItemDatabaseGeneric
{
    static object locker = new object ();

    SQLiteConnection database;

    public ItemDatabaseGeneric()
    {
        database = DependencyService.Get<IDatabase>().DBConnect();
        database.CreateTable<Item>();
        database.CreateTable<Person>();
    }

    public IEnumerable<T> GetObjects<T> () where T : IObject, new ()
    {
        lock (locker) {
            return (from i in database.Table<T>() select i).ToList();
        }
    }

    public IEnumerable<T> GetFirstObjects<T> () where T : IObject, new ()
    {
        lock (locker) {
            return database.Query<T>("SELECT * FROM Item WHERE Name =
            'First'");
        }
    }
```

```
        public T GetObject<T> (int id) where T : IObject, new ()
        {
            lock (locker) {
                return database.Table<T>().FirstOrDefault(x => x.ID == id);
            }
        }

        public int SaveObject<T> (T obj) where T : IObject
        {
            lock (locker) {
                if (obj.ID != 0) {
                    database.Update(obj);
                    return obj.ID;
                } else {
                    return database.Insert(obj);
                }
            }
        }

        public int DeleteObject<T> (int id) where T : IObject, new ()
        {
            lock (locker) {
                return database.Delete<T> (id);
            }
        }

        public void DeleteAllObjects<T> ()
        {
            lock (locker) {
                database.DropTable<T>();
                database.CreateTable<T>();
            }
        }
    }
```

Since the ID field is needed in these methods, it must be added as a constraint to the type parameters of some of the methods. This means you need to upgrade to your data model(s) with an interface that requires an ID (Listing 9-25).

Listing 9-25. Generic Model Interface That Includes an ID Field (IObject.cs)

```
public interface IObject
{
    int ID { get; set; }
}
```

Apply the interface to your models, inheriting from IObject:

```
public class Item : IObject
```

You already have an ID field in the Item class, so there's no need for further changes to it.

Add a Person class as a new data model, inheriting from IObject and including an ID field to implement IObject (Listing 9-26).

Listing 9-26. Person Data Model Class (Person.cs)

```
public class Person : IObject
{
    [PrimaryKey, AutoIncrement]
    public int ID { get; set; }
    [MaxLength(25)]
    public string FirstName { get; set; }
    [MaxLength(25)]
    public string LastName { get; set; }
}
```

Create an advanced repository class that consumes the generic database class. Use methods that are specific to the types of data being handled, as shown in Listing 9-27. Avoid any SQLite implementation in this repository, as the purpose of this class is to act as a layer between the business logic and the data access implementation.

Listing 9-27. Advanced Repository Calls Generic Database Class Methods (ItemRepository.cs)

```csharp
public class ItemRepository {
    ItemDatabaseGeneric itemDatabase = null;

    public ItemRepository()
    {
        itemDatabase = new ItemDatabaseGeneric();
    }

    public Item GetItem(int id)
    {
        return itemDatabase.GetObject<Item>(id);
    }

    public IEnumerable<Item> GetFirstItems ()
    {
        return itemDatabase.GetObjects<Item>();
    }

    public IEnumerable<Item> GetItems ()
    {
        return itemDatabase.GetObjects<Item>();
    }

    public int SaveItem (Item item)
    {
        return itemDatabase.SaveObject<Item>(item);
    }

    public int DeleteItem(int id)
    {
        return itemDatabase.DeleteObject<Item>(id);
    }

    public void DeleteAllItems()
    {
```

```
            itemDatabase.DeleteAllObjects<Item>();
    }

    public Person GetPerson(int id)
    {
        return itemDatabase.GetObject<Person>(id);
    }

    public IEnumerable<Person> GetPeople ()
    {
        return itemDatabase.GetObjects<Person>();
    }

    public int SavePerson (Person person)
    {
        return itemDatabase.SaveObject<Person>(person);
    }

    public int DeletePerson(int id)
    {
        return itemDatabase.DeleteObject<Person>(id);
    }

    public void DeleteAllPeople()
    {
        itemDatabase.DeleteAllObjects<Person>();
    }

}
```

Three components are in this more advanced repository: the generic database instance, the item methods, and the person methods. Item objects are passed into the item methods, and Person objects appear in the person methods. The generic database class resolves all of its SQLite.NET methods by using those data types via generics, deciding which tables to read and write to/from.

That is how to refactor your basic repository into an advanced repository, using generics and a data model interface.

If you're looking at the repositories in this chapter and asking where the model properties and caching mechanisms are, you're asking the right questions. Using a repository to maintain in-memory data models is a common technique in web development, but it can be risky given the limited memory of mobile devices and is beyond the scope of this book. The repositories shown here are basic ones designed only to create an app-specific abstraction around the SQLite ORM.

Note   A third option exists for adding methods to a repository: create a generic repository. This is similar to the second option, the generic database class, but without the encapsulating repository class. This exposes a generic DAL interface to your views and view models and is considered by many to be lazy coding and a leaky abstraction.

CODE COMPLETE: Creating a DAL by Using SQLite.NET

Listings 9-24, 9-25, 9-26, 9-27, 9-28, 9-29, and 9-30 contain the complete data access layer code for the advanced repository example invoking the generic database class. The `Application` object containing the static `Repository` property is found in Listing 9-28. This example uses the advanced repository we refactored in Listing 9-27 instead of the basic database repository (Listing 9-21).

The `ContentPage` demo UI in Listing 9-29 walks through various methods in the DAL. The `List` data model with `IObject` implemented is in Listing 9-30.

This example is a Xamarin.Forms project, which uses dependency injection for retrieving the database connection with the `DBConnect()` method as described in "Connect by Using Portable Class Libraries" and as seen in the downloadable code solution called `SQLiteNetPCL`.

Note   From here on out, this book focuses 100% on data access where the only UI is a Label with a Text property containing data access example results. C# is used to display this label instead of XAML: `var label = new Label { Text = "Results" };`

If you're using a shared project instead, skip the DI and use conditional compilation to create DatabasePath, as mentioned earlier in "Connect by Using Shared Projects" and as seen in the downloadable code solution called SQLiteNETSharedProject.

Listing 9-28. App.cs Using a Static Application Property for the Repository

```
public class App : Application
{
    static ItemRepository repository;
    public static ItemRepository Repository {
        get {
            if (repository == null) {
                repository = new ItemRepository ();
            }
            return repository;
        }
    }

    public App()
    {
        MainPage = new NavigationPage(new HomePage());
    }
}
```

Figure 9-8 shows the UI output of the ContentPage called DataAccessPageRepository (Listing 9-29), a quick demo of the data access layer using the advanced repository.

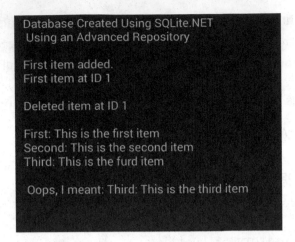

Figure 9-8. *UI display in the demo data access page shown in Listing 9-29*

Listing 9-29. DataAccessPageRepository.cs Is a Xamarin.Forms ContentPage That Uses ItemsRepository

```
public class DataAccessPageRepository : ContentPage
{
    public DataAccessPageRepository()
    {
        var label = new Label { Text = "Database Created Using SQLite.
        NET\n" };

        label.Text += " Using an Advanced Repository\n\n";

        App.Repository.DeleteAllItems (); // clear out the table to start
        fresh

        var item = new Item { Name = "First" , Description = "This is the
        first item"};
        App.Repository.SaveItem (item);

        var firstItem = App.Repository.GetFirstItems();
        label.Text += firstItem.First().Name + " item added.\n";

        var id = 1;
        item = App.Repository.GetItem (id);
        label.Text += item.Name + " item at ID " + id.ToString () + "\n\n";
```

```
App.Repository.DeleteItem(id);
label.Text += "Deleted item at ID " + id.ToString () + "\n\n";

item = new Item { Name = "First" , Description = "This is the first
item"};
App.Repository.SaveItem (item);
item = new Item { Name = "Second" , Description = "This is the
second item"};
App.Repository.SaveItem (item);
item = new Item { Name = "Third" , Description = "This is the third
item"};
App.Repository.SaveItem (item);

var items = App.Repository.GetItems ();
foreach (var i in items) {
    label.Text += i.Name + ": " + i.Description + "\n";
}

label.Text += "\n Oops, I meant: ";

item.Description = "This is the third item";
App.Repository.SaveItem(item);
id = 4;
item = App.Repository.GetItem (id);
label.Text += item.Name + ": " + item.Description + "\n";

this.Padding = new Thickness(10, Device.OnPlatform(20, 0, 0), 10, 5);

Content = new StackLayout
{
    Children = {
        label
    }
};
}
```

Listing 9-30. Item.cs Contains the Item Class Implementing IObject

```
public class Item : IObject
{
    [PrimaryKey, AutoIncrement]
    public int ID { get; set; }
    [MaxLength(15)]
    public string Name { get; set; }
    [MaxLength(50)]
    public string Description { get; set; }
}
```

Database Creation Options

The most common options for creating your SQLite database are as follows:

- *Use SQLite.NET*: Use the SQLite.NET API to create the database and tables as described in "Creating a Database" in the section "Using SQLite.NET." Use SQL for features not covered in the ORM, such as foreign keys and indexes.

- *Include a database*: You can include a fully created database with your app, a good option if you want complete control over details of the tables and their relationships. Use a tool such as the Datum or the SQLite Manager Firefox extension. Then remember to have your app copy the database into a writable directory before using it with code like this:

```
if (!File.Exists (databasePath))
{
    File.Copy (dbName, databasePath);
}
```

SQLite provides a local database to help you maintain state between user sessions and have important data on demand. Many apps also require interaction with a server-side data source, such as a SQL server or other data source on a remote data server.

Web Services

Web services facilitate communication with a remote datastore and synchronization with the local SQLite database. They allow the Xamarin app to pull down data from the remote data source and push it back up when needed.

Many options are available for building web services when using the Xamarin platform, but here are a few of the most common:

- **REST:** A common approach, RESTful services can use HttpClient, HttpWebRequest, WebClient, or one of many third-party libraries, including Hammock, often coupled with JSON or LINQ.

- **Windows Communication Framework (WCF):** The standard Microsoft web service approach is supported in a limited fashion by using BasicHttpBinding in the Silverlight library.

- **SOAP:** An older, standards-based approach for data transmission over the Web, Xamarin supports SOAP 1.1, Microsoft's SOAP implementation, and ASP.NET Web Services (ASMX), albeit with an incomplete implementation.

Detailed exploration of web services is beyond the scope of this book, but the fundamentals are similar to web services used in web, and especially desktop, apps.

There are heavier-weight options that provide out-of-the box data solutions, handle the fine points of security, and can save on development time. These enterprise cloud data solutions are the industrial-grade platforms for remote data integration.

Enterprise Cloud Data Solutions

Optimization of the performance and user experience of mobile apps has increased the demand for full-featured, server-side mobile app solutions. These solutions include mobile-accessible cloud storage, authentication, and push notifications. Build, test, distribution, and analytics are also useful features. Here are a few of the most popular solutions.

Microsoft Azure Mobile Apps

Azure Mobile Apps is a service suite providing baseline features like SQL Databases, mobile push notifications, brand-name authentication via Facebook and Twitter for consumer apps, and Azure Active Directory (AAD) for enterprise apps. Access to these features is condensed into the Azure Mobile SDK, an API used by mobile developers to access the Azure cloud feature set, including local/remote data sync. Serverless nanoservices that instantiate on demand are becoming more common as mobile back-ends and Azure Functions provide these services that are easily implemented in mobile dev architectures.

Azure Mobile Apps is a suite of services that provide back-end support to native and cross-platform mobile apps. It offers features important to mobile app developers including

- Cloud storage

- Offline data sync

- Authentication

- Push notifications

Cloud Storage

Mobile apps need server-side virtual storage with cloud databases and tables that can be instantiated and destroyed on demand. Azure SQL Databases provide cloud storage that is easy to set up and low maintenance, requiring no administration of physical disk, partitions, or logging. They have automatic backups and software updates, and automatic tuning and threat detection. The Azure SDK provides a straightforward way to create SQL Database table references from within a mobile app and conduct CRUD transactions. Azure SDK meets your mobile app's data access needs by querying, filtering, sorting, and syncing data to a local database, such as SQLite. Use the Azure SDK in your mobile app or server-side code to obtain references to your app's Azure SQL Database URL and tables. Execute CRUD transactions against your tables, and filter and sort by row, column, and id. Access to Azure tables can also be achieved using Visual Studio App Center (VSAC).

> **Tip**   Microsoft Entity Framework is another enterprise-grade cloud storage option worth considering.

Offline Data Sync

Sync data local-to-cloud using a SQLite database, an Azure SQL Database, and the Azure SDK. In your mobile app, use a local SQLite database and bind it to your Azure cloud data source. All writes go to the local SQLite database. Sync the databases with push and pull methods. Data is sent to the Azure SQL Database only when explicitly synced using the SDK's async methods. Remote data sync from multiple client apps raises the risk of conflicts. Handle sync errors using a try/catch exception handler or by implementing a sync handler interface.

Authentication

Azure Authentication integrates with Azure Active Directory (AD) and third parties such as Facebook, Google, MS Account, and Twitter.

Using standard OAuth workflow, the mobile app retrieves an authentication token from an authentication provider to access a protected service. This token is used to create an identity for the mobile app which is passed to the target mobile service. The acceptance of this identity finalizes the authentication. The mobile service then executes the desired function and returns requested values (if any) to the calling mobile app.

Push Notifications

Due to the secure and proprietary nature of mobile push notifications, OS providers each utilize their own Push Notification Service (PNS). Cross-platform development must integrate with two or more services which can become unwieldy. Azure Notification Hubs provides a single notification hub for server-side notification generators to integrate with. Provide Azure Notification Hubs with access to the platform-specific PNS then push messages to the hub using platform-specific methods in your mobile app, as specified in the Azure SDK.

Use Azure Notifications Hubs to broadcast notifications by user, device, or platform, in real time or scheduled. The hub's service scales to millions of devices and supports all major push platforms including iOS, Android, Windows, Kindle, and Baidu.

Azure Mobile Apps is a full-featured service suite custom-made for mobile development, providing containers, built-in and from-scratch services, access to data sources, maintained and administered maintenance-free on the Azure platform. Developers can take advantage of Azure Mobile Apps using the Azure SDK for Xamarin apps. Get started using the managed client SDK package for Mobile Apps from NuGet called Microsoft.Azure.Mobile.Client. More detail can be found here: `https://docs.microsoft.com/en-us/azure/app-service-mobile/app-service-mobile-xamarin-forms-get-started`.

Visual Studio App Center (VSAC)

Build, test, and deploy mobile apps in a DevOps environment using Visual Studio App Center (VSAC). DevOps practices using VSAC help development teams keep builds and releases organized as they are distributed to collaborators, teams of testers, customer beta testers, all the way into app stores like Google Play and iTunes. This suite covers the automation of time-consuming tasks such as builds and build signing within a streamlined workflow. Learn how to test on multiple physical devices by creating device sets and choosing from over 2500 devices and over 400 configurations of iOS and Android versions. Set up and manage multiple applications, organizations, testers, and teams using App Center Build, App Center Test, and App Center Distribute. Read more about VSAC in my edX course at `www.edx.org/course/devops-mobile-apps-1`.

IBM Mobile Foundation

The IBM.MobileFirstPlatformFoundation NuGet library provides a bridge into IBM's enterprise-grade mobile application platform product as part of a suite of enterprise mobile solutions. IBM Mobile Foundation (formerly IBM MobileFirst) provides a range of mobile app development features including security, cloud data access, enterprise integration, and application management. IBM Mobile Foundation security offerings include secure authentication using SSO and multi-factors. Transactions can use SSL encryption, local data can be encrypted, and there is some protection against reverse-engineering. The platform's cloud data access feature set provides remote data access, storing user preferences, and data synchronization. Enterprise integration features include unified push, SMS notifications, and optimized access to enterprise services, such as web services, REST services, SAP, and more. Application management functionality provides a full range of app release management features including distribution, versioning, analytics, push notifications, remote disabling of apps, and error logging. These are some of these features available using the `WL.Client` namespace in the IBM MobileFirst SDK. Read more about IBM Mobile Foundation with Xamarin here: `https://mobilefirstplatform.ibmcloud.com/tutorials/ru/foundation/8.0/application-development/sdk/xamarin/`.

Summary

Xamarin.Forms data binding was built upon the foundation and experience of the third-party MVVM libraries used with Mono for years, MvvmCross and MVVM Light Toolkit, and was also inspired by WPF XAML data binding. Leveraging this powerful lineage, the Xamarin team at Microsoft has forged Xamarin.Forms into an advanced and mature API.

Data binding gets data into and out of your data model through your views. Moving that data into and out of your database can be accomplished with SQLite-NET. Some Xamarin developers prefer SQLite-NET because of the ease of the built-in ORM. The SQLite-NET ORM wraps all the standard CRUD transactions in handy LINQ-friendly methods. SQLite supports foreign keys, and those have to be done in SQL or in an included database.

That's everything you'll need to populate your data models and couple them with a local SQLite database.

With that, this book concludes. I hope you've found what you came here for or something equally useful. I continue to see amazing things built with Xamarin, in social media, industry, finance, government, transportation, and many more. Xamarin is how cross-platform apps are built today, and I wish you all the best in building yours!

Index

A

AbsoluteLayout, 74
  adding label, 107
  bounding objects creation, 107–108
    binding location, 110–111
    binding size, 110–111
    coding, 111–112
    points, 109
    rectangles, 108–109
  SetLayoutBounds views, 106–108
  SetLayoutFlags, 109
Absolute location and size, 100
Action menu, 261
AlignItems, 82
Attached property syntax, 62, 65–66
Authentication, 413
Automatic data binding, 350
Azure Mobile Apps
  authentication, 413
  cloud storage, 412
  features, 412
  offline data sync, 413
  push notifications, 413–414

B

Behaviors
  attached properties, 214–216
  commands, 217–218
  Entry control, 216

  implementation, 216
BindableProperty object, 380
BoxView, 31–32
ButtonRenderer class, 315
Button View, 26, 28
  adding, 239
  ListViewButton.xaml, 239
  ListViewButton.xaml.cs, 241

C

CanExecute method, 204
Cascading styles sheets (CSS), 119
  CancelButton style class, 176
  ContentPages and Grids, 177
  CSSPage.xaml, 177–178, 180–181
  description, 174
  feedback page, 178–179
  properties and values, 183–185
  selectors, 175, 182
  StackLayout, 177
  Styles.css, 179–180
  Subject and Feedback, 176–177
  SubmitButton style class, 176
Catalog, 87
CenterAndExpand, 80
Cloud storage, 412
Collection syntax, 62, 65
CommandParameter property, 239
Constant constraints, 99, 100

© Dan Hermes 2019
D. Hermes and N. Mazloumi, *Building Xamarin.Forms Mobile Apps Using XAML*,
https://doi.org/10.1007/978-1-4842-4030-4

Constructors, 55
 complete code, 58–59
 default, 56, 58
 factory method, 57–58
 non-default, 56, 58
Content property syntax, 62–63
ContentView layout, 112–114
Context Action
 button, 242
 ListViewContextAction.cs, 244
 ListViewContextAction.xaml, 243
Controls.xaml, 188
Control templates, 202–204
CustomButton view, 308
Custom ContentView Control, 201–202
Custom controls, 116–117, 305
Custom dark theme, 172–174
CustomGroupedList, 250
 data-bound fields, 251
 ListViewGroupedTemplate.cs, 252–253
 ListViewGroupedTemplate.xaml, 251
CustomList, 233
CustomRendererExamplePage.xaml, 309
Custom renderers
 Android
  [assembly] attribute, 311
  chocolate-colored button, 312
  CustomButton.cs, 313
  CustomButtonRenderer.cs, 310,
   314–315
  statements, 312
 ContentPage, 308
 custom element, 307–309
 defined, 303
 ios
  [assembly] attribute, 316
  complete code, 317–318
  CustomButton, 317

CustomButtonRenderer.cs, 316
 statements, 316
 platform-specific projects, 306
 properties, 310
 visual representation, 305
 Xamarin.Forms elements, 307, 318
 Xamarin.iOS, 304
Custom row template, 233
Custom themes, 171–174

D

Dark theme, 167–169
Data access layer (DAL)
 Application object, 406, 407
 C# app, 394
 ContentPage, 406–409
 Item.cs, 410
 repository
  CRUD methods, 395
  generic database class, 400–402
  GetPerson and SavePerson
   methods, 400
  ID field, 403
  ItemDatabaseBasic.cs, 395–398
  ItemDatabaseGeneric.cs, 401–402
  ItemRepository.cs, 404–405
  multisource, 399
  Person class, 403
  properties and caching
   mechanisms, 406
  static property, Application class,
   398–399
 static Application property, 406–407
Data binding
 data layer and presentation layer, 349
 definition, 349
 and MVVM, 349

Xamarin.Forms
  automatic, 350
  BindableProperty object, 349, 380
  BindingModes, 381
  data source property, 349
  Editable ListView (*see* Editable
    ListView)
  INotifyPropertyChanged (*see*
    INotifyPropertyChanged
    interface, data binding)
  item data model, 351–354
  MVVM (*see* Model-View-
    ViewModel (MVVM))
  nontrivial data binding, 350–351
  read-only ListView, 366–368
  string formatting, 381
  trivial data binding, 350
  value converter, 381–382
DatePicker, 187, 191–193
Default constructor, 56, 58
Device styles, 163–165
DisplayActionSheet, 273
DisplayAlert method, 271–272
Drill-down list, 262
  App.cs, 282
  DetailPage.xaml.cs, 282
  DrilldownTableView.cs, 286–287
  Item.xaml.cs, 281
  ListItem.cs, 280
  List View
    by item, 278–280
    by page, 283–284
  MasterDetailPage, 287
    fly-in menu, 291
    initial detail page, 290
    NavigationDrawer.cs, 288
    NavigationDrawer.xaml.cs, 288
    TableView, 285
    title and description, 280
Droid project, 313
DroidTextValidatorEffect class, 326
DynamicResource, 134
  background color, 134–135
  constructor, 136
  DynamicResourcePage.xaml, 137–139
  DynamicResourcePage.xaml.cs, 139–140
  HandleSubject method, 135
  PageBgColor, BtSubmitColor, and
    BtCancelColor, 135
  user interaction, 135–137
Dynamic style inheritance, 155–156

E

Editable ListView
  adding rows, 369–371
  ContentPage demo app, 377
  INotify interface, 369
  Items property, 375–376
  ListPageUsingListViewModel.xaml, 378
  ListPageUsingListViewModel.xaml.cs,
    379–380
  ListViewModel.cs, 375
  MVVM, 375
  ObservableCollection, 369
  properties, 371–374
  row deletion, 369–371
Effects
  PlatformEffect, 322
  RoutingEffect class, 322
  Xamarin.Forms, 321, 324
EndAndExpand, 80
Entry view, 30–31
Enumeration value syntax, 62–63

Event handler syntax, 62–64

Explicit styles, 146–147

eXtensible Application Markup
      Language (XAML), 3
  attributes, 43
  basic syntax, 43–44
  vs. C#, 3
  classes, identifiers, and references, 60
  code behind file, 67–68
  constructing objects, 61
  data types, 60
  event handlers, 68
  generated file, 67–68
  local variable, 68
  property values, 66–67
  XML document, 43

F

FactorMethodsPage.xaml, 344–345

Feedback page, 122
  Entry view, 120
  Grid and StackLayout, 120
  HandleFeedback method, 121
  NavigationPage, 122
  Placeholder property, 121
  placeHolderText, 122
  view formatting properties, 123–125

FillAndExpand, 80

FlexLayout, 73
  Direction set, 84
  patterns, 86–87
  position views, 82–83
    AlignItems, 85–86
    Direction set, 83–84
    JustifyContent set, 84–85

Focus() method, 199

Frame layout, 74, 115–116

G

Global resources, 142

Grid layout, 73
  adding space, 96
  coding, 97
  fit available space, expanding
    views, 92–93
  fit views, 90
  GridUnitType, 87, 90
  multicell view, 94
    spanning columns, 94–96
    spanning rows, 95–96
  proportionally, expanding views, 93–94
  rows and columns, 87–90
  setting exact size, 91

GroupedList
  headings, 247
  ListViewGrouped.cs, 248
  ListViewGrouped.xaml, 247

H

HasShadow, 115

HeightProportional, 111

Hierarchical navigation
  back button click event, 269
  drop-down menu class, 269–270
  home page, 264–265
  InsertPageBefore, 267
  navigation bar, 263
  navigation buttons, 263
  navigation icon, 268
  Page.Title, 267
  PopAsync pops, 267
  PopToRootAsync pops, 267
  PushAsync, 266
  RemovePage, 267
  second page, 266

I

IBM Mobile Foundation, 414

ImageList, 230

Image view

    Aspect property, 33–34

    GestureRecognizer, 34–36

    local images, 33

    monkey, 32–33

Implicit styles, 148–149

InitializeComponent method, 308

INotifyPropertyChanged interface,
      data binding

    ContentPage, 356–357

    definition, 354

    Entry view, 357–358

    ItemPageUsingTitleViewModel.cs,
      358–360

    TitleViewModel.cs, 355–356

iOS and Android, list view, 221

ItemSelected, 222

Item selection

    alert display, 223

    ListViewStrings.cs, 224

    ListViewStrings.xaml, 224

ItemSource, 220

ItemTapped, 222

ItemTemplate.SetBinding method, 225

ITextValidatorEffect class, 328

J, K

JustifyContent, 82

L

Label view, 23–24

Light theme, 169–171

ListItem data model, 226

ListView

    adding image, 229

      image cell, 229

      ListViewImageCell.cs, 231

      ListViewImageCell.xaml, 231

    automatically scrolls, 254

    binding data model, 225, 227

    binding strings, 220

    buttons

      add button views, 238

      context actions, 242

    caching, 256

    customizing list rows

      complete code, 236

      custom template, 232

      ListViewCustom.cs, 237

      ListViewCustom.xaml, 236

    group headers

      customizing list, 249

      GroupDisplayBinding, 245

      IsGroupingEnabled, 245

    image cell, 229

    jump list, 253

    ListViewDataModel.cs, 228

    ListViewDataModel.xaml, 228

    optimization, 257

    pull-to-refresh, 255

    selecting item, 222

Local images

    Android, 33

    iOS 9, 33

M

MaxLength property, 325

MaxLengthPropertyChanged method, 336

Mobile UIs
   controls, 10
   layouts, 10
   lists, 10
   modals, dialog boxes, and alerts, 10
   navigation, 10
   screens, views, and pages, 10
Model-View-ViewModel (MVVM)
   INotifyPropertyChanged interface, 361
      creation, 362–364
      implemention, 362, 364–366
      wrap data model, 362
   ViewModel, 360
MyBehavior, 214–215
MyCommand, 204, 206

N

Native views
   Android, 339
   declaration, 337, 340–341
   factory methods
      arguments, 343
      EditText, 341
      UITextField, 341
   iOS, 338
   namespaces UIKit, 338
   Xamarin.Forms, 337
   XAML page, 337, 344
   xmlns, 338
Navigation, 262–263
   carousel page, 300
   drawer, 261
   hierarchical (*see* Hierarchical navigation)
   modal, 261
      ActionSheet, 273
      DisplayAlert method, 271–272
      full-page modal, 271

springboard (*see* Springboard)
state management, 262
   application object, 277
   disk persistence, 275
   global properties, 276
   page parameters, 274
   static global class, 275, 276
TabbedPage
   data-bound, 294–296
   iOS tabs, 292
   navigation pages, 296
   TabPage.cs, 293
   TabPageDatabound.cs, 295
   TabPageDatabound.xaml.cs, 294
Non-default constructor, 56, 58
Nontrivial data binding, 350–351

O

ObservableItem class, 372–373
Offline data sync, 413
OnAttached method, 323, 326
OnDetached method, 323, 326
OnElementChanged method, 309
OnElementPropertyChanged method, 309, 331
OnPropertyChanged event, 365
Opacity, 198
Overriding resources, 143
Overriding styles, 149–151

P, Q

Page, 87
Picker, 187–190
PickerSelectedIndexChanged method, 190
PlatformEffect
   properties, 322
   structure, 323

Platform-specific UI approach
   architecture, 6–7
   complex screens, 8
   consumer apps, 8
   high design, 8
   single-platform apps, 8
   Xamarin.Android, Xamarin.iOS, and
      Windows Phone SDK libraries, 6
Portable Class Libraries (PCL), 386
PositionProportional, 110
Property element syntax, 61–62
Pull-to-refresh feature, 255
Push notifications, 413–414

R

Read-only ListView binding, 366–368
RecycleElement, 256
RecycleElementAndDataTemplate, 256
RelativeLayout, 73
   absolute location and size, 100
   coding, 104–106
   constraints, 98–99
   RelativeToParent constraint, 101–102
   RelativeToView constraint, 103–104
   setting view location and size, 99
RelativeToParent constraints, 99
RelativeToView constraints, 99, 103–104
Renderers, 303
Resources, 126
   definition, 127–128
   dictionaries, 126, 140–142
   DynamicResource, 134–140
   lookup behavior, 143
   MergedDictionaries, 143–144
   overriding, 143
   StaticResource, 128–131, 133–134
   styles, 151–153

RetainElement, 256
Rotation, 198
RoutingEffect, 323–324

S

Scale, 198
ScrollView, 36
Selection controls, 187
SetBackgroundColor method, 305
SetNativeControl method, 309
SetPropertyName methods, 214
SizeProportional, 110
Slider, 188, 196–197
Spanning columns, 94–96
Spanning rows, 95–96
Springboard, 297
   gesture recognizer, 299
   Springboard.xaml, 298
   Springboard.xaml.cs, 298
   tap-gesture, 297
SQLite, 347, 410
SQLite.NET, 348
   DAL (*see* Data access layer (DAL))
   database creation, 384–385, 410
   database path
      Android project, 387
      implementation, 385
      iOS, 388
      PCL connection, 387
      shared project, 385
      Windows Phone, 389
   locking, 384
   .NET Standard, 386
   PCL setup, 382
   shared project setup, 383
   table creation
      attributes, 390

SQLite.NET (*Cont.*)
    Delete method, 391
    Get method, 391–392
    Insert method, 391
    Item data model, 389
    lock keyword, 393
    Update method, 392
  web services, 411
Stack, 86
StackLayout, 73, 234
  coding, 81
  expanding and padding views, 79–80
  horizontal orientation, 77–78
  HorizontalOptions, 75
  nesting layouts, 79
  padding property, 74–76
  vertical orientation, 76–77
StartAndExpand, 80
state management, 262
StaticResource, 128
  background color, 129
  hardcoded values, 129–130
  LocalDesignPage.xaml, 129
  StaticResourcesPage.xaml, 131, 133
  StaticResourcesPage.xaml.cs, 133–134
  styled feedback page, 131
Static style inheritance, 154–155
Stepper, 188, 195–196
StepperValueChanged, 196
String formatting, 381
Styles, 119
  background color, 145
  definition, 144
  device, 163–165
  explicit, 146–147
  feedback page, 162
  implicit, 148–149

  inheritance, 153–156
  lookup, 145
  MyResources.xaml, 157
  MyStyles.xaml, 157–160
  overriding, 149–151
  property setters, 145
  resources, 151–153
  StylesPage.xaml, 161–162
Switch, 188, 197–198

T

TextCell, description properties, 227
TextValidatorEffect
  Android platform effect, 326–328
  attached properties, 335–336
  complete code, 331–332, 334–335
  EditText, 326
  Entry controls, 325
  events handling, 331
  ios platform effect, 328–330
  RoutingEffect, 325
  UITextField, 326
Themes, 119, 165
  App.xaml, 166
  Custom themes, 171–174
  Dark theme, 167–169
  four-step process, 165–166
  Light theme, 169–171
  LoadApplication method, 166
  style options, 167
Third-party MVVM libraries, 347
TimePicker, 187, 193–195
TimePickerPropertyChanged method, 195
Triggers, 207
  coding, 211–213
  event, 210–211

</Entry>Data, 209
MultiTrigger, 209–210
property, 208
TargetType, 207
value converter, 213
Trivial data binding, 350
TypeFace class, 341–342

U

UIButton control, 315
UIFont class, 341
UIKit.UITextField, 328
Universal Windows Platform (UWP), 43
User interaction (UI) controls
Xamarin.Forms views, 187–188
DatePicker, 191
focus, 199
general-use property, 188
handler event property, 188
opacity, 198
picker, 188
rotation, 198
scale, 198
selection views, 199
Slider, 196
Stepper, 195
Switch, 197–198
TimePicker, 193
visiblity, 198
User interface design, 73–74, 119

V

Value converter, 381–382
Views (Xamarin.Forms), 23
background color, 25
BoxView, 31–32

build and run, 38
buttons, 26, 28
coding, 38–40
entry, 30–31
fonts
FontAttributes, 26
FontFamily, 25
FontSize, 25
multiple attributes, 26
platform-specific, 26
HorizontalOptions and
VerticalOptions
alignment, 29
AndExpand pads, 30
LayoutOptions, 29
size of controls, 29
image (see Image view)
labels, 23
Padding property, 37
ScrollView, 36
StackLayout, 24
Visiblity, 198
Visual Studio App Center (VSAC), 414

W

Web services, 411
REST, 411
SOAP, 411
WCF, 411
WidthProportional, 111
Windows Presentation
Foundation (WPF), 43
Wrap, 86

X

Xamarin
Xamarin compiler (XAMLC), 68

Xamarin.Forms, 1, 303
    Android and iOS operating systems, 1
    architecture
        cross-platform solution, 4
        customization, 5
        hybridization, 4
        platform-specific UI layer, 5
    basic design, 8
    business apps, 8
    cross-platform solution
        Core Library, 15
        multiple projects, 16
        Visual Studio, 16
        Xamarin.Android, 14
        Xamarin.Forms, 14
        Xamarin.iOS, 15
    customization, 9
    custom renderers, 9
    effects, 9
    learning Xamarin, 8
    mobile UIs, 10
    native OS libraries, 2
    native view, 9
    open-source Mono project, 1
    properties and methods, 9
    sharing UI code, 8
    simple cross-platform screens, 8
    Telerik's UI, 9
    Xamarin.Android and Xamarin.iOS, 2, 7
Xamarin.Forms project, 306
    App.cs, 16
    application lifecycle methods, 17
        OnResume, 18
        OnSleep, 17
        OnStart, 17

    app's main page, 21–22
    ContentPage, 18–19
    Core Library, 21
    Xamarin.Android, 19–20
    Xamarin.iOS, 20–21
Xamarin.Forms UI
    layouts, 11–13
    pages, 11–12
    views, 11, 13–14
Xamarin.Forms views
    coding, 199–201
    CommandParameters, 206
    commands, 204–206
XAML compilation, 68–69
XAML Standard, 69–71
XAML syntax
    classes and members
        attribute value, 47
        namespaces, 47–48
    constructors (*see* Constructors)
    markup extensions, 48
        array, 50–52
        reference, 53–55
        static, 49
        type, 52
XML syntax
    attributes, 45
    elements, 44
    hierarchy, 45
    namespaces, 46
XProportional, 110

Y, Z

YProportional, 110

Printed in the United States
By Bookmasters